Saddles

of

Barringer

Tennessee Gunns

Copyright © 2020 by Pete Lester aka Tennessee Gunns

All rights reserved. No part of this publication may be reproduced, distributed, or transmitted in any form or by any means, including photocopying, recording, or other electronic or mechanical methods, without the prior written permission of the publisher, except in the case of brief quotations embodied in critical reviews and certain other non-commercial uses permitted by copyright law.

For permission requests, write to the publisher, addressed "Attention: Permissions Coordinator," at the address below.

Burkwood Media Group
P O Box 1772
Albemarle, NC 28001-5704
www.burkwoodmedia.com

Printed in the United States of America

Dedication

With love, this novel is dedicated to my family, Debra, Drew, and Carson. Written for all Rough Riders, near and far, past, and present.

For my Uncle Kenneth Lester, an educator and veteran, who painted his house every summer and understood the meaning of being conservative.

To a fellow Army soldier and friend, Mark Lassere, and his wife, Lysa, thank you for showing us a wonderful time in the French Quarter. There's no place better to meet good friends and have coffee and beignets than at Café Du Monde. Much of this book was inspired by that exciting family trip to New Orleans in 2019.

Acknowledgments

In 1999, a number one song by American-singer-songwriter, Brad Paisley became popular about the relationship between a father and his son, the song
"He Didn't Have to Be"
influenced the content for
Saddles of Barringer.

⟷

The creation of a novel doesn't happen without dedication and a team of good people, who make books available for all cultures. For me, special thanks goes to Burkwood Media. The talented team in Charlotte, North Carolina has a vision to ensure my work is available to an evolving readership and finds strategic ways to partner with major retailers like Walmart Books, Amazon Books, Goodreads, Barnes & Noble and many other international bookstores; they ensure my work remains relevant, shepherding the marketing in coffee shops, libraries, and on social media. Each day, I say a prayer for your families and your presence in my writing career.

Introduction

During Thanksgiving of 1999, Pete pinned a town he'd never been to before on a map and decided to relocate. The following Christmas, the Lester family moved from Hewitt, Texas, to Troutman, North Carolina, in Iredell County, formerly known as Barringer. In 1868, by the requirements of the North Carolina Constitution, counties were divided into areas, sixteen townships formed in Iredell County, and one was Barringer Township.

In 2017, when Pete's GPS kept telling him he was in Barringer, he became curious about the name, and a year later, he penned the outline for his second novel, *Saddles of Barringer*. Through uncovering old maps of Iredell County, from the late 1800s, and researching old documents, the memory of old townships, such as Barringer, a once forgotten name in Iredell County history will be now kept alive through this Southern Fiction novel.

Truman Capote was right, "We are drawn back to the places we've lived."

The best part, it's the good people we meet along the way that makes the journey worthwhile.

I

Deep in the Heart of Texas, 1994

As nine thousand screaming fans dressed in cowboy boots and felt hats stood in denim and leather, the smell of buttery popcorn and corn dogs, mixed with designer cologne, lingered throughout the dusty arena as the almost lyrical and familiar announcer sounded over the airways.

"Let's give a great big Waco welcome to the newcomer on the circuit, #88 J.T. Woods." The crowd roared. "Folks, this cowboy is from Bryan, Texas, and let's cheer him on." The announcer sipped his coffee, handling a ceramic Lone Star mug and watched with his big, prominent lobster eyes. "You'll find bad blood between crazy bulls and cowboys, especially in this part of Central Texas. Somewhere between prickly pear cactus and tumbleweeds are where bulls lose their cool with cowboys." He stood and sang, "Deep in the heart of Texas!"

The crowd cupped their hands together, shouting and whistling as the clean shaven, tight-laced bull rider lowered his skinny legs atop the bull, to be called the next rough rider.

Opening the door behind the announcer, a thin man with a handlebar mustache entered the room, sporting a big grin, "How have you been, Big Ray Brown?"

"Hey, look who made it to the Man versus Bull Showdown," said Big Ray, sounding to the crowd. "This sturdy commentator and former bull rider needs no introduction, he's an all-around good guy from Luckenbach, Texas, former Bull Riding Champion, Max Sheridan, everyone."

***

When the war in Vietnam was over, these two bull riders met and started announcing together on the Texas rodeo circuit. Like brothers in a foxhole, they covered each other and finished each other's sentences, too. Max plopped into a leather seat, adjusted his hat and bolo tie, pointing his hawk eyes on the bull rider and found his microphone. The jumbotron glowed in the dim light of the dark arena, spotlights, and cameras spun, and angled to the next cowboy.

"Hey, Big Ray, it's good to see you again," shaking hands with his friend. "I'm over the hill but bull ridin' never stops, here in Waco, Texas."

On a night hotter than a Texas versus Oklahoma football game, the two guys positioned themselves inside a small, air-conditioned booth for the event. Max added a sharp Texan accent as he leaned over the table with a rapid fire, auctioneer style voice, while Big Ray stuck to his slow, country drawl. Big Ray flipped his wide Stetson hat and nodded, as he let Max Sheridan take the lead.

With a scratchy voice, Max said, "Bull rider #88 has a lengthy career ahead of him, folks," pulling his microphone closer to his chest. "Don't think for a minute when he touches that felt hat and hits the ground, he's finished. We'll see that cowboy again soon."

Dropping his glasses on his nose, Big Ray scanned the arena, then anxiously shifted his seat because he'd been tumbled as a bull rider hundreds of times, getting the air knocked out of his lungs was part of the sport.

"But he's got some points to gain to catch Ringo Bare," said Big Ray in a deep voice. "That #21 Ringo Bare, is hated by bulls as much as a fiery branding iron is when it hits the hide of a bull."

"Yeah, and that bull rider is from Temple, Texas," added Max, tugging on his hat, "and he's on the top of the leaderboard."

"Indeed, he was trained by Temple's finest old school bull rider." Big Ray checked the crowd for his old friend. "It's the legendary Clem Cline."

"He's a warrior." Max shook his hand in agreement. "Up next, that's #70 Lance Bridges on a wild one-ton steer. When the broad bull leaves the earth, he's rockin' like a Fort Hood tank!" The room heated up as Max toweled his face, turning on the table fan and making himself comfortable for the night.

"That's gotta hurt that bull rider." Max gritted his teeth. "That bull will wreck ya, folks, and I mean throw you off his back without concern for life or limbs." He tapped his pen on the table. "Not many cowboys can hang with Barn Breaker for an eight second ride. Tough draw for the cowboy, he'll get him next round."

"Eight seconds seems like an eternity on the back of a mad bull," uttered Big Ray. "My back still aches from being a Marine and being kicked a dozen times at Rodeo de Santa Fe."

Adjusting his hat, Max's right hand shook as if he was the next cowboy up. "Next weekend, we'll see J.T., Lance, and a host of other cowboys, making a name for themselves in the heat of San Antonio."

Big Ray thumbed his calendar.

"Huh, that's Easter weekend of 1994, folks."

About that time Max eyed his gold watch. "It's seven o'clock on the Friday before Easter," correcting Big Ray. "You can count on a large crowd, down in Bexar County. This circuit has gone big time folks, so buy your tickets now and make the trip to San Anton."

The crowd was as quiet as a midnight church when Lance Bridges slammed his forehead into the arched head of the massive animal. Then he crashed in the dirt and bounced. Two clowns rushed to secure him, hiding behind barrels while another smaller clown, dressed in bright, fat red suspenders, shuffled his feet to distract the bull from hooking the injured cowboy.

"That's another rough ride." Max gripped the program with both hands. "Trying to stay on board Barn Breaker is a difficult task, he's about as wild and crazy as Bodacious when he was in his prime, wrecking the last 23 out of 25 bull riders."

Big Ray stood and canted his head, "And he's one tough cowboy from Oklahoma City, folks."

The veteran announcer poured more coffee and leaned over the microphone, "Bull riding, well, it's different from all the rest of the events in Waco," said Max, curling an experienced grin. "It's not like ropin' calves or barrel racing."

Big Ray squinted his eyes in agreement.

"It's a rough and tough sport."

Rolling his chair under his desk, Max turned pale as a bag of flour. "Barn Breaker wants to takedown a clown or two before he leaves Waco."

The announcers muted their microphones and spoke to each other for several minutes, in a low voice while the paramedics loaded up Lance Bridges on a long stretcher, who was hurting and seemed lost.

"Hey, that cowboy tumbled and took a horn to the shoulder, didn't he?"

Max turned to Big Ray in a muffled voice, "They saw off longhorns for good reason, and it's not just to make the animal look mean in this sport."

"Life savers, all right."

Unboxing equipment next to his legs, "The modern day bull rider will wear a thick vest and a hard helmet with a face mask for his own protection," said Max, pacing in the announcer's booth, which wasn't much bigger than a minivan. "Rider's take safety first and bull ridin' seriously on the circuit."

Big Ray rubbed his chest with compassion. Max made the sign of the cross on his heart, closing his eyes for a moment of prayer. Unmuting their microphones, the announcers regained their composure and ended their short break.

"Hope Lance is alright." Max intensely raked his thin beard. "Boy, these cowboys are taking a beating tonight, here in Waco."

"We'll check on #70 in a few minutes," nodded Big Ray.

They both checked the monitor with shocked eyes. From flat on his back, Lance Bridges gave the slow thumbs up signal as the crowd stood and applauded the courageous bull rider.

"Hey, he's all right, folks." Max told the crowd, watching the paramedics ease Lance away. "We'll check on him a little later." The crowd continued to stand and cheer, in a respectful manner.

"All eyes are on the next cowboy from Temple, Texas," said Big Ray, tugging on his western star bolo tie. "In this Man versus Bull Showdown, a bull rider will take several hard shots and get trampled in less than eight seconds." He clicked his pen.

"At Lorena," said Max, adjusting the microphone, "two weeks ago this hard-nosed cowboy hung on the leaderboard to win with an outstanding score of ninety-three, ridin' Devil's Slingshot II, hanging on for dear life, but he conquered the bull."

"It's #21 Ringo Bare, he's the local crowd favorite," reported Big Ray, locking his eyes on the bull and the cowboy. "He's having a great year on the circuit," nodding his head and checking his notes. "Here's a little back alley fact about this bull rider, he not only rides bulls, but makes western saddles, too. You can buy custom-made saddles, ball caps, and shirts by Ringo Bare, that is, if he has any merchandise left, at his sovereign tent and trailer."

"I have one in my barn," said Max. "That saddle fits my hind parts like a high-dollar recliner from Monkey Wards."

"When he's not making saddles and riding bulls," chuckled Big Ray, "you can find Ringo Bare for autographs at Clem Cline's Restaurant, hugging a primal cut of brisket, I bet?"

Tipping his hat from the chute, Ringo heard the music thundering as he felt confident above the animal. The crowd watched with concern as Ringo Bare positioned himself, heel on the bull, free hand on the rail, dropping into the bucket chute, and warming the rosin in a pair of gloves he made himself. Far from docile and displeased with the smell of any cowboy, bucking, and turning inside the chute, the crowd lowered their voices. Warming the ropes, Ringo adjusted his legs and hind parts, tight to the bull, as the music played. His hand still gripping the top rail and his boots straight, Ringo wasn't about to disappoint his fans and break an ankle in the bucket chute.

Young kids scooted to the edge of their seats as Ringo rocked forward and backward, finding his seat on the hide of the bull. Some ladies covered their eyes with the program each time the bull rattled the chute. Thousands of fans waited in silence, following what had happened to the last two brave bull riders, it was just as serious when a cowboy hopped on War Wagon or any other big bull in Waco. Risk. Reward.

Yanking and spinning the rope between the belly and the shoulders of the heavily muscled, red coloured Australian Charbray, Ringo's arms pulled the rope, and his heart beat out of his chest. The cowboy offset his long arm to the right of the bull's back, thrusting until he satisfied himself atop the animal's back, wrapping the rope around the back of his hand as Clem Cline watched his protege at work.

"Ringo!" yelled his friend Taz Ridley. "You ready?"

"That bull rider is ready!" said Clem Cline, who didn't make it to all of the events. Cattle kept him busy.

"Cowboy up!" said Ringo, muscling his legs, settled down as the bull compromised his limbs inside the bucket chute. "All bulls are different and deadly." Ringo told himself, "but they can be conquered."

He slapped and yanked the rope and slapped it again. The cowboy gripped the hair on the back of the bull and Clem Cline wasn't sure if it was for good luck or to piss the bull off, but bull riders did it for both reasons.

"I'm buckled up!" said Ringo.

"Good, let's ride." Clem Cline told him.

"Let's go, bull ridin'!" Ringo smiled.

Watching Ringo, a Spanish man with dark hair and big hands held the gate and counted down in his own language. Ringo bit deep down into his mouthpiece, nodding his head atop the bull as the steer raised up, rattling the gate, and shook Ringo like a horsefly. The cowboy had a death grip on the handle rope, tossing the tail of the rope over his left leg, thrusting forward, and locking his legs, making a slight bend in his knee and knew his heart was jumping out of his shirt.

"I'm feeling it." Ringo made another adjustment to his rope. "Let's ride."

"Stay over his head!" Clem Cline pointed at War Wagon with his cane, shaking his head with a big smile. "You got him." In a tense motion, Clem Cline gripped his own wrist.

The bull rider grunted, electric guitars sounded throughout the packed arena and the crowd chanted, "Ringo! Ringo! Ringo!"

"Cowboy up. Cowboy up!" sounded Big Ray, who stood, in excitement.

"Cowboy up, Ringo." Max Sheridan added, squinting his dark eyes behind his glasses.

Along with the rest of the crowd, Big Ray Brown and Max Sheridan tapped their boots to the rhythm of the music and like everyone else, glued their eyes on the star of the show. Fans waited for the gate to open for War Wagon.

"Let's go make some money, boys," said Ringo, slapping his wrist one last time and nodding to the Spanish man to open the gate.

The gate opened wide, the crowd was amazed at the size of the bull, muscled, and bucking wildly, and dirt flung underneath the mad bull, turning a hard right, quick left, leaving the ground, bucking, and kicking. The ride was like fire out of hell scorched his hooves and burnt his legs.

Big Ray placed his hand on his watch, out of habit. "Ringo needs eighty-eight points out of a hundred on this ride, a straight arrow to take the lead and the money."

The mad bull cut left and then right underneath him, dropping his head, spinning around, and stretched his frame above the earth. Ringo held his position. Clowns readied themselves for the sound of the horn, arched and hidden behind wooden barrels.

"Ringo Bare versus War Wagon!" said Max Sheridan, who took off his brown cowboy hat to see the finish.

"Oh! Wow!" Big Ray Brown squinted his eyes. "Ouch!"

The crowd let out a faint sigh and the horn sounded short of the ride, receiving a score of zero.

"Wow!" said Max, tugging on his shirt pocket. "He didn't hang on and paid for it, didn't he?"

"That was head to head contact." Big Ray sat with his eyes closed. "The big bull stomped Ringo's foot and that man is in pain, folks." The announcer told Max. "Looks like a semi-truck slammed into a scarecrow in mid-air, didn't it?"

"I've been there, and it's a hard collision." Max pressed his palms against his forehead. "Contact between bull and cowboy, like the one we just watched, could end a bull rider's career. The summer of 1978 was my last ride, and I lived to tell the story."

Max wiped his face in sheer agony, falling back in his chair, passionately slapping the table in disappointment for Ringo's injuries.

"That's why they call him War Wagon." Big Ray flexed his hands. Everyone stood.

"Ringo Bare, he's one tough rider, forged like steel and a crowd favorite in this town." Max watched the paramedics check him out. "And to take a crushing hit to the head, makes a young rider's ma'am nervous and the newspapers take note how dangerous this sport really is, in reality."

"I believe his helmet and mask saved his life, right?" Max rubbed the top of his hand with his cowboy hat. "Man, he's rough and tough to handle a shot like that and Clem Cline trained him to be as tough as raw leather."

"Yeah, it still hurts, though." Big Ray rubbed his chin. "I'm no doctor, but his foot looks crushed on the big screen." He sighed. "Let's take a look at the jumbotron to see the big ride again, how it happened, rolling in slow motion."

Max rolled his hands over and over, moving them up and down his arms, like he walked out of a deep freezer, checking his watch for how long Ringo Bare had been down on the ground.

"He's gonna need some help," said Max.

"He'll be back." Big Ray breathed into his hands. "From this angle, the bull rider was too far over the bull's shoulders to make a correction. That's when the collision happened." Big Ray closed his eyes and shook his head. "Lots of pain in the foot when the bull impacted his leg, Max."

Churning inside, Max pressed his fist on his chest amid the replay and frowned. The announcers shared empathy for Ringo Bare and hoped his injuries weren't as bad as they looked on the television and back at home for his fans.

2

Coveted Cowboy Stew, 1997

The same year "Dolly the sheep" celebrated her first birthday, was the same year Ringo Bare turned twenty-seven, and the same year his forty-nine year old father, Doctor Gilbert Greenway, climbed to the top of Clem Cline's windmill to view five-hundred head of cattle and a dozen horses from another angle.

Doc promised to fix the windmill once his workload slowed down in the tattoo removal business, and it did that summer. With a new blade and some oil, the windmill turned, without resistance, in Temple, Texas. He'd promised to pick up grain in Gatesville for Clem Cline, by the close of business, too. The sun dropped low behind the furthest row of mesquite trees on the Cline's ranch, Doc rested and stared out to the left of the tall windmill, where he and Ringo's farmhouse stood, the one they'd rented from Clem Cline since 1982.

The rumble in his stomach troubled him, so he took a short break and couldn't wait to latch on to a slice of Mrs. Cline's homemade cornbread and a bowl of Ringo's coveted Cowboy Stew, the recipe he'd encouraged him to fix on the fourth of July. Hungry as a coyote, Doc's taste buds remembered the last two bowls he had with crackers after replacing a section of fence on a cold April Sunday. That was the day Clem Cline's wife, Rita, dropped off old-fashioned, golden cornbread and a bowl of whipped butter for Ringo.

Fascinated by the colors of purple and blue that hung over the Temple skyline, blended by a streak of pink and blue, stretching across the western end of Clem Cline's ranch, was where Doc made the windmill operational again. Resting on the rusty tailgate of his 1970 Chevy, he soaked up the last warm rays of the day and knew Clem would be happy to see the windmill spinning on a windy day. From the bottom of his green Army thermos, Doc emptied the last bit of tea on his dry tongue and coated his sun chapped lips, watching the night conquer the day.

His favorite companion followed him across the ranch, Doc stroked the horse's head and knew he was hungry, too.

"Are you tired, Old Tony? I'm tired. Let's go home."

Suddenly, the windmill spun its first rotation since Desert Storm, and Doc took pride in being able to climb the thirty-foot tower and tend to the needed repairs. In a short celebration, he halved a red apple, the size of a baseball with the red-brown bay gelding that nudged his shoulder for a snack.

"It's sundown, Old Tony, and you need grain." He petted the horse's brown face and gently thumbed the white star on his forehead and called it a day.

After his classic Chevy failed to crank, Doc rode the horse bareback as his silhouette made him look like an Apache Indian, who'd traced his way from San Saba to Temple on a long day's ride. Into the first minutes of dark, winding his way back to the only glow of light he could find and the closer he got to home, the stronger the smell of Cowboy Stew filled his nostrils from the farmhouse. Ringo had made enough stew for a camp of hungry cowboys, taking a break on the Chisholm Trail.

Doc started Ringo's Ford truck, honked the horn, and yelled, "Hurry, let's go!" Doc waved at him. "Get in."

Walking from the kitchen to the truck, Ringo laughed as he looked inside the cab and plainly said, "Where's ya Chevy, Doc?"

Adjusting his glasses, Doc brushed his nose and with a sour face, he had to eat his words about driving Ringo's truck.

"Bull Rider, I'd rather ride a mule than drive a Ford, but I have no choice, you see, my Chevy is down and out, parked under the windmill."

"What's the rush, anyway?" Ringo leaned inside the cab. "I'm cooking my famous Cowboy Stew. Let's eat first?"

"Let that stew simmer on low!" I need your help with handling bags of feed in Gatesville. I jammed the crap out my lower back on the last step of the windmill ladder."

"You'll live, for sure, old man," Ringo handed him a bowl. "Here, eat up," slamming the truck door and placing a slice of cornbread on the seat, he snickered. "Listen, that's the sound of a 350 Chevy, laughing at your truck."

"No. Don't say it, I don't want to buy this truck from you."

Laughing until tears fell down his dry, sun-chapped face, Ringo stopped while he was ahead and chewed his food.

"Nothing better than cornbread and some bacon," said Ringo, slapping his belly. "I saved you some, and just for you, there's a little heat in the kielbasa sausage. Out of practice, I guess, it's been a long time since I used that stove. I'll stick to the grill, it's much easier to handle, less buttons, too."

"The bacon came from that big hog Clem Cline killed last month. Hope you didn't overcook it, like you did that London broil last fall."

"I didn't."

Doc lifted his nose, in a curious way, "Is that beer on your breath or do you need a shower?"

Turning his head toward the window, Ringo mumbled, "I had a few while I cooked the stew."

Halfway to Gatesville, Ringo became curious and fumbled with the radio, taking a deep breath, and talking about beer and stew, a few things he was proud of doing.

"Put on a few pounds, didn't ya, hot-rod?" asked Doc while glancing at Ringo's gut.

"Damn it, Doc, I've gained a few pounds because my foot doesn't work right, and I'm less active after the injury. You and Clem need to leave me the hell alone about my weight."

"You should stay away from double-decker burgers and large fries, milkshakes, and cases and cases of beer."

"To make you happy, I'll burn some calories loading feed for you this evening, how about that?"

"You were once a lean, mean bull riding machine and now twenty pounds heavier, you turned into a heavy milk....."

Interrupting him, Ringo raised his hand, "You better not call me a milk cow again."

"Because you traded your Longhorn bulls for three Jersey milk cows, doesn't mean you join the herd, does it?"

Ringo hit the dashboard, "Don't speak to me." He blasted the radio and looked out the window.

Killing the radio, "Don't be disrespectful," replied Doc. "Hope the cornbread chokes you."

They arrived at the Gatesville Feed Store, Doc unfolded the local paper, and didn't like what was printed. Ringo loaded twenty bags of feed, sweating by the fourth bag, and had no idea his picture was on the sports page. Doc trashed it.

3

Where's Ringo Bare?

Three years had passed since War Wagon busted up Ringo Bare's foot, ending his bull riding career. Big Ray Brown called it 'The Ride to Remember' over the airways. That's what the newspaper printed in July '97, and without a doubt in his mind, Doc Greenway kept his word after a year of helping him through physical therapy and crutches. Ringo walked out of the hospital in his own cowboy boots.

Sharp dressed in a suit and sporting his thick recognizable mustache, Doc took care of Ringo after the bull smashed his foot, and after several surgeries, his foot was repaired somewhat. After he came off the bull riding circuit, saddles made by Ringo Bare collected dust and didn't sell much. Doc didn't give up on Ringo and knew he was the best in the country at saddlery. The good doctor needed to display his products in a place with less competition, far away from the imports of Mexico and Central America, would be the key to his success and confidence.

Despite what the newspaper printed, Doc wasn't afraid to challenge Ringo and knew the article would piss him off if his eyes locked on the page. Doc denied the article and believed Ringo could live without current events for one day. Life was tough for Ringo and Doc, distancing themselves from the dysfunction of the media and how they'd "Poked the Bare" for years because he wasn't riding the circuit any longer. Doc needed a new purpose for his adopted son.

***

Three hours later, the night was as dark as the Inner Space Cavern, deep underground in Georgetown, Texas. Doc rolled the windows down on Highway 36, where he was passed by four fire trucks. Emergency crews diverted traffic from the road leading to Clem Cline's farm, flagging a line of cars, as a tall man in a reflective vest stopped their truck.

"Where's the fire, young man; what's the hurry about?"

The man stood against the mirror and pointed at the smoke, "Sir, I heard Clem Cline decided to burn two barns."

"It's about damn time," said Ringo, leaning out the window. "We live beside Clem Cline, could we bypass this traffic?"

"Follow the last fire truck." The man waved.

Ringo rolled up his window to avoid the cloud of smoke outside the truck and drove as fast as he could to the stop sign.

"Clem finally decided to burn that old fallen barn, did he?" pointed Doc. "Lots of trucks for a controlled burn, though, huh?" Smelling the billowing smoke in the air, but too far to see the barns or the firemen working, Doc said, "Yeah, I'm surprised he didn't ask us to help him with the fire."

Dropping his head, "He did." Ringo covered his face. "I forgot to tell you what night he was going to burn it down."

"Holy cow!" shouted Doc. "He's burning two barns, tonight, alright!" Pressing on the pedal, Ringo suddenly slammed the brakes, and yelled, "That's the barn and our damn house on fire!"

Doc ran to the fire line, three men stopped him a hundred feet from his front door, the place was ablaze, and firefighters kept him behind the yellow tape. Four fire trucks aimed hoses on the flames, two from the ground, and two others powered water from tall ladders, trying to handle the blaze, but it was out of hand.

"Where's Clem Cline?" shouted Doc, moving through the large crowd of spectators. "Clem! Clem Cline!"

Waving from the ground, "He's over here." His wife cried out.

"I'm alive, Doc," coughing up a lung. Clem held Rita's hand and gripped a saddle horn with the other. "Got a little smoke in my lungs, but I'll live, I guess."

"What happened?" asked Doc, placing both hands atop his head, stomping his boots into the dry ground and kicking the dirt. He sat and turned his long face to Clem for the answer and watched it burn.

"Listen!" The thin, pale man caught his breath. "My wife and I pulled up about sundown," trying to remove black soot from his pale skin, "and the kitchen and living room were burning through the roof."

"I ran in the front door," said Rita, crying.

"I busted the back door down with a sledgehammer, I tried to think like you, Doc, and grab something of value first and get the heck out, before we burned alive."

"You shouldn't have gone in there." Doc told them, hugging the gray-headed man. Rita bawled, rubbing her dark eyes.

"He tried." Rita told the men. "All my Clem could carry was Doc's Army uniform and Ringo's saddle."

"At age seventy-three, I did my best, gentlemen. Forgive me, will ya?"

"That's not Ringo's saddle," said Doc. "That's your half-brother's saddle. "Uncle Kenneth made three saddles, back in Barringer, the year before he got pneumonia and died. The one in your hand, it's the last one he made."

"I'm glad I risk my life for my brother's saddle." Clem pulled the saddle across the grass beside him. "Good. It was worth the risk then." He wiped his red eyes.

"You did fine." Doc told him.

"Doc, I wished we could've saved more saddles." Tears rolled down the old man's wrinkled face. "All that leather stacked up in the corner, Ringo, it's gone." Clem scratched his head. "I was just too slow and too damn old, nephew."

"Thank God, you saved Kenneth's saddle, though," said Ringo. "You got out with your life, Mr. Cline, and that's what counts."

"He shipped the saddle to Ringo for his sixteenth birthday several years ago." Doc pulled Clem and Rita to a standing position.

"You did well," replied Ringo, in a deep voice, pacing around. "Mr. Cline and Mrs. Cline, I'm sorry, but the fire, it's all my fault."

"What's your fault?" asked Doc.

Pounding his truck, Ringo said, "I hate myself, right now! I burnt down the house with the hot stove, it must've spread from the house to the field to the barn, too." His face was filled with anguish, as if a bull had rolled over on his leg.

"What are you saying, boy?" yelled Clem Cline.

Light reflected off the stream of tears rolling down Clem's long face, using his sleeves to dry his salty eyes, he was curious.

Ringo dropped his head, "I must've left the stove on too high, Mr. Cline, it's all my damn fault. I'm terribly sorry."

"O' Heavens!" said Mrs. Cline. "It was an accident, boy."

Kicking his hat, "Yeah." said Ringo. "It was my damn accident, though!"

He threw his hat inside his truck and watched their home burn and collapse. In that moment, Ringo's demeanor fell to an all-time low, as if he stood at a graveside burial, and maybe it was his own, he thought, starting toward the fire.

"Get back, boy!" yelled the fireman.

"He wasn't even home," said Mrs. Cline. "How could he have done it?"

"Chef Ringo, here, was making his coveted Cowboy Stew, and he doesn't know what the word sober means. He wrecked his truck last month and burnt down our home this week. He's a damn drunk kid, that's all he'll ever be." In a rage, Doc pushed Ringo against a fire truck. "It's your damn fault, boy!"

"I screwed up! I did this, get the hell off my case, Doc!"

"Damn it, Ringo!" waving his hand in Ringo's face. "Everything we owned was in that house!"

Like a linebacker, Doc tackled Ringo in the tall grass, and yelled, "What the hell is wrong with you, Son?"

"You're not my damn father, anyway. I'm just a kid that was dropped on your doorstep! Why do you even care?"

Ringo rolled Doc over on his back, cocking his arm to hit him, and about that time, a lanky fireman blocked his punch with his arm, separating the fighters.

"Break it up!" A short fireman shouted, with his arms up. "Grab Ringo! I got Doc."

Two firemen blocked Doc's arms, standing in front of them, and throwing up their hands to help. Suddenly, Ringo broke free from the fireman and headed for his truck.

"Where the hell are we going to live now, Ringo?" said Doc, shouting through a group of firemen.

"Far from you, Doc!" Ringo rushed toward his truck. "Don't worry about me!"

Mrs. Cline sniffed, and her lips quivered. "Boys! Boys! Boys!" She raised her hands. "Stop it, right now!"

Walking over to them, and in a muffled voice, Clem said, "You'll stay in my motorhome," putting his arms around Doc and Ringo, you two men can live in my motorhome until you get a bigger place. I don't want any bad blood between us over this fire, you got that gentlemen?"

"I'll buy the motorhome and the house from you, Uncle Clem." Turning and watching the home smolder, "No, I can't pay you a dime yet. I had $50,000 in a cash box under my bed and …it's …it's up in flames now! Damn it!"

In a mincing voice, "I snatched four photo albums from the bedroom and a jewelry box full of gold watches for you," said Mrs. Cline. "I screamed and rushed out and didn't see the cash box." She sobbed and wiped her nose.

Grabbing his head, "I meant to deposit that money today." Doc rounded his fist. "Well, that changes my freakin' life forever."

Standing beside Mrs. Cline with his arms open in tears, Doc hugged her and kissed her rosy cheeks for trying her best.

"You're a brave soul, Aunt Rita." Doc comforted the lady. "We'll get this worked out, right, Ringo?"

Slamming the door to his truck, Ringo drove away. In a broken way, Doc sat in the doorway of Clem Cline's motorhome until after midnight watching the house he'd rented since Ringo was in sixth grade smoldering. If he'd been a drunkard, he'd made sure a fat bottle of whiskey was empty, but he hadn't touched a drop since Ringo came to live with him.

The worst part was, as teenagers Clem and Kenneth helped build the home for their grandfather, a two-story farmhouse with a back porch wide as a theatre stage. Grandpa Cline spent the rest of his days playing guitar and drinking coffee on the back porch. With no resolution in mind, Doc held his uncle's saddle in his lap, rocking back and forth, picturing what could have been done differently with Ringo on the night of the fire.

"It was all wrong." He told Clem Cline. "The way I handled that boy, it was all wrong."

"This situation can be fixed, Doc. But if it becomes too much for my wife, you might have to leave for a while."

Ashamed of himself, Doc tossed and turned all night listening for the sound of truck tires crunching gravel in the driveway. There was no sign of Ringo anywhere. Then Doc's mind flashed back to how he first came to know Ringo and his mother, the glamorous Pomona Bare.

4

The Yellow Umbrella, 1982

With no plans on his agenda but rest and relaxation, Doc found a table with a big yellow umbrella and unfolded a newspaper atop Hotel Monteleone, where the swimming pool smelled like fresh chlorine, and the water matched the sky. After scanning the sports page of *The Times-Picayune*, his attention turned to the dark puffy storm clouds that ceilinged New Orleans at sundown, blocking the sun dancing on the water, and how it had postponed his reading session. Above him the skylight dimmed like the color of an old-fashioned black and white television in a retail store, moving in and out. Doc folded his newspaper, angling his eyes to a beautiful woman seated on the other side of the pool, laughing and giggling, glued to an interesting story herself. Every few seconds, he'd glance her direction and become fascinated by her good looks. For a moment longer, he admired the entertainment, and her tanned legs were smooth and glossy, noticing her, head to toe, and again, in no particular order.

The only two people left at the pool were him and the lady reading in her sundress, lost in a good book, he guessed. Often seen behind dark glasses, Doc became mesmerized by her beauty, turning to the blonde basking in occasional golden rays of light that disappeared between two dark clouds and faded behind a stretch of silver ones. At dusk, drops of rain fell as the clouds shielded the sun, the type of gentle drizzle that elated construction workers but a lady fresh out of a high dollar salon would feel otherwise in the absence of sunlight. Without delay, she dog-eared her page in a panic.

"Oh, my hair, my hair, it's going to be flat," sounded the lady. "It wasn't supposed to rain this evening in New Orleans."

She spoke to Doc, as if he was her good friend.

A magnificent lady, who appeared to be in her thirties, stood in a soft yellow sundress collecting her things in an anxious manner, clutching her book, and jumping as thunder sounded. Her smile melted with each step around her lawn chair, glancing at Doc as if it were a cry for help.

Just as if he lifted the pin on the 18th green at Pinehurst, Doc pulled a long wooden umbrella from the center of the table and covered her. Walking the lady from the patio to the door, protecting the style of her blonde hair and leather shoes, she was elated.

"You are so kind," the lady responded in a soft voice.

Nodding in admiration, Doc stood beside her.

Catching a glimpse of themselves in the glass door, they stopped and soaked up the moment. Still spinning in Doc's hand, the yellow umbrella covered them both, standing as if they were a couple. Her eyes widened as she twisted her curly blonde hair, touching his hands with her long, painted nails, the color of a pink flamingo, and they smiled at each other. In an uncommon gesture, by their side, their hands met, warm and subtle, Doc felt a stunning lady in his grasp.

Because of Doc's quick thinking, her hair was still in place as if she'd walked out of a salon minutes earlier. The lady's pink lips turned a smooth grin at him, and with sincere gratitude the pool boy applauded in Doc's favor.

"My idol," said the young man.

Then Doc collapsed the umbrella and handed it to him, who had collected others himself. Expecting nothing in return for his good deed, and if he'd won the war on chivalry, the lady waited for him in the foyer of the hotel.

"No one has ever looked out for me like that," said the lady in a sexy voice, touching her butterfly necklace.

"You're welcome. No one with blonde hair as beautiful as yours should ever have to style it twice in one day."

"He's "Man of the Year" in my book," replied the pool boy, shaking Doc's hand. "Well done with the umbrella, sir."

Handing the young man a few dollars for his respect and to return the umbrella to the table, Doc slapped his arm. *His crew cut could sustain the dampness*, he thought.

"Not many men would've made the extra effort to share that much concern for others." She adjusted her dress.

"Chivalry isn't dead, my lady," nodding his head and walking by her down the hall. "You have a nice day, miss." Doc paced to the elevator.

"How about an umbrella in my drink at the Carousel Bar?"

Stopping in his tracks, Doc turned his head and tipped his dark glasses, and held out his arm, "I do have a sudden interest in umbrellas, don't I?" Wearing his lucky navy-blue shirt, and his favorite boat shoes, taking her arm, he said, in agreement, "It's my treat, though." Doc grinned. "Nowadays, umbrellas are my specialty."

She laughed. "You can cover me up again someday."

Doc took her arm and they walked like high school sweethearts, charting a course for the bottom floor, in style.

"You might be the last gentlemen in the Big Easy."

The pool boy followed them. "I was going to grab the umbrella!" Rain showered the city. "Lady, he brought you inside just in time," pulling the door tight. "I haven't seen this much rain since I was in Manhattan."

"That's what I'll have then," said the friendly lady.

"What?" asked Doc, watching it rain.

"A Cherry Manhattan," hooking her sunglasses on the neck of her sundress. "That will cool me off."

In the elevator, arm in arm, Doc noticed she was one radiant lady, and the care she'd taken to make herself unforgettable, marked his memory, even years later.

Clearing his throat, Doc said, "That drink isn't served with an umbrella, though." Laughing, Doc felt a close connection with her early on, tugging on his arm.

"I feel like everyone is staring at me when my hair is as flat as an ironing board. Seriously, thank you for looking out for me."

"You make other women jealous, I'm sure, and I didn't catch your name, little lady."

"Pomona Bare." She winked at him while checking her hair in the elevator mirror. "And you are a saint from New Orleans, I'm sure of it."

"Gilbert Greenway, and my friends call me, Doc."

"A doctor with an umbrella, can you dance?"

"Like Frank Sinatra on Saturday night."

"You may be the last perfect man, Doc." She raised her soft voice, "Well, I will follow you to the Carousel Bar." From ear to ear, she shaped a giant smile. "Take me for a spin and let's dance afterward, will you, Doctor Greenway?"

"I'd rather hear about you." At that moment, he didn't mind that she was too friendly with him, he preferred it that way.

***

Years had passed since Doc felt like a hero in a lady's eyes, but he never forgot her unpredictable personality or the sweet, subtleness in her voice that warmed him, even when she was angry. Each time it rained, Doc needed another "Big Yellow Umbrella Moment" in his life, standing in the pouring rain with his hands toward the dark sky, wondering if he'd be struck by lightning or live another day?

Three days passed since he'd seen Ringo, the phone didn't ring at the Cline's home and no messages were recorded. Dark clouds unfolded over Texas, tornados, hail, lightning, and more torrential rain storms were predicted. Doc waited and watched for Ringo, hoping the insurance adjuster and the bull rider would pick up the phone, and say something.

"I need something big in my life, God. I don't know what it is, but something good would help. What do you have for me next, huh?"

He stepped inside the motorhome and poured himself a hot cup of coffee, turning in his mind, thoughts of Pomona, and he remembered sweet night after sweet night with her in New

Orleans. His heart was stuck in a time he couldn't let go of, reliving the wonderful times they'd shared in the Hotel Monteleone and other places, like Austin and San Antonio; places they'd made love, still meant something to him, at least.

***

After a week of dating Pomona, Doc met her son, a skinny, blonde kid, sporting a dusty cowboy hat and worn out boots.

"Who's this young man?" asked Doc, ruffing his hair.

"Ringo Danny Bare, my son. He's twelve."

"Doc, I had him out of wedlock, my sophomore year of college."

The doctor made no judgment of her and knew the pain of his own father, a man he disliked for not loving his own kids. With each rainstorm, Hotel Monteleone flashed in his mind and the confidence he had with Pomona Bare on his arm, became one of the highlights of his life.

When they entered the room at the Carousel Bar, the thin bartender in a black tuxedo pointed at two seats, Doc felt like a movie star beside Pomona.

***

Those days are gone. He told himself.

Sitting in Clem Cline's motorhome with the door ajar, he petted the Cline's German Shorthaired Pointer, counting only twenty-one days Pomona lived at his home, he recalled. Ringo had lived there since the summer of 1982, and the way she left was a memory that haunted him each time he needed an umbrella.

Saddles of Barringer

Waving his hand, Clem covered Rita with an umbrella as Doc opened the truck doors for the elderly couple, who were headed to Temple for breakfast on a rainy morning. Suddenly, a deadly bolt of lightning struck the ground where Doc stood minutes earlier complaining to God about his life. Apologizing to God, Doc thanked Him for not striking him dead.

Not an umbrella, nor a blazing fire, nor the decade they've been apart could take away the fire that still burned inside him for Pomona. Down deep, Doc hoped they could reconcile their differences and become a family again. Each time it rained, New Orleans and Pomona flooded his heart. In the distance, a rainbow arched, and a warm ray of sun shone through the clouds, meaning brighter days ahead. Seeing something in the barn, Doc walked to where he thought he'd seen her dancing in a yellow sundress and holding a small umbrella, the image of Pomona was gone when the rainbow disappeared. Something of his imagination, he thought, and he hoped to see her again.

"Where is Ringo?" he asked himself.

5

Watermelon Wine

Sometimes I'd rather fight a black bear with boxing gloves on than deal with my brothers and sister. Doc admitted to himself.

In 1970, spectators remembered seeing Gilbert fight a black bear at the Central Texas State Fair. That was also the year Ringo Bare was born in the backseat of a Chevy car, less than twenty miles from the city limits of New Orleans, the sort of experience a man could do without knowing.

Long before he was known as Doctor Greenway, he wrestled with a black bear with a pair of leather gloves he'd made to defend himself when he needed them. Gilbert Greenway won. And the best news, Gilbert did it for $10. The man couldn't pass up a profitable deal of that nature, he told people, and he loved a good challenge.

In 1971, when the leaves were golden brown in the Big Apple, a $500 bet was offered to Gilbert to drive a borrowed Ford Fairlane from Brooklyn, New York to Long Beach, California, he took it. The odd part, the car wouldn't go into drive, so he spun the vehicle around and drove coast to coast, cruising in reverse. The car owner told Gilbert he could have the junk Fairlane for being a daredevil and handed him the money five days later. His neck ached for a week, he recalled.

At a hotel in New Mexico, he surrendered to a beautiful senorita for a neck massage. Doc recalled the wild night and told little about the details. "She had a red palomino tattoo on her leg," said Doc to Clem Cline. "I'll say nothing more about her other ink or where it was located."

The next morning, he headed to the hottest part of Arizona on bald tires, the car was running like a dream, and the next road sign read "Welcome to Sunny California, "and so he kept on driving across the desert.

Admired by his friends, Gilbert was referred to as a "One Man Show" for most of his life, he was as free as a mountain lion on an open prairie. No gold ring wrapped his finger on weekends and he'd never been married, "a true friend of the field," was how he shared it. He dated more often than he shaved. *I hope to marry a nice lady by his 50th birthday*, he told himself, and he said, "it may not be in the cards."

***

In Ringo's absence, Doc wasn't a bit cocky, the kid he grew to love was all he thought about and how he'd been a fool for causing a scene in front of the fire department and especially in front of Clem Cline and his wife, Rita. Nearing his horses, Doc sat on a wooden bench he'd made out of leather and mesquite wood and fell asleep.

While dreaming, Doc spoke to the bull rider.

"Rodeos are popping up in places like Huntington, West Virginia and Archdale, North Carolina, Ringo." Doc brushed his hair back with his hand. "And other towns need horses and saddles, too. I have a *great* idea."

"So, what's that mean for us?" Ringo wiped the sweat from his forehead. "I can't ride bulls anymore to cover the rent." Dust and hay fell as Ringo descended the ladder to the barn floor. "What are you going to do for work? How can we make a living working at rodeos since we have no home, and you gamble most of our money away?"

"Since your injury," pointing at his foot, "you made a little bit of money making saddles, hmmm.... cowboy."

Doc handed Ringo his water, leaning against a post.

"Yeah, I can cover expenses for events and pocket a few dollars making saddles, I guess." Buttoning his checkered shirt, Ringo gulped water from a bucket at the well.

"Let's advertise and go big time with western saddles."

Curling his notorious Paul Newman style grin, Doc raised his brow and nodded, hoping Ringo would agree.

"You mean turn this hobby into a saddle business?"

"Exactly!" said Doc, slapping straw off his pants. "But make it a national business, not some small, two bit brand on a leather keychain. Much, much bigger."

The two men paced to where they could both see the baby blue sky of Texas in the doorway of the barn and disagreed.

"Doc is there something fiery in the water you're not sharing with me?" standing back within arm's reach of his father. "Or do I need to ask your barber in the morning?"

"Okay. It's a big deal running a business," said Doc, removing his gloves. "You had a name for yourself as a national bull rider, right? Then that carried over into making saddles and belts and girly leather key chains for the ladies and some boots. Now it looks like you have some talent in your hands and head, good for more than holding a beer, don't ya think?"

"Hey, watch it now," he said, pushing his shoulder and laughing.

"To start, we don't have much money."

"We market our saddles for events and paint our name on a semi-truck, huh, like that Strauss guy, Levi? We'll make the money back that I lost in the fire."

Doc took another drink of tea. "Great idea."

"You have lost your mind, old man!" Ringo slung his hat against the barn door. "There's people who already do that kind of work and the imports are killing the market."

"But they're not as good as you at making saddles. Plus, my uncle's place in Barringer would be ideal land for a saddlery shop since our home burned, in some mysterious fire."

"Barringer! Barringer!" Ringo paced. "I'm not moving to Barringer! There's no need to live in North Carolina. Texas is where it's at, Doc. Texas is the Great Wild, Wild West."

"Yeah. We can leave Texas and buy Uncle Kenneth's land in Barringer, it's near Troutman, and there's a big lake full of bass. We can make saddles and buy the property from Uncle Clem. He's the owner now since Kenneth died."

Doc walked over in front of Ringo with his arms crossed, picking straw and hay from his clothes, like he did a hundred times after he hit the dirt after a big bull tossed him around like a rag doll. He imagined Ringo showing his saddlery business to crowds of people, recreating himself in the media, and settling down, too.

"I've sold saddles in Lorena, Dallas, and Abilene. There's no need to leave Texas for some potluck land in North Carolina." Ringo's face was tight as a barbed wire fence.

Placing his hand on Ringo's shoulder, Doc said, "I'm not sure if you know it or not, but North Carolina has the World

Champion Bull Rider in Archdale. There's thousands of registered horses and bulls chewing on hay each day in Carolina. That means, there's an immediate need for good saddles, son."

"I'm well aware of who he is, and what his championship stands for, and that they do need saddles. But why do we need to leave Texas to sell saddles? The Lone Star State has five times more cowboys and cowgirls than both Carolinas combined." His face turned red.

"What they need is a new name in the saddlery business, right? The name is Ringo Bare. The business is Saddles of Barringer."

"You're dreaming again, Doc. Big dreamer, that's all you are, just a big-time dreamer from New Orleans."

"Dreamer? Listen, there's a few names in saddlery, but Ringo, you are the world's best. Are we going to do this deal or not?" He covered his hand with a glove and poked his side.

Rolling his straw covered hat in both hands and beaming at Doc's dusty gloves, Ringo belted out a laugh when he saw Doc's hand wiggling in front of him.

"Come on, bull rider, here's my skin," said Doc, smiling, like the cowboys do it, and let's grip to the elbow."

"Where the heck have you had your hand, Doc?" Ringo laughed, hesitating. "Looks like you've had it up a bull's butt?"

"Do you want to start a damn saddle company or not?" Doc still offered his hand. "Maybe you like being a has-been bull rider, Ringo?"

Turning and biting his tongue, Ringo cursed Doc under his breath and climbed on his big, red tractor, and stared at him.

"I'll make the damn saddles!" yelled Ringo. "You fund the company, old man. Okay? I'm broke." He pushed the clutch and beat his hat against the steering wheel. "I'm not a has-been, Doc!"

Ten steps later Doc cupped his hands, "I can do my half, if you can do your part," shouting over the loud tractor engine. "I mean, if War Wagon didn't break your damn spirit and crushed your *cojones*, too." He turned, walking back to the barn.

"Kiss my ass, Doc!"

Distancing himself from Doc, Ringo wheeled the tractor down Hewett Drive in his normal rage.

Waking up from his dream, Doc rubbed his eyes and shook his head, dazed, and confused at how real the dream was, and it could happen, he thought.

"Saddles of Barringer," he mumbled, half asleep.

***

Weeks passed since Doc had seen Ringo, dark bags, and wrinkles, formed under his eyes and too many nights of sleep were lost. His dream of making saddles never left the back of his mind, happening three times in one week. To utter a few words and deliver a sincere apology for what happened the night of the fire, was his wish, not a dream.

He'd kept a lump in his throat. Nervous and worried that Ringo wasn't coming back, disappearing into nothingness like his mother had done. Tired of talking to himself and staring out the flat grimy window, Doc eyed the long gravel driveway, in the hope headlights beamed from the grille of his Chevy truck, even after midnight. He'd fix him a hot meal and pour him an ice-cold glass of tea, that is, if he'd just come home.

The next day after another sleepless night, busting with a stomach full of uncertainty and sweaty palms, he held the phone after Ringo had been M.I.A for three weeks.

"Officer, I'd like to report a missing person," said Doc.

The policeman asked a few more questions.

"He's stout as a brahma bull, tall and muscular, like a Quarter Horse, Palomino blonde hair, sports a thin movie star mustache, and smiles like a Billy goat."

"Anything else?" The officer questioned him.

"Yes. He's my best friend, and my son." Doc gripped the back of his neck. "Let me know if you find him. Also, his foot was broken once, and he might limp."

The door opened to Clem Cline's house.

Holding out his hand to Doc, he spoke with a loud voice, "I've broken wind stronger than you, Greenway."

Doc stood and laughed until he cried.

"Never mind. I found him, officer." Doc hung up. "Boy, I'm glad to see you."

They hugged, pressing so hard they felt handprints on each other's shoulders.

"This dry Texas climate sucks. Allergies have hammered me bad ever since you left," said Doc with watery eyes.

"Were you about to put my picture on a milk carton?"

Clapping his hands, Doc shadow boxed Ringo, laughing, and moving his feet in a convivial manner.

"Where have you been keeping yourself?" Doc opened the refrigerator. "How about a ham sandwich, my boy?"

"San Saba." Ringo nodded. "Yes, sir, I'm starving."

Pouring tea, Doc handed him a glass. "You've been working on the pecan farms in this horrible rain, haven't you?"

"Yeah, dreaming the whole damn time about making saddles at Uncle Kenneth's farm in Barringer Township." Smiling, "I never had a dream like that before." Ringo gulped the drink.

"Me either."

"A lady I met at the pecan farm told me about some delicious Carolina bread pudding. Have you tasted it?"

Doc smiled, handing him a sandwich and some chips.

"Hey, we'll eat Carolina bread pudding when we cross into the city limits of Barringer." Doc leaned back in his chair, letting Ringo tell him about what he'd done and the friends he'd made over the past three weeks on the pecan farm.

"I love bread pudding." Doc smacked his lips.

"You say the word," nodded Ringo, "and we are gone."

Crunching his chips and chewing his sandwich like he hadn't eaten in a week, it appeared they were a team again. Doc stopped moving and listened to all his stories, strange or not. He spoke of ladies with tattoos, men who juggled, and horses so beautiful and black, it seemed like a dream.

"Words and dreams don't make a man, Ringo, it's hard times that make men." Doc rolled up his sleeves. "You got the same winning spirit you had when Clem Cline taught you how to ride bulls as a teenager; good, use it again."

Doc spoke plain and simple to the saddle maker.

"I've got more fight in me than a mountain lion."

"Hey, I got big news for you, Puma Bare." Doc tilted his head toward Ringo. "I'm going to Barringer, like it or not, in the morning!" pointing his hat at Ringo.

"What time?"

"Before the first rooster crows." Doc tapped the kitchen table. "This wagon rolls out at 5 a.m."

"I'm going to see Selena tonight. But I'll be here before the first rooster crows, you can count on it."

Taking one last look at Clem Cline's ranch, Doc stood in the open doorway of the barn, where he built the barn, board by board, cutting his hands on raw lumber, and he knew he'd miss the place. He remembered working with Ringo from daylight until the tangerine sun disappeared in the western sky, and not far from the barn was where Ringo kissed a girl for the first time in his classic Ford truck, just like Bud and Sissy did.

Before Ringo left on his date with Selena, he saddled up his horse and turned to Doc who was working in Clem Cline's barn, "I've been your son since I was twelve, but I don't feel welcome here any longer after the fire." His horse moved left. "I'll pack up my saddles and duffle bag, get the hell out. Mr. and Mrs. Cline has yet to walk out of their home or talk to me since I've been in the motorhome."

"Mrs. Cline died the week you left; buried her in Waco. Uncle Clem Cline lives with his son in Austin now. He rarely gets to Temple anymore and things have changed for him."

"What happened to Mrs. Cline?"

Standing tall, Doc stopped what he was doing and gripped the pitchfork with both hands while Ringo mounted the horse.

"The day the house caught fire, Mrs. Cline found the jewelry box and the photo albums under the bed and.... she stole the money box and gave it to her sister in Killeen."

"She stole $50,000 of our saddle money?"

"Yeah. Mrs. Cline was full of lies and that's what caused her to have a heart attack. She died two days after she told the truth to Clem Cline, and the old man wanted to tell you himself, but he moved before he had the chance."

Ringo turned the horse, trailing toward the fence where Doc leaned against the railing and dropped his head.

"Is that all Clem Cline told you?"

"She died in the ambulance and wanted you to know that she was wrong and was sorry about the mess she caused you."

"I'm glad she confessed. I'll miss her oatmeal cookies."

Dismounting his horse, Ringo walked under an apple tree and found shade beside Doc, a man in a dim state. Color drained out of Doc's face, like he'd seen a ghost.

"Mrs. Cline admitted burning the house down with a candlestick in the kitchen, too. She wanted to sell the ranch and Clem wouldn't have any part of it. She got mad, burned the damn place down."

"I've had nightmares for three weeks and everyone called me a big, fat drunk behind my back because of what happened." Ringo was sullen. "And it was Mrs. Cline, who burned down the house, huh?"

"Yeah. She did it."

"I'm glad the truth came out, clear my name in the newspaper now."

"I'm sorry about losing my temper at the fire." Stroking his beard, "That was wrong of me, son. We'll grow from how she hurt us and forgive her. Uncle Clem is devastated and his son, Mike, said he had not eaten in two days."

"Everyone turned against me and that's why I left town."

"The money was gone, but Clem Cline, being the man that he is, paid me from his pocket."

"We have enough to get the saddlery business off the ground, if that's what you want to do? Our trucks are too old to make the trip to Barringer, so we'll leave them here, drive the motorhome to North Carolina."

Ringo pulled out a bottle of watermelon wine from his saddle bags. Doc laughed. "I haven't seen the stuff since Tom T. Hall was on the radio."

Ringo saddled Doc's horse for him, and they raced to the windmill, still spinning under a pearl-blue sky, where Ringo finished the bottle of watermelon wine by himself. Doc didn't drink a drop. Talking about the decade they'd spent together in Temple, had a hundred laughs from a dozen stories before sundown, and they sold their horses to the neighbor that evening and walked back home. Bitter no more, the duo returned to see a setting sun that cast long shadows of the tall barn at dusk, melting away their last evening together in Texas.

The next morning, Doc fired up the motorhome at their agreed time. Ringo was nowhere to be found, rolling the motorhome to the end of the driveway, Doc saw headlights.

Parking his Chevy truck at the mailbox, Ringo jumped in the motorhome with his ball cap pulled over his blonde hair. "Good morning, Doc Greenway."

"Your jeans are ripped and where did you get that damn black eye, Bull Rider?"

"I had to take Selena away from her new boyfriend, he must not have liked the way I kissed her."

"Big fight, huh?"

"He has two blackeyes with his muffin and coffee this morning."

"Is that mauve lipstick on your collar?"

"I sure hope so."

Leaning back in his seat, Ringo laughed and in a little while he dozed off, dreaming about the night beneath the sky with Selena, the only lady he'd been in love with since sixth grade. Her tawny skin was the result of being the descendant of an Apache Chief that once commanded the land where the pecan trees grew in San Saba. Ringo would've married her, too, if things were different. And he did ask her, but she turned the bull rider down, and told him, "I want someone on the circuit."

6

Teddy Roosevelt's Saddle

From the time Ringo was a teenager, old enough to hold a blade, stand over a cutting table, the boy was taught saddlery, enhancing his craft in a world Doc saw as a new generation of enterprise, even ecommerce. Not only in traditional western places, like Montana and Arizona, was there a need for more saddles, but in much smaller towns and online, too. Few people knew saddlery better than Doc, and in the autumn of '83, young Ringo became his faithful apprentice. Doc was Ringo's hero, too, stubborn, and defiant as a mule.

Some years later, after Ringo's injuries healed, he photographed saddles in America and Canada, taking notes of popular styles and what people were buying and why they bought them. Doc hoped to connect with customers beyond El Paso and tap into the Kentucky Derby market, and branding in geographical oddities, especially in Carolina. However, his memory was locked on the famous Teddy Roosevelt saddle, so much so the saddle became an obsession, far more than in a ghostly dream.

***

After Ringo's "roaming mother," a worldly lady, who dated Doc for less than a month in the summer of '82, was impressed by his good character, she skipped town. Pocketed three hundred dollars in her tight blue jeans from Doc's wallet, and Pomona Bare drove to Corpus Christi. Next, she landed on South Padre Island, and Doc imagined himself at work, lathering her with a tropical tanning lotion in South Texas. He deeply missed her.

Three months passed; Pomona didn't return to pick up Ringo as she promised. From one of his friends at Christmas time, Doc heard she'd made it to the shore of Galveston. Five Thanksgivings had passed; not even a birthday card reached Doc's mailbox, nor a phone call was made to Ringo. Dark days clouded Ringo's heart, who had no family at his side but the man he'd grown to admire, the only father he knew, Doc Greenway.

One day, Pomona showed up without notice, it was '87 or '88, and the bluebonnets were in bloom, so it must have been springtime in Texas.

"Hey Gilbert," said Pomona. "Have you been a good father to my son?"

"Well, if it isn't the wicked witch of Texas."

"Ringo, come here, my son."

In a rage to leave Doc again, Pomona rammed her fist at Ringo. "Get tough, Ringo, and with a bloody nose like that, it's a bitch at a bus stop, boy."

"Why'd you hit me?" cupping his face. "You broke my nose!"

She laughed and jumped into her convertible Cadillac, waving as she pulled away, Ringo said, "Mom, stay with us!"

"I love ya, Ringo and Doc. I'm uneasy, gotta go."

The boy stood and watched the car leave Clem Cline's ranch onto the highway, feeling his heart shattered again.

"What'd she give you, son?"

"Gold money clip and a coin."
"Keep it. I bet that's all you'll ever see from her."

Remembering what she wore, Doc glued the image of skinny blue jeans and a pink Dolly t-shirt, tied around her waist into his mind, even snapping a photograph. The boy stood with a hole in one pocket and a quarter in the other, holding an empty money clip in his palm, and the only part that shined on Ringo was a polished Rough Rider belt buckle, one Clem Cline had given him. Ringo had something he was proud of, for once. From that day forward, Ringo's fear wasn't bucking bulls or wild horses that broke him out of his sleep at night, indeed, it was more internal, the thought of abandonment took his breath and shook him to his core.

Fat tears of anger slowly rolled down his face, a sure sign of a broken heart, embedded in his memory bank, like branded cowhide. Another calendar year flipped over, and in 1985, Doc told him how she failed as a mother, with a phone booth on every street corner in Texas. No phone calls were made. Tears soaked into the overgrown pocket of Ringo's shirt, but he didn't ask about her beyond his sixteenth birthday, nor mention her name. He'd stopped mentioning her name during grace and especially didn't inquire about her on Mother's Day, either.

Without a second hesitation in his Creole heart, Doc lifted Ringo off the ground and onto horses and then bulls, seeing how rough and tough he was.

"She doesn't deserve you, Ringo. I'll take care of you and for sure, you're my son now!"

"You are my guardian saint, Doc."

The boy found abandonment to be as cold as a Texas ice storm and as lonely as a runner stranded at third base in the ninth inning of game seven of the World Series. Brokenhearted, the boy found a seat at Doc's table where he had vegetable soup and beef from Clem Cline's refrigerator and on starry nights, Ringo gazed through the pane glass living room window for weeks, cleaning it so he didn't have to see his own face. After Doc walked in the house about the time the boy reached deep in his pocket and flipped the quarter that landed in large hands, now driving, he said, in good spirit, "Look, Doc, it's heads, and finally a turn of good luck, right?"

"Heads!" called Doc, examining the coin. "That's right," roughing the boy's long blonde hair. "You're my good luck charm, Ringo," he admitted, while sitting at the table. Later, Doc spoke to the Lord aloud, "God, how am I going to take care of this kid, feed cattle and horses on the ranch, and handle my practice, and make sure this kid does well?"

"I ain't no kid!" Ringo wiped the dirt and mud from his face. "I can work better than ten of these old men."

Doc's sun-dried eyes glowed. After that day, if there was ever a big decision to be made, Ringo flipped a quarter, in hopes of "Heads." Doc educated the boy, teaching him about life on a ranch and how to fish from a boat, break a green horse while Clem Cline introduced him to bigger bulls. Much bigger.

Without much hesitation, Doc took Ringo under his wing, like he'd cut the umbilical cord himself with his pocket knife. The boy didn't live on the crutch of cruelty, nor dipped his heart into a pail of pity while he was by Doc's side. On the contrary, Ringo was made into a fine young man and admired by many young ladies in Bell County. After seeing the refined woman of Texas, Ringo couldn't believe why Doc dated his mother in the first place.

By the time Ringo was sixteen, he learned to drive, and the legend of a map became his friend, towns, and parishes of where Doc grew up in Southern Louisiana, he memorized. When Doc was out of town on business, sweet Samantha, only two years older than him, taught Ringo how to not only ride the trails and handle a pistol, but his manners at the dinner table had also improved before Doc said grace at the next meal. The cool lady made Ringo take an hour to eat a five-minute meal. They shot beer bottles and kicked rusty cans around Clem Cline's ranch, acted out parts in a Mark Twain novel and at other times felt like Samson and Delilah, and they kissed more than once. Because of his mother, he didn't trust women. At night, they dined on the balcony as they pretended to be on a date in Mexico, beaming at the orange sun dancing on the water of her parent's home on Belton Lake, just the two of them. They became good friends; good, close friends.

In Doc's spare time he told Ringo about the culture of New Orleans, a town with pretty ladies, horse carriages, and haunted hotels. He wanted to see it and dreamed about it, too. By the time Ringo was seventeen, Doc taught him how to cook a pot of gumbo. In the summer of '88, he won a few buckles riding bulls in Texas and Oklahoma and got his start.

"Incredible, boy, your jambalaya is as good as a Bourbon Street bowl."

"I hoped you'd like it."

Even though Doc spoke of parties and card games with his friends while he lived in the Big Easy, Ringo never saw him drunk. Not even when Ronald Regan left office. By the firepit and grill, with the flat clouds rolling in front of a blazing sky, being pushed away by the western wind, was where Ringo learned the difference between Creole and Cajun and how to play the saxophone and tap his foot, in time and rhythm.

By the spring of 1994, Ringo was a professional bull rider. Then Doc did what he said, and three years later, Doc officially declared his retirement. In some humble manner, he was comfortable in doing so, but it was said that he was the banker's favorite customer. Neighbors described Doc Greenway as a "good friend when you need one."

On the contrary, Doc's colleagues disapproved of his line of work, he could care less about opinions and told them to stop spending their hard-earned money on ink. Ringo was mystified about why he dabbled in tattoo removal and why he had a deep interest in saddlery, too?

"There's nothing more attractive to a woman than a man seated in a saddle atop a horse," explained Doc.

"We finally agree on something." Ringo tipped his cowboy hat.

"That's a cinema fact, Jack," uttered Doc, riding his Quarter Horse from the barn to the trail.

"Is that why you make saddles for ladies?" asked Ringo.

His teeth shone and the doctor nodded, keeping stout enough to make most Marines feel ashamed. People noticed that Doc never aged and kept his hair cut too short. On most days, Ringo didn't know whether or not he had any hair atop his head.

He'd made a great living in Central Texas, in an unusual way, but he loved what he did, felt it was time to see the countryside from the point of a saddle. At Doc's retirement party, they called him "Doctor Saddle" and he loved his nickname.

"Some people are just destined for fame." Ringo told him.

"The best people see their path and keep paving it," said Doc. The good doctor sat at his desk for the last time, flipping through bad tattoos, funny photographs he'd collected, and removed over the years, and sighed.

"Look at this one, I removed this tattoo last year." Doc handed the picture to Ringo. "This was inked around the leg in July 1945, 'Birds on a Highwire,' she called it," falling back laughing.

The eyes of Ringo bugged wide, laughing, "Looks like a flock of turkeys on the Texas highway." Ringo turned his head, hurting in the gut from his own comments.

"I just remove bad tattoos, keep my opinions to myself." He said with a bright face.

"You are a magician when it comes to card tricks, too." Ringo flipped through old photographs and the bull rider shuffled through a stack of old pictures, still laughing.

"Here's a soldier with an Army Rough Rider tattoo on his shoulder." Ringo showed him.

Doc grabbed it from Ringo's hand, "Hmmm, well, I remember this guy, had a bad ass tattoo of a Rough Rider on a horse, and the artwork was so great I refused to remove the tattoo, and the man kept it."

"Who were the Rough Riders?"

Saddles of Barringer

"Boy, haven't you learned anything from your education?" Doc asked, tugging on his bolo tie. "You'll find high schools in Baileysville and hockey teams in Cedar Rapids, named after Teddy Roosevelt's Rough Riders, it's a military story, and a good one, too."

"I'll look it up later on the internet."

"You might learn something from the Rough Riders," tapping his fist on Ringo's chest. "The Rough Riders will go down as Army legends. Listen, they were the first Volunteer Cavalry, and all of the Rough Riders were volunteers."

Doc shuffled through hundreds of tattoos and photographs of clients he'd removed at his retirement party, which also happened to be a 50th birthday party.

"Look at her legs." Ringo touched the polaroid as if the picture was real. "Once a bright red rose, and now a wilted, dead flower in a rose garden with a green stem, dropping three weeping petals."

Doc pitched a photograph across the table. "Here's a picture of a ladybug inked in 1969. Wow! Twenty-eight years later, this woman has a red UFO on her thigh." His nose ran, laughing until he coughed and turned red.

"Let me guess, she wanted it removed before her class reunion, didn't she, Doc?"

"How'd you know?" tapping the table.

"I dated Tina, her granddaughter, and she wanted that UFO on her right leg until she found out it was a ladybug from Woodstock."

Gasping for air, Doc fell against the wall in amusement. Doc Greenway was a clever businessman. His offices were in

Temple and Waco, both located beside ABC stores and between a bar and two pubs, and one thing about Doc, he loved to laugh.

Years of making dark ink disappear from old, wrinkled skin added up and the more out of towners dropped in his Waco practice from North Carolina, the more he mentioned moving to his Uncle Kenneth's farm in Barringer. When he'd accumulated his goal in the bank, boxed up his laser for the last customer, and after removing a Navy dagger from a man who'd accepted Christ, the Sunday prior, then he was finished.

Doc considered a handful of possibilities, even declining the ownership of a minor league team in South Texas. The year before he retired, Doc interviewed for the role of college president in Kansas, a position he proudly turned down.

For decades, Doc collected a small percentage as a silent partnership from a thriving pecan farm in San Saba, the one Ringo worked at for several weeks, which was his grandfather's old family investment. Ironically, the place had 'driven him nuts' when his dividends dropped.

***

During the drive to New Orleans, Doc had time to think as he watched Ringo sleep off leaving Selena behind. The fight that gained him a busted lip and a black eye, was a clear sign of his rebellion to leave Texas.

Two weeks into his retirement, and two cups of coffee later, it hit him as the postman accidentally delivered a copy of *Million Dollar Magazine* to Doc's mailbox that he kept. Without lifting his head from the pages, Doc read it cover to cover, pacing around the porch, like he'd uncovered the Holy Grail and God spoke directly in his ear, soft and clear. He folded the booklet under his arm and immediately planned his next journey to Barringer, North Carolina.

By the end of the week, Doc hammered out a FOR SALE sign for his practice, the only real estate he had to his name were his offices in Central Texas. He bought new clothes, smooth shaved his face, for a new look and a new destination, along with a haircut and mustache trim, making himself satisfied, he was ready.

His days of removing undesirable ink from arms and ankles were behind him. Now a wanderlust and intrigued by biographies, he became jealous of men who traveled full time, and owned homes in a number of towns, thumbing through a thick roadmap, he planned his route. Stuffing his green duffle bag and covering his head, not with his normal cowboy hat, but with the finest Big Bailey fedora he could find. The Irish hat was a rare find in Waco, offering him a more traditional style, one of his ancestors.

After breakfast, silent as a government agent on a covert mission, Doc left a dusty trail behind, turning his mind to his past, country roads and ranchers, he thought. To him, a picture of genuine solitude, far and away, pleased him and disturbed Ringo. However, Uncle Kenneth's farm meant something to Doc, part of his past, and to him, the grass was greener on the other side, and he expected it to be that way in Carolina.

At a truckstop on Interstate 10, Ringo swung open the motorhome door and Doc's big hands caught it, not knowing what was on his mind, the bull rider asked, "Where have you been?"

"Buying you a bacon sandwich and some soda inside the truck stop."

"What are we doing in Beaumont?"

Ringo had known Doc Greenway long enough to understand his silence, like when he took off to Kruger National Park, South Africa for the summer, and the time before that when he camped on Ruby River, Montana for ten days, to find himself. Doc loved to travel, most of the time it was away off the beaten path, to clear his head, naturally.

"Headed to New Orleans."

"The Big Easy, huh?" Tabling his ball cap, Ringo continued, "I'm just now beginning to like you as a father, anyway," turning at him. "Now Louisiana?"

"You better love me for what I'm about to do for us, sonny boy."

Ringo leaned on his elbow, waving, "What do you have planned and does this include yours truly?"

"Something big, I promise, and no, I'm not dying," taking a big deep breath. "I'm finally getting a chance to live beyond my work." Doc carried a big smile. "But if I do happen to die, I'll haunt your ass 'til you get my cowboy boots made for Father's Day, which was a month ago."

"How'd you know about the boots?"

Ringo scooped up the last bite of bacon on his plate.

"My horse told me."

Ringo followed him outside to hear the rest of his hidden agenda, and to see if it matched his own thoughts.

"Be serious for a minute and stop walking."

His father rested in the shade, stretching out his legs.

"Got something to talk about?"

"I notice you always look away when you hate to say something that you know I might disagree with." Ringo gulped his root beer float. "What then?"

Doc walked away. "I'll tell you later."

"Damn it, Doc, what good is it to have you run off and leave me!" Confused. Blood boiled inside of Ringo's flushed head and face.

For the next hour Doc avoided Ringo. Next, the bull rider hustled to the back of the motorhome, where he thumbed through the article Doc had dog-eared, and left on the bed.

"New Orleans Millionaire Buys Estate in Barringer," said Ringo, moaning. "Bingo!"

He glanced at the good doctor to see his reaction. Their eyes caught in a certain stalemate like two opponents in the boxing ring or two big bucks ready to lock horns in the Devil's Backbone of Texas. Folding the paper in his hand, Ringo commented, "You've been acting a little weird lately."

"What do you mean, Ringo?" Tabling his fork beside his soda, "A man of knowledge needs exploration, and you must not be afraid of geography. A new adventure and a new town might wake you up, slap you in the face about your talent."

Gripping his saxophone, "Your gambling gets you in a whole lot of trouble, from town to town."

"Gambling?" Doc's head turned. "Cards, you mean?"

"You play poker in your sleep, old man."

"Okay. We are going to New Orleans to gamble, and take a break, so there you have it."

"I'll stay on Bourbon Street and you gamble your damn retirement away!" blocking his path to the back of the motorhome. "I said, I'd move to Barringer and that was our deal and now you are taking us out of route to Louisiana, to lose it all."

"I didn't want to leave Clem Cline, and now that he's a widower and an old man, there's something I need to do."

"What's the big something?" The bull rider leaned against the sink.

"I need to find a nice lady friend and settle down."

"That's bull crap and you know it! You'll never settle down. You're too damn stubborn, full of pride and selfishness. Mom left because you wouldn't marry her, right?"

"That's my business!" Doc snapped back.

"Who's the lady in New Awlins then?" Pacing around the small kitchen, Ringo's neck turned warm and red, like when a bull threw him.

Taking a seat, Doc canted his head slowly toward his son, like he had just finished one of his tattoo removals where the patient was in pain. Without thinking, Doc bolted and charged. Then Ringo's reaction made him counter his feet and Doc fell, hitting the floor like he found his bed, watching dust cloud the backroom, Doc's head bumped the door and the article about Showman Wagoner landed on his back.

Ringo checked on him and left him face down for a few minutes until he was able to clarify his thoughts and re-evaluate his absurd idea to gamble his money away in New Orleans. In some strange and unusual fashion, Ringo was curious to know after all these years why he wanted to go home. With some familiar labor to his back and legs, Doc worked himself up with the help of the doorframe, returning to his favorite kitchen chair.

"A half-nude beach in Gulf Shores would suit my experience just fine," said Doc, unfolding the magazine.

"If we make it past the Big Easy," snapped Ringo, who had slipped into the driver's seat, headed to New Orleans in the motorhome.

Failing to show Ringo the article in the magazine or elaborate, covering his real purpose for the move, Doc tucked the paper in his rear pocket, and as fast as he could, Ringo snatched it from him.

"I looked up my mother's information online in Lawton, Oklahoma, she wants to see me." Ringo nodded for confirmation.

"Ringo, she drove right by Temple when she moved from Texas to Oklahoma, Son! Interstate 35 goes right by our exit. Do you think she thought of us when she drove through our town?" Doc scoffed, taking the driver's seat, and clicking his belt. "She probably stopped at Clem Cline's restaurant, had dinner, and the woman didn't even call us."

"She told me, she wanted to stop."

"She did? Ha-Ha-Ha!"

"But she was afraid you'd run her off again."

"She wouldn't tell the truth inside a church." Doc rubbed his head. "Pomona must be low on money, if she wants to talk to you."

"I'll never see her now since we're movin' to Barringer."

Ringo sighed and fell back.

"Do whatever the hell you want to do, but I'm rolling to New Awlins. Then Barringer." With a deep breath, Doc wadded up the newspaper, threw it against the windshield.

"Don't you think I have a right to see her?" Ringo shouted. The young man turned his head toward Doc.

"Hell yeah, you have the right, just don't give her the privilege of seeing you. I'm sure she saw you on television when you took that big spill with War Wagon."

"I'm sure she did."

"Damn it! She never even called you. Pomona knew you made it big, even world famous, and it would have been easy for her to watch you ride in Oklahoma City." Doc slapped his hands.

"You gave me everything, Doc, but it might be time for me to get out on my own."

"Don't you forget who cared enough about you to take you in when she left your butt on my doorstep and stole my money to stay at the beach house, shacking up with some sailor."

"You are right. She took off with a man she barely knew." Ringo agreed, musing at him. "The shirt on my back you bought. Trucks, horses, saddles and everything else, you bought 'em. I have pulled my weight, though."

Doc slapped his shoulder, "I remember the circuit."

"My circuit days are over, Paw." Ringo laughed.

"And I never ask you for a penny because I love ya, Son. Plain and simple. Love is a rare thing, and I don't give it freely."

"Love is a cold damn word. If it's not sincere and often, it's the coldest feeling to have, especially not knowing."

Nonetheless with a handshake as the bond that sealed the deal, Ringo was destined to head to the East Coast with Doc. The bull rider felt uneasy and unsettled. He asked Doc a number of questions about Barringer, having traveled on the circuit, he'd heard good things about the town, but would not admit it to Doc. Deep down, Ringo wanted to see the town for himself, plant his boots in the clay soil of North Carolina.

"We'll stop for fuel soon, if a lady in distress stops us, then that's a sign to stay in New Orleans, huh," said Doc, jokingly. "Take a gamble and nothing will be a signal, okay?"

"Don't you mean a smoking hot lady in a short dress?" Ringo grinned while moving in the passenger's seat. "If she drops her sunglasses, twisting and bending her legs in stilettos, like she needs to be in a New York City play, we'll turn and go back to Texas?"

"You know me too well."

"It looks like lady luck is waiting for us in Nawlins."

While Doc drove, Ringo practiced playing the saxophone in the back of the motorhome, and the music didn't bother the good doctor because he was rather good with the style of jazz his father grew up listening to in the Big Easy. The entire trip Doc talked about playing cards and finding a good game downtown. He was addicted. Ringo knew he couldn't leave a bad habit behind in Texas and start anew.

With a pocket full of cash, Ringo observed his father. He asked rubbing his chin. "Where the heck are we going, anyway?"

"Downtown Orleans."

"Is this about an old girlfriend?"

"I need to see a few people. How about I drive you around my hometown?"

"I want to see your hangouts and hear a few stories."

"Only a mile from downtown, you'll find my black and gray house, it's a shack of a place, I bet?" Doc held the steering wheel in anticipation. "In the 1960's, the home barely had heat, and when the wind blew from the south, we had fresh air through the curtains."

"They look like boarding houses in a magazine, though."

"It seems that way, doesn't it?"

"Your parents died, didn't they?"

"Yeah. Mama is gone to heaven and daddy isn't with her. I have two brothers and one sister. My baby brother is still in town, hanging around."

Casing his saxophone, Ringo occupied the passenger's seat again as he made his way close to the historic city, which towered in the distance on that particular evening.

"You never mentioned you had siblings."

"Frank, he's retired from the Navy. Well, Chuck, he'll be drunk somewhere in town if I can find him?"

"Your sister?"

"I lost track of her when I joined the military. Then I went to Tulane University, I didn't see her again. I think she lives in Sturgis, South Dakota. To her, I was the bossy brother she didn't like to answer to on weekends. But she liked Chuck better than Frank and she liked me the least of all, I guess."

"I don't have any sisters or brothers that I know of."

"I'm the oldest, Frank, Le Joie and little baby Chuck."

"What does Le Joie mean?"

"I called her Le Joie as a kid. To me, it means the joy of Sunshine. She was unforgettable and beautiful, too," replied Doc, rolling down the window.

"Sounds French."

"Her real name is Melody."

"That's musical and sweet."

"I have a picture of my sister in my wallet from high school."

Doc lifted his hip to remove his wallet, pulling out a thick leather trifold, untucking a creased photograph of a young lady.

"Blonde hair, dark brown eyes, hey, I might keep this photo. Melody is hot, Doc." Ringo teased, dropping the photograph into his shirt pocket.

"She was in the military ten years ago. I lost track of her again after Sheppard Air Force kept her overseas. In 1988, Frank mentioned her in a Christmas card, saying she finally moved to her favorite city in South Dakota."

"What else do you have planned on this wild adventure?"

"That would spoil my surprise, now wouldn't it?" Doc turned and tilted his Big Bailey fedora, like a proud Creole. "It's a damn good secret, though." He pointed at the next exit. "I'll let you know. Ringo, it's like Creole cooking, you don't know what's in the pot, but it still tastes good, doesn't it?"

Ringo belted out a laugh in a Southern Louisiana accent, a better-known Cajun language, just to piss Doc off, of course. To Doc, there was nothing worse.

"Why don't you share what we are doing in New Orleans?"

Rolling up the map, Doc fanned his face and plucked his shirt when the motorhome got too hot.

"I'll let you know and then you'll be filled with knowledge. How about that much for a guy who can tack saddles on weekends and remove tattoos for a living?"

"I can read a map, too." Ringo grabbed the large book, flipping through the marked pages until he found Doc's white napkin. "New Orleans and Barringer, the two addresses I need if you get knocked out or lose your mind."

"That's where we're headed, and I have friends to see along the way."

"Make sure you introduce me, will ya? You have some strange friends and I need to approve of them before I let you hang around them for exceptionally long."

"You mean because they have tattoos?"

"No. But strange friends deal in other things. Like that awful "Who dat say dey goin' beat the Saints," you told me about it last year."

"That doesn't make them strange. It's a working man's saying in Nawlins. Plus, they'll have the spot covered up with a new picture at the end of a losing season, anyway. Then they buy another tattoo, even bigger and more expensive, right before the season opener."

"I'll have to drive just to watch your money and..." taking a deep breath, "so they don't rob you blind."

"As long as they don't steal my Fedora and my Barringer map, I'll let 'em live." Brushing his hat, Doc rolled his fingers off the brim and down his nose.

"They don't need your hat, folks in New Orleans have good taste."

"They have good taste for cherry moonshine and shrimp gumbo."

Rubbing his belly, "I've been hungry since Baton Rouge and starvin' like Marvin. Let's eat, alright?"

"I don't understand how you eat like a grizzly bear and still stay in *somewhat* decent shape, Bull Rider."

"Just a few weeks ago, you said I was fat."

"You lost weight when you were working on that dang pecan farm. I could've told you; pecan farms are hard work. For me, it's the second toughest job I know."

"I'm afraid to ask, what's the toughest?"

"The only job tougher, mining West Virginia coal."

"Bull riders are pretty tough, too."

"Yeah, boy, it sure looks tough signing autographs and kissing babies for a living."

Pushing his mustache down to his goatee, "I sure did kiss a few baby dolls when I rode the circuit and snapped a few photos to prove it. Some of them had tattoos, and boy, don't I miss the circuit, too."

7

BEYOND THE BAYOU

The Township of Barringer was a small community of three thousand skilled craftsmen, educators, good businesses, and a booming factory or two. Since Kenneth Greenway passed away, the town was without a good saddlery shop. Imagining a peaceful place where leather was still plentiful, Doc told Ringo how two more laboring hands could blend right into the workforce. They looked forward to adding BEST SADDLE MAKER IN THE WORLD to the classified section of the *Statesville Record & Landmark Newspaper*.

Dropping his cowboy hat to block the evening sun, Ringo said, "Everything's better with a bull rider in it."

"As they say in North Carolina, 'Well, bless your little Texan heart, Ringo,' and that's not always a compliment when you hear it for the first time in the Great South." Doc tugged his ear. "If you hear those words spoken into your naive ears, just nod and keep going, be a gentleman."

"It never is."

They laughed as they cruised across the streets of New Orleans, Doc's hat fell off his head as he hit the back of the driver's seat, swaying in amazement.

"Maybe I'll get famous by removing 'Bless your heart' tattoos from a tanned Carolina lady," said Doc, scanning the streets. "So, they can replace it with Saddles of Barringer."

Ringo turned to the pages until he reached the standout article on Showman Wagoner again, gripping his hand, he waited for the right moment. Later, at a fuel stop Ringo flipped through the magazine that impressed Doc enough to grab the booklet.

Clearing his throat and unfolding the booklet, he said, "Harley "Showman" Wagoner, Barringer's first multi-millionaire, moved from New Orleans to Barringer by the Water, a gated community for the elite. You have something against him, right?"

"Yeah. Heck, yeah, Showman is my long-time enemy." Flipping a toothpick in his teeth, Doc squinted his beady eyes, and added, "He followed me around for cards and beat me almost every game. I was victorious only once."

"He's your reason for moving to Barringer then?"

"The story goes, as roadways and the railway divided the resort area into a township, Troutman and Barium Springs, became a resort community in the late 1800s, and by the first war, Barringer Township had faded away, a small grid on a North Carolina map that has recently been brought back to life. You and I will grow with the town, making some money with saddles. In that town, we'll meet him again at the card table."

"I can't wait to see this rivalry," said Ringo, rubbing his hands together and grinning, "and meet this multi-millionaire."

"Barringer, well, they named Showman Wagoner as the Grand Marshall of the downtown parade. It sucks eggs that he has a damn key to the town. It's not like he made a moon landing or unearthed Noah's Ark on a mountain in Boone or something."

And Ringo wasn't sure why, at that point exactly how Showman made his big money, but the magazine printed that he was a high stakes real estate investor, who had acquired lakefront condominiums and handled "private consulting" deals.

"Gambling, it's how he paid his way through Tulane, I heard. Now Showman is buying up houses and warehouses on Eastway Drive in Barringer and rolling in the money."

Thumbing the dog-eared pages, Ringo grinned. "This booklet printed how Showman Wag-O-Ner is the top runner for "Man of the Year" in North Carolina."

"He probably owns the magazine," gripping the shifter until his fingers turned white, Doc was envious. "Don't believe everything you read until you know who printed the pages, got it?"

Ringo regarded Doc as inscrutable.

8

From the Big Easy to Sweet Carolina

Interstate 10 rolled past Louis Armstrong Airport to the left, Ringo admired the landscape of legendary New Orleans for the first time. Jazz music played on the radio, tapping his foot to the upright bass, thumping the speakers and the sounds of a soft sax hummed over the airwaves, he was in heaven. Ladies huddled around a large oak tree on the campus of Tulane University, toting backpacks, and coffee in hand, causing Ringo to take a deep breath, perhaps a bit of jealousy ran through his veins because it was August, and classes were in session. The historic city had been a vivid picture in Ringo's mind, now under his feet until then, leaning forward to see the Big Easy, he was impressed.

His bum foot limited his travels and crushed his confidence, but Ringo didn't want to hobble to class like a wounded horse, one that needed a farrier and a new set of shoes. On the other hand, the Big Easy was one place he wanted to socialize, sample food, and have a good beer. For him, college was postponed, a faraway dream that had passed, the bull rider told Doc.

Parking lots were full of cars at French cooking schools and loud music played, shopping centers were lined with minivans, and to the right stood tall buildings on both sides of the highway. Loving it, Ringo soaked up the city. Much like

Austin and San Antonio, he witnessed a glowing skyline, stretched across a blue backdrop, like the eclectic light painted by Picasso or an illuminated print by Bob Ross.

To his right flowed the Mighty Mississippi River, Ringo mused the river barges, watching the wheel of the red and white steamboat chug along the waterway, and endless lines of traffic stopped on famed streets of New Orleans, a city he'd only read about in novels and pinned on maps.

Before he could examine the turn of the river, they crossed a long, steel crescent bridge, arching over the Mississippi River, wide and muddy, a fascination that had come to life. The city was no longer in pictures and books, but in his line of sight, where Ringo felt alive in New Orleans, a cool vibe hit him to play 'When the Saints Go Marching In' on his saxophone while being stuck in traffic. Tourists strolled along the high banks of the river for a better view of the French Quarter, the majestic Jackson Square, and a church that towered above any he'd ever seen stood in the midst. The blue and pink skyline hung like a curtain in the backdrop, a sensational view to witness on his first night in town.

Doc got excited. "See the church touching the clouds?" leaning over for a better view. "I'm homeward bound and know where I'm at now."

"Your hometown is a beautiful place, Doc."

Dozens of times, Doc visited the lavish church and described the incredible paintings on the ceiling as he waved his hands, trying his best to describe the church, a majestic and spiritual place for him.

"That's Saint Louis Cathedral."

Saddles of Barringer

"Catholic?"

"To the bone!" said Doc, grinning. "Sure ain't Baptist or Lutheran, and The Presbytere Museum, it's to the right of the cathedral."

"I'd like to see them all."

"My goodness," said Doc, gripping the wheel with some anger. "It's hot in here!"

Slapping the dashboard, Doc pressed buttons and slid levers, moving as if operating a candy machine, and desperate to feel the coolness of fresh air on his face.

"Roll down the windows," said Ringo, taking off his shirt. "What's wrong with this dang air conditioner?" Ringo pulled his long hair over his ears, collecting sweat in his armpits and down his flanks.

"It's as hot in this motorhome as it is outside." Doc pressed buttons and yanked the lever again, hoping for a sudden burst of cool air. There was none to be had. "Ringo, I'll melt like a damn glacier, if we don't get some cool air soon."

"This sucks." Ringo fanned himself.

"This is the hottest part of Louisiana, too. There's a dozen red lights before we get to the Monteleone Hotel."

Doc could have worked on the space shuttle, but vehicles were not on his long list of desirable repairs. Within a short time, sweat beaded on his face, rolling down his back into the bend of the leather seat, and he was ringing wet under his fedora.

Handing him a container, Ringo extended his Army thermos, and nodded, "Here's a drink, old timer?"

"I can drive without water," Doc smirked. "From now on I drank water from Louisiana."

"I filled the thermos in the toilet in Lake Charles." Ringo reached out his arm again and laughed. "Might taste like home, just the same, take a snort."

"Good. Texas is in the rear-view mirror now. It's the Big Easy and then Sweet Carolina from here on out."

"No air conditioning," said Ringo, wiping his brow with an ice cube. "Good times never *felt so good* without good ole' air conditioning." Ringo adjusted his seat; he turned his body to the window, soaking up the view.

"Can I ask you something else?"

"You are going to have to speak louder, with the windows down and all these trucks rolling by us."

Ringo looked at Doc, leaning toward his captain's chair. "Why did we have to leave Texas, anyway?"

Stroking his hand over his smooth shaved face, adjusting his hand on the steering wheel, Doc replied, "Sometimes the Lord sends you into hardship and you don't know why you are there until you look back at the storm, he pulled you out of His goodness, didn't He? The Lord saved you from getting killed when you wrecked your truck and the bull was another story, right?"

"This move is for your jealousy or do you have a hot cup of coffee planned with a lady? You tell me?" Ringo yelled over the noisy traffic. "I can't figure you out."

"Isn't it always about coffee with a woman?" Doc coughed and laughed into his hand. "Now you can stop asking so many damn questions."

The young man leaned back in his seat and seemed as though what he said was the truth; good, they were getting somewhere.

"You could have told me that a month ago and I would have supported your "love story" more than handcrafted saddles in Carolina."

"It's the same reason you wanted to stay in Texas, a woman will make you do crazy things, Bull Rider."

Cupping his hands, Ringo's eyes and face agreed.

"What does she look like, Doc?"

"Who?"

"The woman you are chasing in Barringer?"

"I don't know her; we haven't met yet."

"What?"

"That's why we are moving to Barringer, the hope of a Sweet Carolina lady?"

Despite the sweat rolling down their cheeks from the heat that came with New Orleans, Ringo played the saxophone while Doc sang "Sweet Caroline" as red lights halted their journey, one by one, having fun, like father and son.

The young man turned to him, smiling, "You plan to make it big in saddlery and land a few dates, here and there, in Barringer?"

"Yeah." Adjusting his hips as if fire ants were crawling up his backside, Doc was uncomfortable. "You read the article, didn't you?" gazing at the road and then over at Ringo, back and forth, teeth shone.

"I read everything you did, three pages of crap about some rich man named Showman Wagoner, the man you envy and have chased for years ago, I bet? Did Showman steal your woman, too?"

"No. I plan to takedown Showman Wagoner in a cool hand of cards and win a considerable bank for myself. Retire and relax in Barringer, build a cabin on the water in Troutman, or live somewhere extravagant that would piss Showman off, even more."

"You're not good at cards, though."

Ringo's face turned a smile, stale red in color, dropping his sweaty arm over the side, smirking, and laughing.

"I can play." Doc mumbled.

"You will lose your ass; lose what little money we have with us."

"I can play enough to beat him."

"Hot damn!" Ringo leaned back, kicking his legs and grinning, "I will be flat, busted and dead broke again, standing on the doorstep of someone I don't know asking for a nibble of Carolina bread pudding."

"You will be what you stand up for."

Ringo put his hands together as if he were deep in prayer. "God, up in the big heaven, please help Doctor Greenway, who has lost his ever lovin' home and mind," he opened his eyes. "Lord, Doc's a certified poker player and "Pecan" nut, in my book. So, Big God bless his little New Awlins-Creole heart. Amen and amen."

"I don't like to lose, Ringo."

"You haven't been lucky twice in ten years. You can't live on luck, either. Doc Greenway taught me that a man can't live every day on luck. It's skills and talent that makes him who he is."

"Luck and hope are all I have now. Sometimes you have to believe you can ride a bull that's never been ridden." Doc covered his head with his hat, tipping his brim at Ringo. "You taught me that much, cowboy."

Making every effort to press down on the pedal of the motorhome inside city limits, arching his back with some aggression, his voice died in his throat for a few minutes, and he relaxed. Doc and Ringo gleamed at the city lights, taking in the sights and sounds of such traditional culture.

"Let's plan to win against Showman Wagoner, smartass, and I'll win big this time! I'll make that freakin' condom millionaire, a middle-class citizen, just like he used to be when we grew up together."

"It's a condominium millionaire," said Ringo, shaking his head. "Not condoms. It's way, way, way different."

"High risers and overcompensation," said Doc, laughing. "It's all the same."

Ringo drank ice water from his thermos and disliked every drop of it, telling Doc his plan was worse than swamp water and a dash of river mud, mixed with bourbon.

"Are you freaking' kidding me? We moved across the damn country to gamble against an old friend." Ringo adjusted his baseball cap. "Something you could have played on the internet or better yet, you could have lost your ass in Temple, down at Willie's 305 Truckstop, trading cards with a trucker passing through on his way to Laredo."

Doc scooted up tall in the driver's seat ignoring Ringo's comment. After a few songs on the radio, Doc told him about his lady in New Orleans and Ringo was ready to meet her.

"I got one more thing for you before the hotel," said Doc, scanning the nice cars in the city.

"What's next?" turning his face. "Removing a Bud and Sissy tattoo from a homeless guy's butt on Bourbon Street?"

"No way," said Doc, shaking his head. "I don't mess with Texas tattoos. I'll remove a Gilley tattoo, though."

"Who's Gilley again?" Ringo was lost.

"Anyway, I want to try a slice of famous Carolina peanut butter pie on Thanksgiving Day, during a football game."

Ringo held his throat and raised his voice, "Peanuts might kill me, if I eat enough of them."

"Hey, after you try the pie, I'll finish the rest of the dessert for you. Then bury your ass in a mason jar after the game is over." Doc flipped his hand. "Hello, Rodeo World, this is the last remains of Ringo Bare, may he rest in little peanut butter pieces." When Doc laughed, he nearly broke the windshield with his outburst.

"It ain't funny." Ringo chuckled and rolled the map. "Nuts are deadly."

"I've heard." The old man said sarcastically. "Your *peanuts* have terminally ended a few relationships for ya, stud."

"Well, 'Bless your little heart' for understanding a well-rounded young man's legume." Ringo spoke like an old lady

"But what about your love life, huh? You ain't no saint, are ya, Doc?"

***

Doc and Ringo became closer friends on the trip, telling stories, laughing, and even planning the next chapter, but the unknown was the worst part or was it poor planning that made Ringo nervous? Ringo seemed to be in favor of the trip and the idea of partnering in the saddlery business with Doc after they were confined for several hours in a recreational vehicle, which seemed to comfort him somewhat.

People were making money on every corner in New Orleans, from hotdog vendors to musicians singing country music alongside jazz bands, artists painted historic buildings, settled in the shade under wide oaks that hung like divine guardians over the tall fence at Jackson Square.

"Gator shows?" Doc asked. "Helicopter rides are a few more attractions in the Big Easy and it looks like we are in New Awlins for the night, sonny boy."

"Hey, I'm finally here." Ringo was amused. "I made it to the world famous French Quarter."

"Yep."

"Didn't you say you had a friend who gambles downtown?"

"Well, partner," tugging at his black hat, "he doesn't gamble much and if he's dead, that is, he won't be gambling at all. But if he's still living, he does manage to lose when he drinks."

"I bet you're buying him Absinthe, aren't you?"

"You need to join the C.I.A., Bull Rider."

Ringo placed his hand over his heart, "The government is for someone else, for I'm an honest man. I work on one thing at a time until it's finished."

"You might change your mind once a high-profile Duke lady hooks you on a secret C.I.A. mission with her."

"I'd rather eat peanuts and drink Bayou water than be a Blue Devil, though."

"You should be a comedian, work twenty minutes a week. Since that eight second bull riding thing didn't work out for ya."

"Or I could find a rodeo lady, who loves saddles and convince her that I'm the man for her?"

"That didn't work in your favor in Texas."

"Ladies love a man on horseback, though." Ringo was singing and turning the radio to a local station.

Eyeing the bull rider, Doc belted, "You probably picked your best career, and it wasn't being a country singer."

"I could make saddles and make love for a living?"

"You'll go broke, Romeo. Stick to saddlery, finish one thing at a time, please."

"We both need ladies."

"Speaking of family business?" said Doc, parking the motorhome. "Here's my brother's house or my old home."

"He needs to mow the grass." Opening the door, Ringo jumped out of the motorhome, stretching his legs. "Needs some paint, too. That's a giant dog and parrot cage in the window."

"But we're not staying long, even if my brother asks us to be his guests for the night, okay?"

"Thank God for that."

"Our hotel is a few miles from here."
"Good."

Chuck Greenway's house was empty. Down a brick alley and three blocks from Bourbon Street, Doc found a parking space for the motorhome behind a large row of buildings and unfolded big bills, stuffing the rest in a small Army shaving kit, where he tucked it in his secret place within the motorhome. He kept a few large bills for gambling and nightlife, that is, if the evening went well. He was at home in his old neighborhood and felt comfortable. They located a high-end hotel, talking about his brother being a drunken hellraiser disappointed Doc, but it was a reality and a vice. They caught a cab back to his brother's house a second time. Doc needed closure, a long list of bad memories plagued him once again, where he needed a resolution from his brother. One reason for the trip was to see his brother again. He had others, too.

"He's not here." They took turns knocking on the door of the grey and black house. Dogs barked inside the house when the door rattled and clapped from the many hits. "Hey, Chuck, you home?" Doc beamed his eyes through the grim and cloudy door; he once knew as a kid.

"That's a mean dog," said Ringo, looking through the glass. "Where do you think your brother would be after dark?"

Ringo hobbled behind Doc down the street as he extolled the beauty and history of the city where he grew up by foot, just to see if any of his old neighbours were around. Sadly, he didn't recognize anyone.

"I might know of his hang out." He wiped the sweat from his head. "He loves beer more than most people."

"Where's his hangout?"

"Let's go find him."

Recognizing the dark swinging doors from his Army days, Doc knew where his brother was hiding. On streets and narrow back alleys, box trucks made deliveries and business owners were spraying the dust and dirt off the sidewalk with a lemon scented fragrance, no less than a mile away. Larger businesses were lit up in pink, red, yellow, and blue lights, while some of the older establishments, still dark and dingy, operated the same as when he was a teenager. Crowded streets became common after dark, and especially on weekends. Now as pedestrians, Doc guided Ringo through the grandeur of the Big Easy.

"Does he know you're coming?"

"Nope." Stuffing his hands in his pockets, Doc kept on walking, unsettled, mixed emotions, and too many thoughts crossed his mind. "I don't call him. You want the truth, Ringo? We haven't spoken in years, he'll be surprised."

"You don't like Chuck, do you?" His father walked fast and by his silence, he must've realized what slumped shoulders meant.

"The Famous French is what I like to call it, where ladies like to show off their tattoos for a handful of beads. It's risky after dark, so let's not get separated."

"It would be a great memory, either way." Ringo hobbled into a weaving line of people. "I could get the feel of this place."

"Why Ringo Bare..." grabbing his shoulders, "from deep in the heart of Texas, we gotta get you a few necklace beads and some showtime, my boy, right?"

Stopping inside the doorway, "This store has gold, purple, silver, green and red beads. There's too many good choices."

"I'll buy Saints cups and throw in some beads for you."

"Make sure she's a "C" cup," pulling his shoulder close to him. "Or better, huh, Doc?"

Doc deepened his voice, covering his heart like the star of a western movie, "These are the times that try men's souls and fill a man's pockets with beads. Let our eyes be merciful on this journey." Laughing and causing him to become speechless, he totaled his purchase.

"You're going to get killed, flashing large bills around town, old man. Let's swing by the motorhome, catch a cab to where we are staying."

They made it to the hotel, a grand structure, not too far from the action of downtown New Orleans and the place was surrounded by several eateries and shops, overflowing with souvenirs and cultural items, rich traditions, and even voodoo shirts were on sale.

"I bought you a Marie Laveau shirt, pops."

"Luke, I am not your father," pushing the button on the elevator. "I don't have children, remember."

"When you get into trouble tonight, gambler," breathing heavily from dragging the luggage racks from the cab, "remember I'm not a member of the Greenway or the Cline family. I'm barely a friend and not even an official partner yet until we sell some saddles, Doctor Greenway."

When Doc brought up the man's father, his neck and cheeks flushed like he'd stood under a bucket of red paint.

"Son, remember we don't know who your father *really* is and since your mother likes to "hold hands" with soldiers and sailors, touching men from Temple to Tacoma, it's unpredictable."

Squinting his eyes, his words reminded him of a bull that pissed him off. "Hope you get a dead man's hand first draw, smartass!"

They stood in front of the room, Doc keyed the lock and dropped his card into Ringo's shirt pocket.

"I'll live forever young man as long as I have cards and good company." Doc held the door. "You just hang tight; you might learn something."

"You need an exorcist."

"Here's some money, Bull Rider, but I better keep the money." Doc flipped large bills into his hands. "Your room is through that part of the suite and please, for God's sake, don't disturb me or say, 'Who dat after midnight' when I bring up a lady to the room."

"Good one. Keep dreaming, Gilbert the Monk." Ringo popped his mouth and frowned. "Look at this room, I need some distance," closing the door behind him.

"And I'll need my privacy!" shouting and raising his eyebrows. Doc checked his profile in the mirror, kicking off his shoes for the television and remembered his days in the city as a young man. Then opened the door of his son. "We may be here a couple of days, so make yourself at home. Try to look sharp and cut that hair before it hits your shoulders. If you are lucky, I'll introduce you to a great friend of mine."

"A lady?"

"Of course."

"I want to meet your crazy brother, too."

"You might not like him." Doc kicked his feet up when he sat. "He's not friendly, a bit of an ass, at times."

"He must be a carbon copy of his older brother, Gilbert." Ringo chuckled, turning a curl on his lip, jumping in the shower.

Splashing on cologne, Doc combed his short hair with his hand and was glad to be home again. Ringo's foot was killing him from the trip and the miles they'd walked added to the pain. After a hot shower Ringo took a short nap, resting his foot and prepared to hobble the streets whenever Doc decided to stop primping.

9

Moonlight on Bourbon Street

Later, Doc spun around with a roundhouse kick and jumped reminiscently, elated to trek through his hometown again. They thumbed a cab to Jackson Square, pacing through the streets, like he was a young Creole late for a date on a redeye flight out of town, Doc looked sharp for his lady. On the other hand, Ringo carefully dodged people, lifting his head to see the sights of the Big Easy with his foot pain pounding and throbbing, he loosened his shoe on a bench.

"Slow down."

"I cannot go any slower," said Doc, who halted. "I'd be walking, now wouldn't I?" Waving his arms like a traffic cop, motioning Ringo to hurry along. "At your pace, grandpa Ringo. Should I get you a rickshaw and a room for retired bull riders?"

"I'll catch up. Never mind, speedy."

"I'll wait. Get that cool leg in gear, let's go…go…go, Bull Rider."

"I can't. My foot hurts too much to walk at your pace."

They found another bench to rest.

"War Wagon made his mark on you, didn't he? Sure slowed you to a crawl, crawl, crawl."

"Go on ahead, Doctor Greenway, that is," getting loud, "if you don't want to help your disabled bull rider friend across the street!" biting his lip and embarrassing him.

"I'll help you, cowboy," said a lady, hooking her arm with his arm. People booed Doc. Finally catching up with his old man at a street crossing, the bull rider added a cocky smile.

The voice of the lady was deep. "Anytime, cowboy. Take my number, and you call me, I'd get that leg stretched out for ya, New Orleans style. I'm a masseuse on weekends."

Doc waved and closed the distance to Ringo's shoulder, whispering, "You know that wasn't a lady, right?"

"Ladies have big hands and even some have voices that sound like bass singers, don't they?"

Laughing at the bull rider, he said, "Man, you and your manly lady friend could have won an Oscar, you know? You two could have an Off Broadway performance, and talk to each other man-to-man after the show."

Stopping at the red light on Canal and Conti Streets, Doc was still laughing and touring him around some of the places he'd been. "Let me give you a clue, Ringo, in New Orleans, giant hands and an Adam's apple are clear signs that you are being felt up by a man. I'm just saying, and don't think I'm being a "drag" when I say that, either."

"Yeah, yeah, yeah. Whatever!" Ringo pulled out the card. "Her-him-his-her first massage is free, though," wiping sweat from his forehead. "Just keep up with me, old man. My plan worked to get you to slow down, didn't it?"

"Don't let me "drag" you around this French town."

He belted out a laugh. Dodging people and handing dollars to bums, the gentlemen became popular with their generosity as well. Being scolded was a normal practice from police when Ringo stepped on the lush green grass. Right before they reached their destination Doc and Ringo were side-by-side, like father and son, friends even, and partners, too, gleaming at Canal Street.

"I was arrested at a bar on Canal Street in the early 70s. It was when I was on leave from the Army."

"No way!" shouted Ringo, looking at his face for a lie. "What for, Doc? Please elaborate on this story!"

"Drunk and disorderly charges and something else."

Belting out a laugh, Ringo howled at the thought of Gilbert Greenway strutting down Canal Street, sporting long hair and flapping his bell-bottom jeans and a dark comb in his back pocket.

"Tell me about it." scanning Doc's big smiling face.

Rearing his head back and biting his lip, Doc said, "I fought two men at one time. It was sort of a big fight."

"Did you win, Creole?"

"My friends said it was a tie, even though I had three too many beers and saw stars a few times from being cracked in the head with a sucker punch."

"What were you fighting about?"

"They didn't like two things I did." Doc chuckled and cracked his knuckles. "One was dating their sister and…"

Walking up beside his father, Ringo pulled him to a halt, and cleared his throat, humming, "And what was the second?" They stood on the street corner. "That is, if you don't mind me knowing some of your good stories?"

"It was unfortunate that their heads came into contact with the heel of my zip up boots after they caught me with their sister."

Hugging Doc's shoulder and laughing, the man could keep him amused. "You used to be a cool lady's man?"

"Used to be?" pushing his shoulder. "Like a bad windstorm hitting a pig farm, I made their tails curl up during the fight just like a tornado does in Texas. Then I kissed their sister again and we left together. Least I don't hold hands with a Drag Queen, named Betty Blue."

"You said there was something else, more than kissing their sister, I bet?"

"Oh, yeah," laughing and walking at the same time. "They saw me giving their sister a belly shot, which caused the big fight."

"What's a belly shot?"

The doctor's jaw dropped, thinking the bull rider may have been kidding him, and needed to get out of the barn more often.

"It's when the lady lays flat on her back, a shot of liquor is poured in her belly button and the man consumes the drink."

"You mean, they caught you resuscitating her navel?"

"Some people join the Mile High Club, but here," poking his shoulder, "in New Orleans, we have the Belly Shot Club. It's a long standing Creole tradition among tourists. And no, I'm not making this club up. It happens, and it's a true club."

A pale man walked up beside them and stopped.

"That clean-shaving man is telling you right, the BSC does exist. It's a real treat on Bourbon Street at exactly 2100 hours." Forming a fist, he winked, tsk. "It's called the Nine o'clock Naval Shot." He laughed, walking a few paces, and turned around, outstretching his arms, "Ha-Ha-Ha. I may even be the founding father," tipping his hat and kicking his heel. "But I'll never tell."

Ringo turned Doc around, faced him with a smile and leaned over laughing. "Yeah, but I'll never tell, either." A loud laugh escaped his body.

Aside from Doc's days as a drunken medical student at Tulane, he talked about his time driving a truck in Vietnam and hanging out with beautiful ladies he'd seen overseas. After bending Ringo's ear with amazing war stories, Doc edged him atop the banks of the Mississippi River for a better view, still muddy from northern rivers and streams. To Doc, it was the most pleasant view in the French Quarter, one he wished everyone had a chance to see.

Nearing Decatur and St. Peter Streets, the duo traveled to the apex of a long knoll that wrapped around the riverbank, the place where large steamboats and paddle-wheelers motored and docked. They saw passengers singing and dancing to jazz music, their voices echoed across the water as they passed by Washington Artillery Park, as people swayed to the sounds of a horn, Doc and Ringo loved pure jazz, the clear horn sounded, and then faded away into the distance.

Doc turned to Ringo. "That could be us in a couple hours, huh?" He asked. "Don't get your hopes up about the Belly Shot Club on a paddle-wheel. I'm not sure they let bull riders join the club, anyway."

"I was talking about a relaxing boat on the river."

The two men headed down the steps on the street that led to Doc's favorite place in New Orleans.

"Let's have some fun and mingle," said Doc, hugging him. "Don't get lost and keep up, Bull Rider."

With one last look, Ringo saw hundreds of dancing red, yellow, and green lights reflecting off the wavy water as boats were dots on the mighty river. Much different than the Brazos and San Saba Rivers that Doc had taken Ringo to as a kid.

Upstream a half mile, Doc pointed at the Crescent City Connection, spanning from Central City to Whitney and other places like Algiers and Harvey, the road they'd traveled into New Orleans on was heavy with traffic. After leaving Washington Artillery Park and Jackson Square, they strode down Decatur Street for food and to enjoy the talented musicians.

Ringo stood and looked around for the most famous street in the city, and asked, "Where's Bourbon Street? Are we lost?"

"Nope. Been here a thousand times."

"Well, prep your pipes and buy some beads. They're both a few blocks away."

Masterful at directions, Doc knew his city better than he knew himself, a human road map, and a bloodhound when it came to good dessert and jazz music, too.

"Good." Ringo stood under the shadows of the towering St. Louis Cathedral, humbled to be in such a place, he said, "Point the way, Doctor Greenway."

Adjusting his collar, Doc paced down Decatur Street, and turned around, in a serious voice, "I spotted an old friend, we'll talk awhile, then we'll hike to Bourbon Street, I swear, cowboy."

"Okay, but who are we chasing down now?"

Parting his thin hair with his hands and covering his head with his hat, Doc told him about a young, radiant brunette he was once crazy in love with, years ago. He knew where he could find her, too, as she ducked out of sight.

10

Café on Decatur Street

The duo strolled like searchers to Decatur Street, winding the smell of fried doughnuts, watching a hundred elated customers cover their lips in powder and chatting underneath a green and white canopy that wrapped around the block.

"Here's the famous beignet cafe, I've been keeping the place a secret since we left Texas."

"If you've eaten one doughnut, well…" said Ringo, touching his chin, "you've tasted them all, right?"

"My boy don't be judgmental before you taste the goods. God, Himself has graced you with this twilight evening and even Jesus would enjoy a handful of good beignets with us tonight, if He were here with us for communion." Doc nodded. "Just like all women are not created equally, food is different… much in the same way, my friend."

On that night, under the green and white canopy, Doc introduced Ringo's taste buds to the finest dessert known to man, a legendary establishment, deep in the heart of the French Quarter, cultured and well-rounded, they were comrades, working through their differences. Doc knew a few things well; one was food, of which he knew better than leather and cheap tattoos. Ringo figured the person he was about to meet was a fine looking woman, too, so he was eager to see the lady Doc loved for the first time, years ago.

Out of all the questions Doc had answered over the years for Ringo, one stumped the man, and he questioned him for clarification, "Why do you have a nickname for every lady you have dated?"

"Nicknames help a man remember the lady's real name, that is, if a man has a handful of females on the line, nicknames will help him remember the experience he had, along with her face and eyes and other parts."

"Ain't that the truth, Sir Romeo," a black man seated inside the dining area told Doc as they became friends.

"Right on, brother!" said Doc. They high fived. "So it keeps you from screwing up their real names."

"I think I know exactly what you mean."

"You are catching on fast, to the style of Nawlins," said Doc.

"One woman is enough for any man," said the stranger's girlfriend.

The black man looked at Doc and burst out, "Ha-Ha-Ha," catching his breath in the middle of their amusement.

Doc's voice sounded sincere, "I know Sandy from San Francisco, Maybelline from Mobile, and Fantastic Freda from Fredericksburg, and VV from Vicksburg."

The dark skinned man said, "Let me try?" waving his hand. "I had Bayou Betty and Tina from Tulsa and Mona from Montgomery, who's kinda sassy," laughing. "I nearly married Roxy from Biloxi, who had a nice ...Aston Martin."

The lady on his side slapped the daylight out of his head, grunted, and thumped him in the arm several times.

"Ouch! Stop! Wait!" he sounded. "Hey, that's enough, Lupe, you fruit Lupe. Stop it, woman!"

Doc and Ringo grabbed their chest and laughed.

"That must not be her," said Doc, sputtering his lips.

"You better stay out of this game, Gus." The lady told him in a stern voice, tugging the black man's ear, yanking him to a standing position. "Let's go! You messed up, Gus, get your tail on the bus and you talk too much."

"See how the idea takes hold of your ear, Ringo," Doc said, grinning. "Be thinking about your order, less about name-dropping. See, you got that man in trouble."

"Lupe," said Ringo, smiling, "she'll fix his trouble."

Ringo and Doc stood in line at 813 Decatur for a half hour spouting out nicknames of ladies, to pass the time and some they just made up, and others they'd known. The two of them watched the last moments of a fanning sky melt away into twilight. Their mouths watered watching customers sip hot coffee and load their cheeks full of beignets at Café du Monde. The wind swept through the air and into their nostrils, driving their hunger to an all-time high, stepping up to the glass window, Doc ordered for the both of them and flashed his cash again. Ringo chose his own hot coffee and spotted a seat.

"Put those large bills away." Ringo told him.

"I'm fine," covering his big hands over the bills. "Keep your coffee in the cup. That means, don't spill it on these fine people when you walk by narrow aisles to that open table near the street."

Ringo's mouth was dry from the wait. Both of their stomachs were growling, and the summer heat was making them sweat like dogs at feeding time. The boy hadn't had anything to eat, but a greasy ham and egg sandwich in Lake Charles, and some deep fried potato slices at a gas station somewhere after they'd crossed into the Big Easy. Nothing solid had touched their stomachs but water, by that time of the night.

"What is this dessert?"

"My good friend, it's rich and powdery," mused Doc proudly. "They call them beignets, my son."

"I need a second and a third plate."

"Take your time, Tex. Slow down, Bull Rider. You cleaned that plate in 8 seconds flat."

"You know, I wasn't born in Texas."

"The story goes, your mother moved from North Carolina to Louisiana when you started cutting your teeth so you could chew on crawfish and alligator meat as a toddler." Doc told him, chuckling with powder on his lips and face, too. "So, this trip is taking you home."

"To be honest, Doc," said Ringo, turning a sincere voice, "my mother told so many lies, I have no idea where I was born. Plus, the sad part, I have no one to call and double check her story with."

A short lady with dark hair pushed a second round of treats in their direction, the turquoise plate included six more treats, squared and powdered doughnuts, glowing white squares of goodness underneath Ringo's chin. She added a second coffee and two cold glasses of ice water. At least that's what Doc suggested while they were in line, Ringo was so thirsty he could have swallowed a pint of motor oil and chased it with a slice of crusted bread and a jar of tasty pickles.

Doc cleared his throat when the server looked down at him, adjusting her glasses, curling a friendly smile under his hat. The second server's skin was the color of soft mocha, her eyes were blue, and Doc thought she was a fine looking female.

A loud voice shouted from his right side, "Gilbert? Gilbert? Gilbert!" a thin lady, out of Doc's league ran in his direction. "Is that you?"

Rubbing his chin in a curious manner, Doc stood with endearment, arms wide open to accept her warmth, something he'd missed. Ringo stood beside him, smiling and big eyed at her beauty.

Shuffling his feet like a tap dancer in her view, Doc said,

"I'm still dancing and playing cards in the flesh." Two tables of people cheered him on, taking a quick bow for his arrangement of steps and mobility, Doc was proud.

"Honey!" The lady shouted, "It's so good to see your sexy smile in New Orleans. It's been too long, Gilbert Greenway. I stopped looking for you two years ago."

"She must be a blind friend," said Ringo, licking the white powder from his fingers.

Doc had fast feet and he kept himself busy enough to stay lean and mean, changing little in a decade.

"Who's this good looking young man beside you?" The eager lady hugged and kissed Doc first, then Ringo found he was surprisingly next in line, by association.

"No. She has perfect vision," said Ringo, reaching to greet her with a big hug and kiss himself.

Doc proudly gripped Ringo's shoulder.

"Let me introduce you to Ringo Bare from downtown Temple, Texas. He's the best guy I know. Indeed, I'm proud of him, and more importantly, he's my son."

"Hey, young man, I'm Mary "Moonlight" Daffin," kissing Ringo's cheek, adding an outline from her rosy painted lips. "To me, you look like a young Doctor Gilbert Greenway, Ringo."

"I hope that's a compliment."

"My Gilbert was handsome thirty years ago; he's still a sexy stud today in his fifties."

"I'm just five-zero, doll. No more."

Both Mary and Doc leaned back in their chairs laughing and catching their breath, still a bit in love; good for them both. Ringo watched Doc endure a dozen kisses and hugs, like newlyweds on a honeymoon in the Bayou.

"I can't believe you're here, kissing me."

Doc interrupted her, "Ringo, Mary and I met in 1978 while I was in med school at Tulane."

"It wasn't 1978. The first time we were together was in 1968, and Gilbert held my heart in his hand from across the room." She pushed him, kissing his lips, turning Doc red as a beet in a mason jar. "We were making love when the headline news reported Robert Kennedy was assassinated. You said, 'I'll never forget making love to you, Mary' and you sure forgot your first lover, didn't ya, Gilbert?"

"That's right." Doc held her hand. "I have an empty stomach and my sugar might be low tonight, I guess."

"I'm your Sugar Baby now."

"Lively lady, unchanged and unattached," Doc whispered to Ringo. The cowboy was amused with what he saw, moving his eyes about the voluptuous woman from the south.

"I do remember that night. We saw each other again in the 70s, though, when I was playing in a band one summer. I was in the Army Reserve, I believe. That counts, doesn't it?"

"Nope. Making love three times in thirty years doesn't count any more than walking on the moon with Michael Jackson." She folded her arms, pressing her big lips together.

"He will do better tonight, Mary," said Ringo, being sarcastic. "Won't you, Doctor Loverboy?" winking at him and chewing a mouthful of food.

Covering her laugh and picking up where she left off, reaching under the table, and tugging at Doc's shirt, who became bug eyed drinking his coffee cup in one hand and feeding himself beignets with the other. After three beignets, smeared lipstick and some embarrassment, Doc never stopped smiling.

"Come to think of it," said Doc, "I still have your picture in my wallet and a piece of your heart in my heart."

"I'm free after my shift ends at nine o' clock, if you have time for a Bourbon Belly Shot, Doc?"

"Mary, you were on the market when we first met and you are still available, why?"

Mary wrapped her hands around Doc's head and sighed. "Lucky for you, huh? I've missed you, baby." Her lipstick stuck to Doc Greenway's face in three separate places before he stopped her.

Calming his smart mouth down, Doc relaxed after he visited with Moonlight Mary, downing his dark coffee, and swallowing a third plate of beignets. Mary spoke of their misadventures and years of partying together on Bourbon Street. Ringo soaked up the lady's love stories as if he was on jury duty, taking mental notes, building up a case to tease Doc later, watching the lady's hand disappear underneath the table again atop of Doc's hand. Ringo was amused by the stories he'd heard for the first time and wasn't surprised, either.

While the last drops of brown coffee rolled around in Doc's white coffee cup, they spoke of their younger and better days, even retelling a few stories. With tears in her eyes, Mary hugged them both and returned as the kitchen manager. The lady had bright pale skin and a slender figure with sandy brown hair, friendly as a new puppy at a birthday party, dismissing all judgments after Ringo had a chance to know her better.

Taking a drink of water, Doc cleared his throat, "She can drink whiskey sour, shoot pool, and ride a bicycle to Bogalusa all at the same time. She's an awesome lady."

In all seriousness, Doc squinted his eyes when he told Ringo, drinking more and more water as he spoke. The evening was so hot the ice melted in less than twenty minutes. Ringo held the glass against his forehead to cool his flesh and became content with being in New Orleans with Doc. He told Doc how he was having a blast.

Ringo slapped his knee and turned to catch air for his lungs. "She's a beautiful lady, Doc; You gotta marry her, right now."

"She can fight like a tomcat on crack," pushing his empty coffee cup to the center of the table.

"Why not marry, Mary?"

"Do you want more beignets?" Doc asked the young man and avoided his question as if he hadn't heard a word of the conversation.

"Nope." Ringo shook his head. "I'm full and busting my pants open now from the best dessert I have ever had. Thanks, Doc."

"We will do this again soon."

Ol' Doc lightened up after "Moonlight Mary" saw him, the beginning of the Big Easy romance had revived his spirit when she waved at him from across the room. He didn't say if he would meet her after work or not. Ringo listened to more of Doc's NOLA stories and carried on laughing as Doc recalled his days in his hometown. Mary left to care for her teenage daughter. Doc spoke about North Carolina and all the opportunities he planned to nab when he pulled into Barringer. He counted his winnings at the card table, missing his horses and the ranch back in Texas, the one he didn't know if he would ever see again. After coffee and dessert, they walked at a steady pace that both of them could handle, side-by-side.

"You could have driven to Waco for a good card game or flown to Carolina and lost your money all in a week's time?"

Doc adjusted his hat. "This is a life changer for you, Ringo. I can't describe your future if you don't give yourself a chance to live in the moment you've made for yourself."

"I'm not sure if it is for me, though."

Ringo turned in disagreement with Doc's ideology as his cheeks brightened in having to deal with uncertainty, rubbing his face and talking about his new experiences and what could be expected on the other side of the country.

"This trip will make you better." Doc told him as they stopped at a corner pharmacy for a soda and to cool off with cold air conditioning blowing into the street.

"I'm still young and look forward to seeing Barringer."

"All great men need to be pushed into the unknown just to see if they can stand or fall under pressure. I'm a predictable guy," said Doc as he looked around the city. "I eat the same meals each week and serve myself my favorite drinks, too."

"Bread, brisket, and beans," said Ringo, echoing his answer between buildings. "And your last favorite dish is sliced tomatoes, with salt and pepper, covered in red onions on wheat bread. You may need to broaden your diet and have a cold beer once in a while."

"Bread, brisket, beans, and tomatoes; that's all I need."

"At your age, it wouldn't hurt you to sample some port before you're fifty-one and relax."

"I stopped getting drunk a long time ago."

"Like every doctor, you need to follow a good regiment, right?"

Doc tipped his hat to the ladies walking by him on the sidewalk, who carried strong drinks and tugged at their beads with a friendly smile.

"All women are different and special," said Doc, surveying the crowd. "Some black. Some white. Some with accents from other parts of the world, like Germany, Japan, and Mexico. All women are wonderful, and if we will just listen to them, we'll make ourselves better men, for doing so."

"New Orleans has a wide selection."

"You just need to find a good lady and keep her." Doc waved at a nice looking lady dressed in cut-off jeans and a red, white, and blue shirt. "Life moves constantly; you have to be flexible."

Ringo gleamed inside a rock and roll bar, where sorority sisters were dancing and having fun, which may have been part of that constant movement Doc spoke about as they observed their mobility.

"You mean, like the sweet ladies dancing?"

Doc's eyes bugged wide, and his head tilted. "That red head has some range, doesn't she?"

"She's smooth."

"Risk makes you proud and you'll have regret in most of the things you do." Doc sipped his tea, bought chocolate pies at the pharmacy, and had one while they walked.

"You're going to lose your money at a card game and I'm going to be caught in the middle without a saddlery shop. That is my worry on this risky trip, not yours."

Doc whispered, "Are you some fortune teller in training? Can you predict my days now?"

"No. Just leave me out of your dreams and misery, Doc, how about that?"

"Your trashy mother left you and I'm all you got, Ringo Bare. The best and worst person in your life, well, it's me."

"I have a mother, she's traveling now."

"She's a whore and a night owl, if that makes it more politically correct for ya, cowboy?"

"She'll be back when she gets ready."

"She's not coming back!" yelled Doc. "I don't want to tell you that she won't be home soon, but most women of her *nature* keep going and going, and in the end, hate themselves for going from man to man. They've emptied their heart, little by little, and become callus to real love."

The young man's head dropped, and he didn't understand why she'd left him when he was twelve.

"God forbid that she's settled down with a good man," said Doc. "But some women spend too much of their life trying to find money and pass up peace and understanding for partying and chasing a good time."

"Maybe my mother would like to start over?"

They stopped at the corner of Bourbon Street and Saint Ann Street to rest Ringo's throbbing foot.

"Son, her *kind* starts over every weekend. Some people can party and live for the party, but they never fill the empty hole in their heart; she's one of them."

Doc and Ringo finally understood each other as they walked and talked, and Ringo heard what Doc had on his mind. Though, not always in agreement, while touring the French Quarter, but communicating more than they ever did in Texas. Talking about life, and regrets and the hope of walking the right road in life, wondering about 'what ifs and maybes and forked roads' that lead them to where they were that night, "living out a midlife crisis." That's what Ringo told him, followed with a respectful nod.

"Bull riders have the same emptiness of being unsatisfied," said Doc, stuffing his hands in his pockets. "Being a good bull rider, it's chasing a dream and you might get busted up for being the best, but you did it with pride and courage, didn't ya?"

"Yeah. I had big plans and I ruined it."

"There's an emptiness in some women that can't be filled with love or with the best bottle of Andy Oliver wine. And there's a winding path in a man's heart just the same, he chases dream after dream, too. But if a man's not careful, he'll give up too soon, wasting his life, a sad life of regret, too."

"I'm not sure of my purpose or my big dream," nodded Ringo. "But I'll give Barringer a try, I guess."

Doc stood at the corner wondering what direction to go and what advice to offer him, something that might give him some confidence, and prepare him for North Carolina.

"Most of all," said Doc, staring at Ringo, "make sure your dreams have morals and your journey exhibits, not just character, but your best character."

They walked inside a restaurant that had good music, tapping his leg, Ringo realized something. "So, are dreamers wasting their time?" Ringo turned to Doc, letting his lungs release a long sigh.

"The majority of the time, it's because of jealousy or stature, or love, or money, Ringo. Dreaming is the best hope a man can have, and dreams change like the weather."

They watched the band practice.

"And then a man makes one small compromise and gets far off track for some temporary satisfaction. Some people make a game out of life, until they get what they want and figure out it was a horrible risk. Lots of people get hurt in a bad game of selfishness."

With a serious face, Ringo asked, "Dreaming is a lot like gambling, I bet?"

"Yeah, winning makes you feel like a champion, but most of the time people end up chasing dreams and compromising decisions, and some are harmful. They settle for a hint of the wrong type of satisfaction, living a life of emotional regret, and yet it's having your mind made up long before a compromise comes, and that's what counts."

Ringo folded his fingers and popped his knuckles.

"They settle and compromise."

"Damn it, boy, you need a prime time television show where people can call in, clear their conscience with Ringo Bare, the All-American Bull Rider."

After talking for a while Ringo's eyes started to blink and his head bobbed in exhaustion, checking his watch, Doc was tired and needed more water.

"It's been a long day."

Ringo followed his father.

"Are you going to stay the night with Mary?"

"She's working overtime, and yeah, I'll say goodbye to my lady. Hey, Ringo, trade me wallets."

With a confused face, Ringo handed him his wallet and they traded. "Why?"

"You'll see why soon. Let's meet on the southside of the church, say midnight?"

"Near the garden?"

"Yeah, see you in thirty minutes."

Ringo walked back the way he came to the cathedral, lifting his head to the grandeur of the structure as he decided to make his way around the church. The darkened skyline was enough to see down the dark, shadowy alleyways, too. At midnight, the sounds of a man playing the saxophone on the sidewalk made him stop in admiration, listening in the "City that never sleeps," was what Doc told him on the road trip.

The bull rider did as Doc said and listened to the pipes when he had the chance, loud and alluring, and then headed to the church to meet him. Walking by a black metal bench that held a homeless man, Ringo placed $20 in his hand and another man attacked him while he slept. Ringo defended the man on the bench, and not forty foot away nodded a talented man who played the saxophone. Ringo broke them up, and the man never missed a beat on his instrument. The bull rider turned to find Doc kissing Mary behind the church garden on Royal Street, and Ringo was hopeful for the couple.

Mary slowly released his hand, looking back to see if he was watching her walk away and she yelled, "I love you, Gilbert." Her sharp voice echoed off the tall buildings, wiping her tears.

"I love you more, Mary," cupping his hands as his deep voice emptied his lungs, a tear rolled down his cheek, too. "I always have, Mary," whispering in a low, broken voice, lifting his heart to his throat.

Walking up behind Doc, Ringo watched the sweetest lady he'd seen in a long while step inside her home and cried over Doc Greenway.

"How come you and her never got...?"

Doc interrupted him. "Don't you say it!"

"I mean, marry "Moonlight" Mary." Ringo chuckled and pulled Doc in close with his hand. "Love her and marry her. Like you haven't thought about it, right?"

"I was poor as dirt growing up and she was filthy rich, driving a sports car, owning vacation homes, you name it and she had it going on in her younger days."

Walking together down Orleans Street, "What does that have to do with love, right here, right now, tonight?" Ringo stopped in the street. "You need to get past this pride thing, make a comeback, Doc."

"To be honest, I wasn't wealthy enough for her when we were younger, she wouldn't have me, and that's the plain and simple truth. It was sad how she judged me, how I lived in my hardship, right down the street from her mansion, too. We can't help who we're born to, but we can swear to do better when we have the chance to make a difference."

"Mary said that to you?"

"She said to call her if I ever reached her level of wealth."

"Look at you, retired, sold our horses for a stack of cash, you're a doctor, and you'll buy that land free and clear in Barringer sometime soon."

With a cold gun barrel pressed against his neck, Doc raised his hands, "Don't move a damn muscle Gilbert

Greenway. You and your friend raise your hands high, nice and easy like."

"Calvin Coolidge Cartwright, I haven't heard that scratchy voice since my freshman year of high school," said Doc.

"Forgive my manners, Gilbert, but I couldn't resist picking on you again, old neighbor. I saw you flashing lots of money at the cafe. Hand me that big, fat wallet of yours, and I consider us being old friends again."

Behind the garden, Doc handed the man his wallet, just as he said to do, glancing at Ringo who had his hands high above his head.

"Take it all, Calvin." Doc told him.

The gunman opened the leather wallet, which was Ringo's custom made wallet.

"Three freakin' dollars!" yelled Calvin. "That's all you got?"

"Ringo Bare, here, this man has all the damn money, Calvin." Doc pointed at Ringo's pocket. "Open your wallet, Ringo, and look at his cash, Calvin. He has big money."

Turning his head toward Ringo, Doc said, "Calvin, that will buy a lot of weed and a classic truck to cruise on Bourbon Street. Look at that green, man."

Calvin Coolidge Cartwright turned his head.

"Smack! Take that you piece of crap!" shouted Doc.

Out of the corner of his eyes, Ringo saw what happened, like a snap of a rubber band, Calvin dropped his gun and fell to the ground.

"Damn it, Doc! I believe you knocked Calvin out cold with that roundhouse kick."

Picking up Ringo's empty wallet, Doc yelled, "Leave the gun. Let's go! I'll have the policeman on the corner, check him out."

They walked in front of the Bourbon Orleans Hotel and Doc reported the gunmen to an officer on the beat and explained everything. Ringo stepped inside the hotel bar and Doc followed him after he was finished with the policemen.

The two men found a table pretty quick.

"How did you know he was trailing us, Doc?"

"Calvin has been following us since we were in line at Café Du Monde. I've had trouble with Calvin Coolidge Cartwright since we were in grade school together."

Ringo flagged the waitress for drinks, drumming the table with his hands to the sweet sounds of jazz music, styling in his own element, at home again.

"At some point, we have to resign from our childhood ways, become men, step up to the plate and get in the ballgame."

After two songs, Ringo gulped his beer and tipped the waitress, then sat straight up and turned to Doc. "Was that directed toward me, Creole?"

"Maybe, it was a general statement; good for us both."

With a note, Ringo requested the band play King Oliver, and the leader told the rest of the members after a short break. They agreed.

"It's time for you to step up in business," said Doc, leaning on his shoulder. "Think about settling down with a nice lady, start yourself a family, and have some fun."

"I hate family. Can you talk about the Rough Riders and that Teddy Roosevelt cat, he seemed cool?"

"One day, you'll wake up from that deep sleep, less paralyzed by your own weaknesses and feel alive with courage, just like the way I do with Mary. You'll love it. Go have some fun doing it, and not just go through the motions in your head."

"I'm not in a relationship and don't plan to be."

Finishing his beer, Ringo leaned forward, tapping to the music, and singing in an impressive manner.

"One day soon, I bet you'll have the courage."

Ice hit Doc's tongue from his soda. His father's words stung the cowboy enough to move him to sing with the band members, Ringo was given permission to handle the saxophone. He played with the band until last call. Over fifty people stood and applauded the performance of Ringo Bare, outside of his practice sessions, that was his first attempt at playing an instrument in public.

Taking a bow, Ringo showed his courage, and conquered his stage fright. Nowhere had Doc heard anyone handle the saxophone with such appreciation and grace than on that night, amazed in the moment, and pleased as punch.

"Hot damn, Son!" shaking his hand. "Where'd you learn to play like that?"

Walking off stage, Ringo grinned, "I played King Oliver with the sax, didn't I? I played King Oliver! I just played King Oliver, the way it needs to sing to a man's soul."

"You're a rebel to step up on stage and buzz this place with your cool talent. Damn, I'm proud of ya, so proud of my son."

More than anything he had courage, and Doc told him so for the first time, in a long, long time, too. It was a cool moment to witness, a special night for Ringo after a long list of bad days behind him.

"What about you, stepping up to the plate with Mary?"

Ringo shook his head with sincerity and slapped his arms, too.

"She's a nice lady. We had a few times in the past, but I'm still bitter, I guess."

Strolling past the bar to the hotel lobby, people were still clapping and shaking hands with Ringo, not as a bull riding champion he once was, more than that, it was something new, graceful, and refined. He stood among the best musicians in the French Quarter and shared his talent, fearless, and a cool moment for them both.

"It's a time for second chances, Doc. Isn't this trip about starting over, stepping up to the plate again, getting in the big ballgame?"

"She had prerequisites. I loved her regardless of what she had or didn't have in the bank or the way she acted. I loved her, anyway."

"It's a great night." Somewhat jealous of the dancing crowd, Ringo embraced the gratitude as a saxophonist, like Sonny Rollins, John Coltrane, and Charlie Parker, and he said, "Once you've played in New Orleans, all life is downhill, Doc."

They stood in the lobby and soaked up the praise, beaming with the acceptance he'd always desired for himself.

"I'm proud of you." Doc told him between hugs and handshakes.

"Let's call it a night, okay?" Ringo added a yawn, "This cowboy is tired, and a soft bed will do me some good."

They toasted glasses and hugged.

The men from Central Texas caught a cab and found their rooms at the top floor of the Hotel Monteleone. Ringo told Doc that his surprise trip to New Orleans was an experience, and more about life's choices than it was about food and sightseeing and old friends. His son said he'd remember his first time eating beignets and playing the saxophone with the best father a man could ever hope for.

II

The Famous Carousel Bar

Fog rolled off the Mississippi River, a cool rain reflected the glare of street lights on the pavement, and it showered until they reached the place Doc had in mind to entertain Ringo on their second night in town. They arrived at the famous Carousel Bar, located within the historic milk white colored Hotel Monteleone, sporting an eclectic flair, and gloriously structured in the Beaux-Arts architectural style. The hotel was designed by a man from Sicily, a structure laced with gold and pearl color, inside and outside, which made the grand establishment a major French Quarter attraction in New Orleans.

"This hotel needs to be in a Hollywood film," said Ringo, standing and looking up at the towering structure. Half asleep and stumbling in the night before, Ringo was too tired to appreciate the hotel's high-class design on their first stay.

They stood on the streets, two dashing men, dressed as if they were fresh from a film set themselves, where the high-rise hotel screamed ritz and elegance, glowing in the night like a dream, and Doc couldn't wait to walk down memory lane.

"This is where I met your mother."

"I could've lived without the thought."

Doc waved Ringo through the golden doors to the bar.

"I must have been in a daze last night and too exhausted to realize your generosity; you picked a good place." Ringo walked inside the hotel with great curiosity.

"Hotel Monteleone, and the hidden gem is the famous Carousel Bar." Doc couldn't resist laughing. "You need to get out of the barn more, see a few nice places again."

"I like this bar, it's more casual than Cactus Canyon. I'm glad I jumped in the motorhome now and got out of Texas."

"Yeah. Let's enjoy ourselves while we're in New Orleans, how about it?"

"This hotel needs to be in Austin, Texas."

"Austin was settled by the Tonkawa and Comanche people." Doc admired the tall clock in the lobby. "New Orleans is pure French, with a dab of Italian design mixed in, and now modernized, commercialized, and Americanized. Different cultures persuade people to try new things and educate them more than they realize."

Elegant golden and white mirrors surrounded them, and Ringo felt it to be an advantage, that made the place look bigger than it was from the outside.

"New Orleans is much different from Austin; I prefer this place with a rich history of hospitality," said Doc, who stood in a place that was full of memories for him, "and it's the only Carousel Bar in the Great South."

"Look! Books written by Hemingway and Faulkner, and the two of them are unhappily beside each other. Ironically, they weren't fond of each other's work, either."

"Two different styles, huh?" said Ringo. "They were a lot like us. Two successful men and yet quite different."

They walked up the steps and scanned the gold colors that lined the traditional Beaux-Arts style, polished marble floors ran from room to room, in such an over the top fashion for guests, that it didn't look real, but it was authentic and traditional.

"Hotel Monteleone screams first class, doesn't it?" asked Ringo, examining books and photographs behind thick glass.

"You were half asleep last night when we checked in and you missed all this good stuff, walked right by it."

The young man noticed the bright chandeliers and paintings and stopped to peer at William Faulkner's picture in the glass case beside Ernest Hemingway's book and photograph. A friendly lady with light brown hair, neatly pinned up above her collar stood behind the counter and answered questions for Ringo while he admired the place. On the other hand, Doc walked past a giant wooden clock to the front desk and remembered his last time in the hotel lobby.

"Welcome to Hotel Monteleone," said the lady, who greeted them. "How long will you be staying with us?"

"We have already checked in." Doc paced around the foyer.

"Well, it's great to meet our guests," she replied. "Enjoy the Carousel Bar."

Walking across the room, Ringo said, "Good idea. Let's see the main attraction."

A few minutes later Ringo was seated at the Carousel Bar and waited for Doc to finish speaking with the lady at the front desk. His father hadn't seen the golden carousel spinning but a handful of times since returning from Vietnam, and one of his favorite times was with Pomona. He kept that to himself.

"I saved you a good seat," said Ringo, who was enjoying himself. "The Carousel Bar rotates every fifteen minutes and seats twenty five customers. That's what the bartender told me and it's a spinning dream, alright."

"What in the world, you drunk already?" asked Doc, who made himself comfortable in a chair. "Are you offering tours now? It was much different when I turned twenty one, had my first drink here, back in the 60s. Back then, they had a cool red and white canopy with lights, but I like the new upgrades. Times have evolved at the Carousel Bar, I can tell."

"I like the mirrors and clowns faces, too," said Ringo, turning around to see the decorations. "Makes it look more like an actual carnival ride, doesn't it?"

"Sure does."

The broad bartender stood in front of Doc, leaning over with a deep voice, and introduced himself as Mark.

"What can I get you gentlemen?"

"I'll stick with a soda," said Doc, flipping through his wallet to pay. "I'll start a tab for the man to my right."

Looking down with dark eyes, the bartender asked, "Could I see your identification, sir?"

"I just became of age, Mister Bartender." Doc laughed.

"What about you, young man?" He turned to Ringo, handing him back his identification. "I'll have a Cliff's Old-Fashioned."

"One of the house specials," said the bartender. "Good choice, coming right up."

The bartender placed two white napkins down with the hotel's picture etched on the front, followed with a soda and a straw.

"Here's your Cliff's Old-Fashioned, see what you think? It's a house favorite," said the friendly man. "Need anything else, let me know." The bartender continued to help other customers.

Doc pointed toward Ringo's glass. "That's a strong whiskey drink," he said squinting his eyes and leaning on him. "Where'd you learn about Cliff's Old-Fashioned, anyway?"

"My good friend Clifford told me about the drink after he got back from a rodeo in Denver." Turning his lip, "Well, Selena said it was her favorite drink, too. I thought I'd try one today in their honor."

"Try it with brandy sometime." Doc referred to a collection of bottles behind the bar. "You might taste a slightly different flavor in the whiskey."

"Hello?" A lady said with excitement in her voice, turning her chair toward Doc.

"I'm sorry about that, miss." Doc apologized. "Did I hit your arm?"

The young lady held his shoulder, speaking with a southern accent, and frowning. Then she smiled and winked. Doc was off the hook.

"Oh, I'm okay." The lady batted her long eyelashes at Doc and waved at Ringo. "I thought you called my name." She laughed, leaning on him in a cheerful manner. "And that's why I turned around to meet you guys."

"Whiskey?" asked Ringo, grinning.

"I'm Brandi, silly, not whiskey. It's good to meet you." Touching his lips with his napkin, Doc shook her soft hand.

Decorated with gold and diamond rings, Brandi flashed her long, red, white, and blue nails, the colors caught Doc's attention as he dropped his head in admiration.

"I'm from Savannah, Georgia." She leaned forward, rotating her chair as far as it would go toward Doc and Ringo. Her pale skin and a heart shaped face glowed in a red tint, if she'd had too much to drink or spent too much time in the sand and sun.

"We're from Texas. Good to meet you, I'm Doc Greenway, and this young man is the famed bull rider, Ringo Bare."

Extending further to find Ringo's hand, she stood and hugged him in a more formal approach to greeting a celebrity, which was one way to reveal her hourglass figure to the bull rider. Without a doubt, he examined Brandi, from her eyes to her thighs, and with few words spoken, she was truly a Georgia peach.

"Oh, where are my manners?" said the lady with bright emerald eyes, intimidating Ringo with her movements. "These are my friends, Mickey Starr and Tipp Starr." The lady looked back and forth at Doc and Mickey after her introduction and smiled at the men. "Doc, could we trade places?" asked Brandi. "I'll talk to Ringo since he's about my age, how 'bout you gab with Mickey and Tipp, okay?"

In his mid-sixties, grey headed, sporting a well-manicured salt and pepper goatee and sun-chapped skin,

Mickey was well dressed. Tipp Starr was in his twenties, slightly taller, had long blonde hair, just like Ringo.

"Good to meet you, Mickey, Tipp," said Doc, nodding and shaking hands with both men. Walking over to Mickey and Tipp, Ringo struck a conversation with the gentlemen. Later, Doc Greenway swapped seats with Brandi.

Mickey spoke with a sharp southern accent, wearing a snug leather vest, buttoned top to bottom, and held an Arturo Fuente cigar from Florida, and smoking it, too. Tipp, a much younger version, had tanned skin, sporting a smooth shaved face, and his long, wavy blonde hair touched his collar. The gentleman nervously tugged his blue fishing polo shirt, pocketing one hand inside his faded blue jeans, and thankfully, like Mickey, he was born with the gift of gab.

"What are you drinking, Doc?" asked Mickey, waving money at the bartender.

"To be honest," touching his chin, "I stopped drinking years ago, but I do appreciate a good conversation, though."

"Smart man." Tipp responded to Doc. "I'll have a soda on the rocks, and make it a double, Mark the bartender."

Mickey leaned to Tipp's ear, speaking in a low voice, and the two men suddenly stood, stretching, and clutching their drinks as if they were done for the night.

"Doc," said Mickey, "Let's go over to the sofa and talk. This spinning Carousel Bar machine wakes my vertigo up."

Tipp slapped Mickey's shoulder, "I'll join you two men since Ringo and Brandi are deep in conversation."

"Yeah, of course." Blowing smoke way above his head, Mickey led the way. "We'll grab that sofa and chair before one of these youngsters beats us across the room."

Leading the way, Mickey headed to a more comfortable spot in the lounge, Brandi and Ringo looked friendly in a short time, close enough to kiss, laughing, drinking, and becoming friends. Doc tapped Ringo on the shoulder and showed him where he would be, near an unoccupied piano, and with less people than at The Carousel Bar. The three men sat in a dim corner and leaned back, curiously observing each other for a moment, uptight and interested about one another.

"What type of business are you in, Doc?" asked Mickey, resting his arm on the sofa, and rolling his glass, hand-to-hand, examining the doctor's polished shoes and pressed slacks.

"I retired from my medical practice last month." He flipped his hat back in his hand. "And I sold most of what I had in Central Texas, taking a few days to relax and show Ringo the French Quarter."

"Congratulations!" said Tipp. "He's looking for the next chapter in his life. That's a man on a "Dream Wheel" right there, contemplating his next chess move, and he came to New Orleans to celebrate his successes, I bet?"

"Sold my horses and cattle, and now I need to part with two office buildings. Ringo is starting a new enterprise in North Carolina next week, so we leave in a few days." Doc handled his glass and sipped his soda.

Mickey finished his drink. "He's a wise man."

"What type of business?" asked Tipp.

"I was working in non-invasive tattoo removal."

"What the heck?" said Tipp.

"Don't people want tattoos on their body?" asked Mickey, puffing on his cigar. "I'm confused, my friend, and please educate me on that type of career, will ya?"

"Some people have bad tattoos or partial tattoos that they're displeased with, and that's where I remove them, using a laser, of course." Doc moved his finger across the inside of his forearm. He had no tattoos on his body. "My next chapter, well, it's starting a saddlery business in Barringer."

"I've got too much business to even think of retiring," said Mickey, shaking his head and waving his cigar around. His gold watch reflected light when he moved his arm under the lamp.

"Saddlery, huh?" said Tipp, touching his mustache. "Mickey Starr has a herd of horses and is buying more good stock, expanding the famous Tobacco Barn."

Doc rocked his head in curiosity. "What line of work are you in, Mickey?"

"Boats. Horses. Land. Cars."

"Opportunities," said Tipp, clearing his throat. "We are in the seafood industry and own Friesian Horses and Quarter Horses, roaming on two-hundred acres, outside Savannah."

"Boats and barns, huh?" said Doc, chuckling and clutching his glass.

Tipp pulled his chair up closer to hear the conversation as the room became crowded. Couples were dressed formally for a party and entered the lounge, and in a short time, all the seats were occupied. The lobby and bar area became much louder than when they first arrived. On that particular evening, a crowd of beautiful ladies locked arms with men, fashioned in bright gold colors and designer fragrances lingered as they strolled by the bar. When the crowd grew, Doc slumped excitedly to hear Tipp tell how Mickey Starr's seafood company had expanded after he returned home from the Korean War.

"That keeps us traveling." Mickey tugged his goatee.

Crunching ice in his jaw, Doc wondered if he was full of crap or not. "Sounds lucrative and I have to confess, I do enjoy a good seafood platter on holidays."

"We supply seafood to fifty restaurants in Southern Georgia and as far north as the Greenbrier Resort, in Almost Heaven, West Virginia," said Tipp. "We're expanding our territory each year since Mickey bought high-caliber horses for the Tobacco Barn. With a big change of heart and some confession, Brandi joined us as Media Manager last year."

A round pale waiter showed up in a bow tie and a black and white suit eager to do his job. "Here's a couple sodas and another Cliff's Old-Fashioned courtesy of the bull rider, with his arm around the blonde bombshell at The Carousel Bar. Oh, yeah, he sends his best, he said to tell you, Doc."

"Appreciate the liquid fire for my friends, Texas Bull Rider," sounded Doc, waving both hands. Ringo tapped his cowboy hat like famed bull riders did on the circuit. "There's a fire burning bright in your arms tonight, Ringo," said Doc.

Spotting a five for the waiter, Mickey grinned.

"We'll have them empty shortly, mister waiter," said Mickey, turning in Doc's direction. "When are you headed to North Carolina to open your saddlery business?"

"Two or three days, when the bull rider sobers up."

"Good deal." Brushing his mustache with his hand, Mickey looked at his grandson, and spoke candidly, "Come to think of it, Tipp and I have business to tend to this fall with Harley "Showman" Wagoner. I have heard that Barringer is a good horse town, serving lots of BBQ ribs. I have a log cabin in the next county."

Doc's face turned sour. "I know Showman Wagoner."

"There's a big bash in Barringer this fall, you and Ringo should join us. The bull rider likes Brandi, and the boy might want to see her again." Mickey toasted each man. "They want our fresh seafood in Barringer on the morning of the event and our trucks will be there long before sunup."

"Might be five or ten thousand people in Barringer that weekend." Tipp chugged his soda. "There's a big party planned at Showman Wagoner's ranch, too. Hope to see you there, Doc."

"Invitation only, though, and it's for the big boys, I've heard." Mickey smacked his lips.

"He'll want me and Ringo to be there, I bet," said Doc, wiping his bottom lip and remembering how Showman's mouth smirked when he won over him at a championship card game in Waco, back in 1991.

Mickey observed Doc, tapping a deck of cards in a pleasant manner. "Showman has been known to dodge the truth and fill a barn full of crap," said Doc, cutting his cards. "If you know what I mean, Mickey?"

"Is that where you two are headed?" Tipp smiled at Doc for an answer. "Good, you and Ringo will be headed to the party in Barringer, and he'll have a big barn burner."

Saddles of Barringer

"Cards and saddles, that's my game." Doc spoke politely.

Mickey told Doc that Showman Wagoner had bought five-hundred Quarter Horses from him over the past three years, transporting the animals from Georgia to Wyoming and Canada. Thoughts tumbled in Doc's head confirming his dream to build a saddlery shop in Barringer, which sounded better the closer he got to North Carolina. Doc told Mickey and Tipp how the rolling hills in that part of North Carolina was prime land for additional farms and big businesses, and how two dozen stables and paddocks were added in '95. Mickey told how Barringer might climb to the caliber of Ocala, Florida, and Lexington, Kentucky soon, calling Barringer "The Equine Capital of Carolina" for stakeholders and auctions.

"I didn't see a ring on your hand, Mr. Greenway," said Mickey, smiling. "You two aren't trying to saddle up with Ol' Showman Wagoner because of his money, are ya?"

Choking a laugh into the ball of his fist, Tipp looked at Doc, who fell back on the sofa grabbing his stomach.

"Heck no!" said Doc, waving his hand. "Ringo is a saddlery master, the best leatherman in the country. The boy has sold saddles to King Ranch in South Texas and saddled the Ponderosa Ranch of Henry Wilson's in Utah."

"So, you are seriously starting a new high-profile saddlery enterprise in North Carolina?" asked Tipp, tapping his glass. "You'll make some money off of Showman Wagner then."

"Hope to. I know you'll appreciate that I rode horses in the Army at Fort Hood," said Doc. "Horses are in my blood, too. We sell saddles to lots of veterans."

"You were in the 1st Cavalry Horse Detachment, Doc?" Mickey leaned forward.

"Heck, yeah. Served at Fort Hood, Texas."

"Good to meet a fellow soldier," said Mickey. "First Team on Trigger the Horse."

"I have ten black stallions at the Tobacco Barn, outside Savannah, and they are stunning creatures to see. You and Ringo need to take a long weekend, stop in Savannah." Mickey pulled something from his shirt. "Here's my card, give me a call and we'll talk saddles, once you get settled in Barringer, North Carolina."

"That's a deal." Doc grinned and shook hands with Mickey and Tipp again.

Crossing his legs, Tipp said, "This is mid-August already, I'm wondering if you could have ten custom-made saddles for us by mid-November?"

Doc was startled. "I'm not sure about ten saddles, gentlemen, it's a new venture for us. That would take a few more hands." Doc scanned the room and thought about what he needed in Barringer to make saddles for Mickey Starr. *It would not be easy.* He told himself. "But I can't pass it up."

"Listen, I'm interested in custom-made saddles with my Circle Starr brand on the fenders." Mickey cleaned his glasses. "Is cash flow a problem, sir?" Mickey whispered. "We can pay upfront, right Tipp?" reaching for his wallet. "If the saddles are high-quality, that is, and not that imported crap we've been seeing at rodeos? We'll need the good stuff."

Snapping his hand, Tipp added, "If we're going to ride our Friesian horses in the New York Thanksgiving Parade, we'll need twenty-five new western saddles for television."

"Now, Tipp, I promised the parade ten horses and that's what they'll get." Mickey spoke with a sharp voice. "I never told that lady twenty five horses. No way!"

"That's several horse trailers and a supply trailer for new saddles." On a white napkin, Tipp penned his thoughts.

"Tipp, here," added Mickey, "he's the man who pushes the numbers for our company. Big numbers, too."

"I have ten saddle trees ready for leather." Doc shuffled the deck. "Mick, we'll work day and night to have your custom saddles ready for the parade. That's a heck of a deal gentlemen."

"Hot damn!" yelled Mickey, slapping his leg. "We'll have brand new leather saddles oiled and ready for television, Tipp." Mickey lifted his head in relief. "I'll pay good money for custom Bordeaux leather and brass horns, too." He nodded in confidence. "Can you handle vintage Bordeaux, Greenway?"

Tipp canted his head and waited.

"It's as good as strapped to the belly of your Friesian horses, Mickey Starr." Doc squinted his eyes and faced his new friends.

"Don't go into battle if you don't know the way out, good soldier. You're first class, Greenway."

"I believe this guy is for real." Tipp's face lifted into the light, beaming a hopeful face at his grandfather.

"Ten custom made vintage Bordeaux saddles are on order," said Doc, handing Mickey a ten of clubs. "You'll need twenty Bordeaux saddle bags for the ladies, Mr. Starr. That will run you gentlemen $35,000." focusing on their reaction. "The question is, can you handle the cost of Bordeaux, sailors?"

Tipp and Doc examined Mickey's face, bright-eyed and glowing, who adjusted his glasses and absorbed the numbers that tunneled into his ears. The old man turned his head like a moving bullet just left the barrel of a gun. Then he tapped the napkins and passed the note to Tipp. Shuffling cards, Doc knew the cost of every rivet, frame, and cut of leather that he needed to close the saddle deal.

"Doc, we'll have $35,000 cash on delivery." Mickey stroked the breast of his vest. "Yeah, for sure, ladies who ride my horses will need twenty Bordeaux saddlebags to match, just to store makeup and personal items. It makes a woman happy to have her makeup kit with her on a horse."

The men laughed.

"Well, well, well, they can't go down the street without makeup on their eyes and face," said Tipp. "And matching saddle bags by their butt, now can they?"

"No. Thank God and Greenway, they'll have them, too. All right, it's a fair deal, sir." Mickey tapped his gold watch and crushed his cigar in the ashtray.

"What do you think, Doc?" Tipp studied his chapped face. "Easy to say, but can it be done, though, in a short time?"

Doc cleared his throat, sipping his soda for a moment and knew the work needed a dedicated team of men and all the time he had over the next few months to complete the Bordeaux saddles for the parade; time was short.

"You still up for the deal, Doc?" Tipp stopped moving.

"Well, well, let's see," said Doc, shuffling his cards. "That's a lot of work, but you'll have the finest saddles on television from Mr. Ringo Bare himself."

"We better," said Mickey, tightening his brow and clutching his collar.

"I'm a man in the money game, boys. Let's play ball with Bordeaux and Bordeaux back in style, gentlemen. Are you good for the dollars on the saddles, Mick?" Doc's face tightened. "Can I get a purchase order from you today or do you need to call your accountant?"

Tipp examined Mickey's big grin to see if he was bluffing, raising his glass against his lips, Doc didn't know Mickey or Tipp from Adam in the Garden. All he knew was the amount of work ahead of him in the next few months and how he didn't have even a shoestring of leather since his house burned to the ground.

"I don't have to call anyone," said Mickey. "I own the bank. Have you heard of Starr National Bank of Savannah?"

"I have now." Doc's teeth shone.

"Now, do you get the picture, Picasso?" asked Tipp.

"I'll take half the money tonight and you can pick up your vintage Bordeaux at Saddles of Barringer, in mid-November then." Doc stood prepared to shake hands. "Excuse me, gentlemen, while I step into the barn and water my horse, let you count your Benjamins."

Doc thought about what needed to take place in Barringer before leather could be custom-made, a new room had to be attached to the barn and he needed to visit a tannery in

Virginia for supplies. His plan was wiring, lights, and drywall from Troutman Hardware. Grabbing his face as if he was removing his first tattoo, Doc was stressed in the mirror of the restroom. His fists slammed the water basin, head swimming, and heart pumped anxiety through his veins. *There's not enough time to do this damn job. Look what you've done now, big shot.* He told himself as he peered in the mirror, shaking because of his big mouth. *I can't back out now, though.*

***

Later, Ringo, on the other hand, was arm in arm with Brandi, signaling to Doc, heading to his hotel room for some pillow talk. Doc flipped his thumb at the bull rider like he had a silver coin in his palm. In turn, Ringo reached deep into his pocket, flipping his coin atop his left wrist while Brandi nosed around the foyer. Ringo smiled and nodded.

"Was it heads or tails?" Doc mouthed the words from the lounge.

The bull rider looked at Brandi who was checking her figure in the golden framed mirror, touching his forehead with the coin, he grinned.

"Heads," said Ringo, nodding and hooking Brandi's arm.

"Good." Doc saluted the lucky man, thinking of himself with Pomona, years earlier.

It was unpredictable, but Ringo couldn't make a decision to save his life without the flip of a silver coin telling him what to do. If the coin would have landed on tails, Ringo would've joined Doc alongside Mickey and Tipp, just to avoid a bad decision. The bull rider trusted the fate of superstition after his mother left him with Doc. As a teenager, he became funny about seeing black cats cross the road, walking under ladders at the barn, and opening umbrellas inside his home. In that strange manner, Ringo avoided bad luck, he told Doc.

Stretching out her arm, Brandi waved at Mickey and Tipp, following Ringo's lead to the elevator. The bull rider took a deep breath as he noticed her lean figure and how her sweet rose perfume cast a spell over him and encouraged him to hug her when he could. His charm caused her to lean deep into his shoulder, even jumping inside his arms on the elevator, shafting and kissing from floor to floor, until they reached Ringo's room on the top level.

Tipp and Mickey stepped into the restroom after Brandi left the Carousel Bar. Doc told how he needed laborers to help with hides, unloading trucks, and building a new wooden shop as soon as he pulled his motorhome into the driveway in Barringer. Mickey and Tipp returned to their seats in the lounge and Doc was deep in thought as he finished his soda and crushed ice in his mouth, humming in amazement about the deal he just made with two strangers from Georgia. To honor their agreement, Tipp returned from his hotel room with cash inside a cigar box for Doc.

"Listen, gentlemen," said Doc, "now that we've ordered Bordeaux saddles, what's next on your list in New Orleans?"

"Mickey and I are buying a well-bred black stallion tomorrow from a farmer in Mandeville."

"A high caliber stallion, huh?" Doc turned to Tipp.

Mickey adjusted his collar and hat in the mirror.

"Is the horse broke, gentlemen?" asked Doc.

Raising his hand to his brow, Tipp answered, "Heck, no! This is a crazy horse and wild as hell."

"Hmmm," said Doc.

"If you have time, Doc, stop in." Tipp handed Doc a business card. "We'll take you to see Conrad Cavender and our stallion, Black Rio, in the morning. We'd like your opinion about the horse, what do you say? And whatever you say about the horse, we'll take it to heart, one horseman to another, if you can make it?"

Tipp stood with his arms crossed.

"Yeah. I'm from New Orleans," said Doc, removing his hat, "I've heard of Conrad Cavender, the man who handles the best breed of stallions in Louisiana. I haven't had the pleasure of meeting him yet, but I'd like to."

Scanning the room and rolling his watch, Mickey added, "In these parts, Cavender is a damn legend; good man, when it comes to handling horses."

"This stallion might be a six-figure horse, unhandled and wild, just shipped in from the Great West Herd. Few men have gotten close to this horse, and to be honest, we're not sure how we can load this horse in our trailer without getting kicked in the head or killed." Tipp's eyes bugged. "Wild as a damn buck and he hates dogs, cowboys and being loaded on a dang trailer."

In a soft voice, "Gentlemen, gentlemen," said Doc, grabbing Mickey's shoulder, "Ringo Bare can break your black stallion in the morning." Doc brushed his hat and reached in his back pocket, "I have $2,500 says he can ride that horse."

"Are you saying that crippled bull rider can handle horses and bulls?" asked Mickey, wrinkling his face, staring at Doc, and laughing.

"Ringo Bare breaks horses? Well, well, well, we are in on that bet!" said Tipp, thumbing through his wallet. Suddenly, he left the conversation to speak to a pretty lady at the bar.

Doc and Mickey stood and looked at each other.

"I understand Ringo is a professional bull rider, Doc."

"He was a professional bull rider, but he had hung his spurs in the barn." Doc stuffed his cash deep inside his hat. "One of the best in the country, less than three years ago, then a bull wrecked his foot in eleven places. He's on rental videos and sports bloopers now."

Mickey lit another cigar and blew rings of smoke that rose and disappeared within seconds, speaking slowly, "I think I have heard of Ringo Bare, big time guy, too, I bet? I don't think he has the Mojo, anyway, since his injury, does he? That young man's day has passed him by, Doc. Romeo, he's definitely not a bronc buster."

Doc placed his hat on his head, curling a tight face, "I said, Ringo Bare can break your horse in the morning, do you want that stallion rode or not?"

"Yeah. Hell, yes. I'll take your bet. But my money is on Black Rio," said Mickey. Three drinks made him a loud man. "I'm going to call it a night, Doc. We'll see you and Ringo at Conrad Cavender's big barn and get that bull rider rested up. I'll have to warn you, though," smiling, "Brandi has her way with men. I've seen it with my own eyes, and I mean, any man she wants, she gets under the covers with. Brandi dated Volt Hendricks, three years ago."

"The superstar singer, Volt Hendricks, huh? Didn't he just move to Barringer?"

"Yeah. He's a bigtime country star from North Carolina," handling his cigar, "and that young man is on my payroll, too. I'll introduce you to him, at Showman's bash."

The two businessmen shook hands and talked about horses and saddles, and watched Tipp crash and burn, holding his cocktail glass in his hand at the end of the night.

"Doc, we'll have a pot of coffee waiting for you in the morning at Cavender's barn. Let's make it nine o'clock." Tipp saluted his new friend.

"Have your money in a cigar box, Mr. Doc." Mickey tapped his watch and disappeared into the elevator with Tipp.

Unlocking his room, Doc heard a lady laughing in Ringo's room, realizing Brandi had found the champagne bottle and a cowboy to enjoy it with in private. Rooms were yellow and white, cozy, and designed with lovers in mind. After a long day, the queen bed was a perfect landing zone, a sweet spot to cushion the fall of any exhausted man and woman.

12

Meet Conrad Cavender

In Mandeville, Louisiana, one of the premier horsemen of Cajun country lived on a ranch with a half dozen wild horses, he'd shipped from Wyoming to his barn. Too dangerous for children and beginners, his horses had to be broken by a professional cowboy before they could be profitable on the open market. The first man he called for a quick sale when Black Rio arrived on his ranch, none other than Mickey Starr from Savannah, Georgia. Thinking they'd been stood up by Doc and Ringo, Tipp and Mickey finished a pot of coffee alongside Conrad Cavender, who stood inside the barn questioning and cursing his friends for inviting a couple of Texas saddle makers to his barn.

Planning to shop until she dropped in the French Quarter, Brandi was gone when Ringo opened his restless eyes, having slept on pillows and cushions on the floor. Finally, catching a cab with Doc to the motorhome, Ringo's head was spinning as they crossed Lake Pontchartrain, nervously Doc drove to Cavender's as fast as he could, slamming on his brakes beside Tipp and Mickey's black truck. Both his friend's waved, pissed at the tardiness of their invited guests.

"We are late, late, late, hangover boy!" shouted Doc. "Look at what your drunken ass has caused us to do." Brushing his hands through his short hair, Doc eyed Ringo with disappointment, rolling his eyes. "These men have been waiting on us all morning and my watch says ten o'clock."

"Ugh! Ugggh!" Ringo stepped behind a tree. "Ugggggh," spitting and stumbling over to a water hose, draped over a galvanized horse trough.

"We're not running a damn rehab center for drunken Texans!" shouted a man, pacing and pointing his cowboy hat at Ringo. "Listen, sober up or get off my property! Some people just can't handle the Big Easy, and you must be one of them," kicking dirt at Ringo.

Lifting his head, Tipp said, "Mmm. Is he hungover because Brandi is a party animal?"

"No. I caused this myself." Ringo told Tipp. Don't blame the hot model."

Leaning between a post and a tree at the barn, Doc was ashamed of the young man in the cowboy hat, sporting a loose bull riding belt buckle from his hips, shirt untucked, and acting like a damn Irish Bum Scottie.

Mocking Jack Nicholson, Mickey shouted, "Boys, you can't handle the spin of the Carousel Bar! I stand thirty yards from a creature who wants to kill me."

Excited to hear his voice, the guys laughed at the old man.

"Did Brandi wreck your night on champagne and caviar?" sounded Tipp, laughing with a cigar in his hand.

Mickey walked over to Doc, "You still think he's a professional bull rider or in recovery?" looking around. "Is he some two bit rodeo clown?"

Taking a deep breath, "Yeah." Doc nodded. "My money says Ringo Bare can ride any damn horse you have, especially that black stallion in the corral. Good fellows, just give him five minutes, he's fine." The men walked away. "Get up! Ringo, you've been summoned to the corral."

Rolling over on his back, Ringo hacked a dozen times. All the men laughed when Doc walked over to rescue the drunken bull rider again, handing him some coffee and started fanning him with his hat.

Coughing and choking, Ringo said, "I'm the best, boys! I'm the.... bla...." pulling himself up with the help of a corner fence, the bull rider continued to clear what was on his stomach.

"He doesn't look the best." Conrad Cavender walked inside the dark part of his barn. "Texas hasn't produced a good athlete since that Air Force quarterback from Dallas, Roger something? Yeah, it was Staubach. Now he was the best."

Walking up beside Doc, Mickey rocked back and forth, smoking his cigar and chuckling. "This is the Mandeville horse trainer I was telling you about, Conrad Cavender. He was quarterback at Tulane back in the 70s."

A pencil stick of a man in dark glasses stood with his hands on his hips, a slice of straw in his mouth, pondering the safety of the bull rider. The wind shifted his straw hat which blocked the midmorning sun from hitting his pale face, having a short, private conversation with Doc before he let Ringo close to the corral. Then Doc reached out his hand with the sun in his face. "Good to meet you, Conrad Cavender. I'm Doctor Greenway from Tulane. Sorry I didn't see you play ball for the

Green Wave; it was my time to serve Uncle Sammy in the Army."

"I've heard about you from Showman Wagoner," said Conrad. "Tulane makes me proud, not for oneself..." sharing the school motto.

Interrupting him, "Not for oneself, but for one's own," blurted Doc.

"Tulane is a great school." Doc slapped his shoulder and became his friend, though, he didn't know how Conrad felt. "That's Ringo Bare washing champagne and brandy from his chops."

"I've heard of Ringo Bare. My wife and I saw him in Waco in 1994." Twitching his lips, Conrad Cavender wasn't impressed with Ringo on that particular morning, stepping away.

Slapping Cavender's shoulder with a giant smile, Mickey said, "I haven't seen their work yet, but these are the saddlery guys from Texas."

"Is Conrad "Strawman" Cavender your real name?" asked Doc.

"Yeah, the one my father gave me, and my mother still disliked it, but he did it, anyway." The rancher spat. "Somewhere along the way they added the article to emphasize my last name. Can you believe that?"

"Yeah. If a man can walk on the moon, I can believe anything."

The gentlemen chuckled.

With a slow voice and turning around, Conrad Cavender asked, "Is Doc Greenway your real name or is that some prefix, you're using to overcompensate, along with that Lone Star recreational vehicle, double parked in my driveway?"

"I earned the prefix." Doc stood tall. "Plus, I added some overcompensation with the fuzzy dice on the visor, like hippy M.D.'s do when they graduate from Tulane."

"Is that bull rider alive, Doc?" taunted Conrad Cavender. "Let's get the drunken cowboy up and away from my mailbox before the mailman wrecks him on his morning drive by."

Conrad Cavender was thin and tall, dressed in denim and tied around his head was a wet, red bandana, sporting a pair of black glasses, and his hat shifted when he spoke. His denim collar was flipped up, not because he was cold, but somewhere along the way he kept his bad boy rodeo image, using it beyond the arena and acted cool.

"He couldn't let go of the nightlife." Doc spoke to Conrad.

Mickey reached in his pocket. "Let's hurry this alone, I've got $2,500 says your boy can't break that stallion."

Conrad Cavender told the men the rules, "the bronc buster must circle the corral three times by two o'clock," a man of few words spoke. "You got four hours before chow time, man from Tulane, I hope you can prepare your apprentice. Get that bull rider a leather bib and let's get started."

"Are you still a betting man, Doctor Greenway?"

"You bet your life on it, Mickey Starr."

Doc loved to bet and couldn't pass on what he knew about Ringo's riding ability. However, he scratched his head and turned toward Ringo, who had his face half buried in the

Louisiana soil. Then Doc turned flush red from the side of neck to the tip of his ears, chewing the thunder out of his gum, and loosening his collar.

"I have my $2,500 to add to the pot, Doc," said Tipp, who emptied his pockets. "That will make it $5,000 from the Starr boys, and let it be known, the stallion breaks Ringo first."

Conrad Cavender had the stallion in an old, round metal corral, the fence was ten foot tall, locked in tight, and even the fastest horse would never escape, no matter how determined the animal was to find open range. Honoring the Old West style, chains or good ropes held the gate, a serious approach to equine management and discipline was adopted by the rancher.

"This is the largest wager I've seen on my ranch since LSU and Alabama played football last season." Conrad Cavender wiped his forehead. "I usually don't allow horse betting on my property, but I'm just damn curious as hell to see how this Texan can overcome his alcohol poison and ride my horse. This kind of craziness just thrills my bones and stops a lot of talk among the younger crowds, who think they can ride a rocket to space from Houston. I could have sold tickets to this fiasco and invited more people, if I'd just known a drunk Texan was going to be my main attraction."

"What about it, Doc?" asked Mickey, walking over to pull Ringo up from the ground. "You got any faith in this boy, or what?"

"I still believe he's the best man for the job, even half sober, gentlemen."

Staring at Doc, Ringo was surprised. Slurring his speech from the pressure of the water hose, Ringo pleaded, "Give me ten minutes, I had a double shot of brandy-Brandi last night." With only a few hours of sleep, Ringo blinked and rubbed his watery eyes. "In my mind, I'm going to Carolina on the Carousel Bar, Doc."

Mickey kept Ringo from falling in the mud.

"Rest easy," said Tipp, hooking his thumbs in his belt loop. "Double shot of sweet brandy-Brandi, huh? That will do it every time. There's no rough rider left inside this guy."

Pounding the ground, the massive black stallion was running wild around the corral as Mickey and Tipp walked over to the gate. They propped their boots on the railing and watched the muscular horse, they were about to buy.

Walking out of his motorhome, Doc raised his money above his head, and shouted, "I got $5,000! I'm still a betting man, boys!" raising up Ringo's limber arm. "Son, hey, can you ride that damn horse, you hear me or not?"

"Maybe? There's a good chance, well, yeah, I guess."

"I'll hold the money." Conrad Cavender used his straw hat as a money bowl for large bills. "Well, gentlemen let the ass busting begin, before it gets hot enough to fry an egg on the hood of my '73 Ford."

"Smart man," said Ringo, "he's a Ford man."

"You got a bridle and a rope for Ringo?" said Tipp, checking the supply room for the items.

"Yes, sir," said Conrad Cavender, nodding his head. "Here, in Mandeville, real cowboys have a full line of horse training gear for Texans, if they can use them properly."

Pulling on Ringo's hand with all he had, Doc yanked his arm, and with great resistance he decided to assist him to the corral gate.

"There's a wad of cash against you, boy," said Doc. "We need it, all of it." letting him fall to the ground to rest. "You got a horse to ride," he urged while helping him up. "Hope you don't die today; I'd hate to lose my saddlery CEO after that $35,000 order from Mickey Starr last night."

Whispering, "$35,000?" said Ringo, looking at Mickey from a distance, who smoked his cigar.

Doc turned the water hose on and sprayed Ringo once in the face, trying to get him in decent condition for the ride.

"Hey, hey! What the hell, Doc?" blocking the water with his hands. "Wait! Wait!" yelled Ringo. "Stop it, Doc!"

Walking inside the corral, Conrad Cavender observed one of the finest horses he'd ever bought or seen for that matter, black and muscular, shiny, pacing like a newly waxed car on the racetrack. The animal was wild and ran in circles, clouding dust, mane bouncing and tail dragging the ground, Black Rio slowed his pace, breathing hard through his nostrils, wide, rapid, and frightening for any cowboy. Knowing he needed a moment, Doc escorted Ringo into the motorhome to coach him. Not a word was spoken in the first few minutes as Doc tried to bring him to life with a cold glass of water and a damp cloth.

Calmly, Doc planned his approach.

"There's a stack of cash out there against you, boy."

Ringo rubbed his hands together, toweling his face, and trying to find an ounce of strength between drinks.

"It's all on my damn shoulders, too, and I didn't agree to this deal, but I'll play along, for the sake of you and your damn money."

"Yeah, yeah, yeah." Doc rubbed his face and looked out the door at the men and then the horse.

"And it's the drunk man's fault if we lose, right? It's "Hangover Hero" to the rescue."

"I bet on you before I knew this would happen."

"I'm hurt." His eyes watered in anger. "Let me call my own shots from here on out, Doc."

"You were once the best in the world, before you got hurt and then found the bottle." Doc lowered his head. "Listen, take what you got on the inside and beat these guys, right now."

"My best days are done, Doc, and stop betting on me to ride."

"Flip that coin, let's see what it tells us, huh?" Doc pointed to Ringo's pocket.

"Where's my coin?" Ringo slapped his pockets. "What the heck?"

"Did you lose the lucky coin your mother gave you when you were twelve?" Doc's face was long and pale. "You've had that same coin since you came to live with me."

"The last time I saw it," said Ringo, pulling out the liner in his pockets, "I was in the restroom and Brandi needed change for a snack. She must've checked my pockets and snatched the quarter." In a sober and sour face, he pounded the cushion with his fist. "Damn it! I was drinking and screwed up again."

"Well, it's in a fine place on the top floor, safe in a snack machine, and she got her candy man, didn't she?" belting out a laugh. "You lost it, I guess?"

"Yeah. I lost it." Yanking on his hair, Ringo's head fell in his hands and his eyes closed.

"You didn't have a big smile on your face last night when you walked through the lobby with Brandi, the coin wasn't on heads, I bet?"

"Nope."

"So you were drunk and lied to me?"

"I'm sorry."

Doc tilted his body away from Ringo, resting his head against the wall. "Be true to yourself and others."

"My day ain't worth a damn." Ringo kicked the seat.

"Your talent doesn't depend on a coin, Ringo. My big money still says you can ride Black Rio, though." Doc slapped the table. "Do this for yourself, not me!" slamming the motorhome door.

"I'm screwed," yelled Ringo, closing his eyes. "Damn it! You shouldn't put money on me!"

The door clapped from the hard wind, turning, and stepping back inside, Doc said, "I'll bet all I have on you until the day I die." Doc cleaned his glasses. "Just ride the damn horse, Ringo, okay? This is a cakewalk for you, son, a stroll in the park on a sunny day."

Washing his face, Ringo pulled his long hair back over his head and broke the bathroom mirror with his fist. Instantly, he regretted his rage. Blood ran down his arm and onto the floor, checking his cuts, and washing his hands, pulling chards of glass from his knuckles. A white towel turned red from dabbing his hand in water and his heart pounded when he realized what he'd done. Ringo found a pair of yellow leather gloves and ran to the corral where a small crowd waited on his attempt, just as if nothing had happened.

In a soft voice, "We thought you were taking a nap, my boy." Mickey welcomed him, patting Ringo's back when he took the bridle from Conrad Cavender's hand.

"Give the horse your best try," said Conrad. "Don't get killed or mess your hair up in the process."

Spooking the horse, Ringo opened the gate, easing inside the dusty corral, the young man saw the liquid eyes of the animal and the bull rider heard Doc's voice coaching him, '*You'll find the soul of a horse inside his eyes.*' Clear and concise as if Doc was standing beside him, gloving his chin, Ringo heard him again, " '*When the horse blinks, you can trust him and then you can trust each other.*' " Ringo stopped in his tracks and faced the animal, the beginning of a bond was formed, and he was locked in his own world.

Much too late to flip a coin or bow out and walk away, turning a lump in his throat, Ringo stood eye to eye with the heavy breathing animal, still in his element, respecting the distance the horse had made between him.

"I'll take him," holding up his hand, "and I don't need an old school lasso and post." Ringo accepted the whip through the fence from Conrad Cavender, gawking over to where the horse paced around him, Ringo found a central position.

Doc had taught Ringo to find common ground with an animal, building a two-way bond of command and control.

Years had passed since gentling a horse, but Ringo still remembered horses as being curious creatures, even half sober and pale as a ghost, but he knew how to take command.

"The horn sounds at two o' clock, Ringo," Mickey said.

His injured hand pounded, and his heart beat out of control, climbing up into his chest and throat, and he quickly sobered up when the horse reared up. The situation made him forget about his sour stomach, too. To miss breakfast was a mistake, shoveling down a sunrise biscuit would have done him some good. In turn, he got down to business, studying the horse's moment, large and swift, more powerful than any horse he'd dealt with at Clem Cline's ranch. Black Rio's long black tail touched the ground when he turned in nervousness and caution.

With three men leaning on the corral, Conrad Cavender agitated Ringo atop his favorite whiskey barrel, a move that was unfair to the bull rider, but a short show and all in good fun. "That horse needs a rider, Ringo." Conrad Cavender jumped off the barrel.

All of it made Ringo nervous as hell and being on television didn't compare to having Doc's money and reputation hang in the balance, much less his own character being judged at the end of the day, too.

"I believe the horse will bust his ass," said Conrad Cavender, whittling in the shade. "Gentlemen, pull up a chair, I'm afraid this might get exciting for us." The horse trainer commented as he dropped his butt on a short whiskey barrel chair. "Drunk Ringo drives Black Rio to the left, then he eyes the animal for respect, a stalemate move," commented the rancher. "The horse turns left, whipping at him, and now it's a standoff for respect, folks."

Leaning against a post, "Who will win?" said Tipp, adjusting his dark glasses and pacing around the corral for shade.

Mickey examined Tipp's face, grinning, and laughing at Ringo staggering for position. Like his grandfather, Tipp propped his boot on the fence by the barn, ducking out of the hot sun under a tree, watching Ringo handle the wild horse.

"Whoa, buddy," said Ringo, easing toward the unsettled horse. "Calm down." The bull rider paced around in a nervous mess, spitting words in a low voice and whipping the top layer of soil for control.

"You gotta rope and a long bridle, boy?" asked Conrad Cavender. "It's on the barrel, so do what you know and use it."

Retrieving the bit, Doc rushed it to his son.

"Look behind you, Ringo," said Tipp, who rang a cowbell to keep from falling asleep. "And Ringo just stepped in a big load of horse crap."

The men chuckled.

"Oh, oh, crap," said Mickey, belting a laugh. "He's down!" grabbing his shirt and rattling the gate. The dog barked and the horses reared and screaming kids ran out of the house to see the action.

"He was born in manure," said Doc, chiming in on the conversation. "It's too damn late to change things now."

Pushing himself up from a stumble, Ringo spread his back leg out, dusting the dirt and crap from his denim jeans and picked up the whip. The horse kicked and reared up, pounding his hoofs in the soft soil, more than once. Ringo found the center of the ring again and squatted down, rubbing his gloves, and roughing his boots in a small patch of grass and dirt. Ringo jumped up and walked toward the animal, remembering how Doc taught him how to handle a green horse, even older, and wild stallions like Black Rio were still manageable, though. Doc taught Ringo the same style of command, and it had worked in his family for decades.

"Mr. Cavender?" asked Mickey. "Did you strategically drop the horse manure, just to distract young Ringo?"

"I don't think he needs any more crap stacked in his boots today. That bull rider acts like he's afraid to break that animal." Conrad Cavender adjusted his thin flannel shirt and found his cowboy hat. "He might be a better fit for a stick horse."

"Oh, Ringo's not afraid of any horse or bull, for that matter," said Doc. "And you can't rush a good trainer." Pacing toward the bull rider, the doctor hoped he was right.

"Did you teach him how to fall into a sack of crap?" Tipp scratched his chin and flipped his sweaty blonde hair back, baking in the Louisiana heat. The men were looking around, laughing, and noticed how the horse was winning the show.

"No, sir." Doc shook it off. "He invented that move himself. Ringo is just getting warmed up." Doc walked back in the shade of the barn with the rest of the crowd.

Doc's face turned red as blood. Embarrassed. Money. Horses. Half-sober bull rider. He was pissed as thunder rumbled overhead, a storm was brewing out of control, edging slowly in the distance. *It was foolish betting money on Ringo's good intentions and past reputation*, Doc thought. After he witnessed Ringo's steadiness, he regretted not putting down more currency or another two-grand for the unknown curiosity of the horse that seemed to be gentle on occasion.

"I need a gallon of sweet tea," said Conrad Cavender, walking to the porch of his ranch style home in disappointment. "Let me know if you boys want any food or drinks, I got chores to tend to this morning. You folks just entertain yourselves and the ambulance is nearby if we need it, Ringo. Hey, gentlemen, the outhouse is in the barn, if you need to powder your Texas nose, or clean your jeans, Bull Rider Bare."

"This might take a while." Mickey watched Ringo over his shoulder, walking with Conrad Cavender, who jumped in a golf cart and toured Mickey around his ranch. "Let's see a few more of your horses you'd sell and meet your family," said Mickey, holding on inside the golf cart.

Tipp turned to Doc with a big smile, holding a cold drink and shaking his head. Then after a few minutes of watching Ringo, he said, "Give us a yell when his rehab is over!" hopping in his truck for a nap.

Raising his hand, "He'll be mounted by lunchtime, Tipp Starr," said Doc, who hadn't given up on his son, not for one minute.

Wiping dust from his face, Ringo was fading as he sobered up. Doc watched him command the animal without weakness, making progress, and the bull rider took off his shirt a half hour into tending to the stallion. Both of them were getting a good workout.

Moving over toward Doc, Ringo moaned, "My head's pounding," clutching his forehead. "Could you find me some good water, Doc, please?"

"Sober up in the cattle pond," said Doc, who found ice water for Ringo inside Conrad Cavender's home and offering a bit of compassion was Cavender's oldest daughter, who would draw Ringo away from the horse if she stepped outside. "Here, there's no room service in Mandeville for hangovers, so drink up!" Doc brushed his lip with his hand and laughed.

Wiggling his hand, Ringo flexed his fingers between commands, and being the good doctor, his strange behavior gained Doc's attention.

"What's wrong with your hand?" asked Doc, grabbing his arm, and pulling off his right glove. "You're bleeding through the tip of your damn glove, why?"

"Hit your mirror in the motorhome, cut it up pretty good."

Rushing to find a water hose, Doc washed his hand and checked for pieces of glass. There was no glass. His knuckles were red with a few cuts, and he'd lost lots of blood.

"What the hell?" Doc crushed his hat into his hand. "Damn it, Son!" He kicked the ground and looked around to see if anyone saw Ringo's injury. "You need to get your crap together!" Doc walked to the motorhome, yelling back at Ringo, "Why the hell did I decide to go into business with a hot head, anyway?"

Turning a lopsided frown and counting all the mistakes he'd made over the past week, Ringo wiped sweat from his face and handled the whip in anger, startling the horse and pulling his gloves on, whipping in a mad rage. Taking a deep breath and leaning on the gate, Ringo scanned the ranch house for anyone else left to make a confession to, but there was no one available. He hoped for a priest, frowning like a desperado on the fence, but he was alone.

"Just me and you, Black Rio, me and you, boy."

The horse became restless at the rattle of the gate and the snap of his whip, spooking the animal and causing the stallion to run. Black Rio stood strong at the far side of the corral, flexing his muscles when he pounded the earth, and his body shook in defense.

"Whoa, boy!" Ringo eased within arm's reach as the horse trusted him. Both animal and man were stressed out, he stared into the black liquid eyes of the stallion, making his first connection with the horse. That was as close as anyone had come to handling the wild horse, other than transporting the animal, from Wyoming to Louisiana, causing more harm than good. No one was around to see that pivotal moment or to see him when touched his head, either.

"We're friends, Black Rio, buddy." He tried to win over the animal with a soft voice and smooth hand.

About an hour of building a bond, Ringo touched the horse for the second time on the nose, a simple trick Doc had taught Ringo to be animal conscious, even to speak the horse's language. When Ringo examined the horse, he could hear Doc's rough voice again in his head, echoing, *'Ease up to the horse, they have a language inside them and a curiosity, too. Get him to speak to you and then you ride him, Son,'* moving closer to the unsettled animal.

While Doc was cleaning up broken glass and blood inside the motorhome, Ringo was making good progress and learning the horse's demeanor, a teachable moment for any rookie. Not sure how to reason with the animal until he learned the animal's language; two hours into working the horse in circles, a herd of horses ran through Ringo's mind as if he were training Quarter Horses for Clem Cline as a teenager again.

The bull rider imagined himself on an Old West ranch, where horses thundered across the narrows of the Brazos River into the dusty town of Waco, hundreds and hundreds of horses pounded the earth on the first Chisholm Trail ride, he was there, at least in his mind, the picture was clear to him.

By that time of day, low in energy, he was exhausted and ready to resign and a dozen times he wanted to quit and find Brandi, and finish another bottle of champagne, but he didn't. Knowing Doc would disown him, Ringo continued to handle the animal in good nature, and not in a heated rush, either.

The Louisiana heat was over a hundred degrees by midday, falling back against the fence from dehydration, Ringo rested, from time to time, closing his eyes when he needed to pray. When the horse moved toward the rope and the bridle, Ringo started to believe in what he was doing, bonding, and connecting with the animal might work, he thought. Sometimes it took days and even weeks to earn the trust of a wild horse, but on that day, his style was different, pacing himself on a southern ranch worked in his favor.

Laughing at himself, "Maybe the coin was on "heads" inside the machine," Ringo muttered. "I might be turning some good luck on this horse," he said. Ringo edged closer to the horse's head, holding the bridle to his ear, and whispered, "Come on, boy, take it, Black Rio," rocking back and forth on his good leg as the stallion jerked objectively.

A dark storm thundered over Lake Pontchartrain, closer and closer, Doc stepped out of the motorhome and checked his watch to see how much time Ringo had left. The wind blew inland, and the bull rider felt the breeze on his wet face.

"You got one hour to ride that horse, Ringo," said Doc.

A gentle rain fell as Mickey, Tipp, and Conrad stood under the eave of the barn telling jokes. Suddenly, Black Rio turned on Ringo's command as he gentled the horse under his own language. Then walking under the carport, one of Conrad Cavender's daughters handed Tipp and Mickey sandwiches and sodas, and she didn't forget to feed her father his portion.

"Thirty minutes left," said Mickey, tapping his arms. "He hasn't even mounted the horse yet, Conrad." Mickey chewed the end of his cigar and even played the harmonica when he was bored of hearing about Ringo's bull riding career from Doc.

"He won't make it," said Tipp, perched atop a set of steps. "The weather is against him and the clock is running out."

Conrad's youngest girl, a tiny thing, spoke in a tender, sweet voice. "Look, the bridle is on the horse, Daddy."

The small crowd stopped gossiping and joking, Mickey checked his watch and nudged Tipp. Conrad, taking ten steps and being the lean horse trainer he was, stood and held his hands on his hips and observed Ringo's style; in amusement, by that point, he told everyone the horse was beyond command for one session. Doc noticed what had taken place and walked to Conrad Cavender's barn, crossing his arms in amazement.

"My boy needs a saddle," said Doc, urging and waving, whistling at Mr. Cavender.

"He doesn't have time," said Conrad, shaking his head.

Mickey cocked his face in a smirk, and shouted, "Get that man a saddle, Conrad!" Mickey flipped his cigar hand. "We have ourselves a showdown." He climbed atop a whiskey barrel for a better view. "Damn it, Doc, Ringo is one hell of a handler, but there's not much time left for him to showcase his skills in Mandeville today."

Stepping inside the barn, Conrad Cavender yanked a western saddle from his dusty supply room and handed it to Tipp, who handed it to Doc, who ran like hell to the corral where Ringo stood in appreciation. The horse spooked when Doc splashed water. Then thunder and lightning cracked and popped in the dark horizon, the black sky rolled in off the coast and the strong wind reminded Doc of the windmill that turned at Clem Cline's Ranch, just the same as it did at Conrad Cavender's ranch, slow at first and then rapidly.

"Open the gate." Doc toted the saddle to Ringo's side.

Clearing his eyes of sweat, Ringo gulped water and handled the saddle. "This stallion is ready for a bronc rider, Doc."

"That horse likes you." Doc told the bull rider.

"He's only got a few minutes," said Tipp, cupping his hands to his face.

Holding his wristwatch high above his head, Doc alerted the onlookers with a wave and a smile, and spoke, "He's got fifteen minutes." A lump formed in Doc's throat, gripping the gate until paint chips crumbled in his hands. "Ringo Bare," in a low voice, sticking his head against the metal gate, "Come on, Bull Rider, he's yours now."

"Fourteen minutes now," said Conrad Cavender, who spat tobacco on the ground. Then he snapped his watch around his hand, counting down the last ten seconds of each minute with his young daughters.

"You got just a few minutes to ride 'em," said Tipp, warning him.

"How many?" Ringo stared at the dark eyes of the horse.

"My watch says thirteen minutes," Mickey confirmed.

Carrying the saddle to the center ring, Ringo rubbed the leather down with his own scent and mixed a handful of dirt and mud on the fenders. The talented bull rider lathered the soil in the saddle and counted on an old trick Clem Cline taught Doc, which was passed on to Ringo as a teenager.

"Attaboy, Ringo," said Doc, poking his head through the gate and jumping in the spirit of the moment.

In some great conviction, with a tear in his eye, Doc stood in a gentle rain, wrapping his hands around the rails of the corral. Hoped. Prayed. Proud. He was emotional in a patronly way.

In a bit of a distraction, Mickey saw Conrad's oldest daughter, who was dressed in blue and brown designer boots and pressed denim jeans, splashing her way through the mud and muck to get a closer view of the bull rider working the animal without a shirt on his back.

She was able to turn any cowboy's head with her alluring bright smile and long brown ponytail pulled around her shoulders. The cowgirl was a barrel racer by day and a cross-country runner in college, whose eyes never lost contact with Ringo, cheering him on as if she had money riding on the cowboy from Texas. Ringo moved the horse to the side where the lady was positioned beside Doc. "What's your name?" Ringo curled his lips, teeth shone, and became elated as if she was already his date.

"Ringo?" said Doc, shaking his head. "Keep your mind on the stallion, not the pretty lady."

"Hey, I'm Bella."

"We'll talk later, Bella."

Ringo became lost in her soft green eyes.

Grabbing two umbrellas from his motorhome, Doc handed Bella her own. Ringo looked past Doc to see the lady in snug denim, who spun her umbrella when she looked at him. Maybe it was to let him know she cared. Her long brown hair was tied with a thin leather string and her eyelashes moved when she smiled at Ringo.

"Black Rio," said Ringo, moving close to the horse, "Big boy, we got visitors, so I need this Cowboy Up."

Easing close to the horse, Ringo felt competent in his bond with the horse and now the lady, too, closing the gap and tightening the bridle rope, the bull rider pulled the rope snug without spooking the horse out of his grasp.

Black Rio paced slowly around the corral and with a sudden hoist of the saddle, Ringo grunted and landed the saddle on the animal's back. With a jolt of the bridle snug, Black Rio kicked the saddle off into the mud.

"Five minutes, Ringo, come on," said Bella. Her soft voice echoed in his head as he picked up the saddle and winked at her.

Covering the soaked saddle with new fuel in his soul from a lady's sweet voice, Ringo rushed the saddle to the horse a second time and examined the language of the horse through his dark eyes, snatching the girth strap, and yanking it underneath the body of the stout horse. The man knew what he was doing, tightening the strap, hooking his left foot in the stirrup, when the horse reared, jumped, and stood straight up, Ringo fell into the mud, flat on his back.

Bella screamed.

"Whoa! Easy! Whoa, Black Rio!" yelled Doc. "Hey, are you alright, cowboy?"

"My pride is broken," replied Ringo.

"Don't scare me like that again," said Bella.

Surprisingly, Doc and Ringo looked at Bella, shrugging their shoulders, like father and son.

When Bella reached for him, her concerns strengthened him into a standing position again, and in some sincere way, they bonded. Ringo steadied himself against the rails, not letting it show how his cut hand was throbbing and foot pounded even worse.

"Three minutes," said Conrad Cavender, pacing in the rain, impressed with Ringo's style enough to strap his glasses around his head.

Slapping hands with Bella between the rails, Ringo smiled as if he was on the circuit again, winking at Bella.

"Get on the darn horse!" yelled Doc, clapping his hands and whistling. "Ringo, let's go!"

The gleam in Bella's eyes fired Ringo's spirit up, and grasping every word Doc said to him, the bull rider heard his father's voice echoing in his head again, *'Read the language of the horse, not the lady and concentrate, Bull Rider'* laughing to himself and remembering his next step with the horse.

Stepping with his soaked boots toward the horse, Ringo steadied himself when Black Rio stood motionless for the first time since he entered the corral, then Ringo tugged the saddle with the straps and flipped the stirrup down again.

"One minute," said Conrad Cavender, spooking the horses in the barn behind him with his grizzly voice.

Nodding as if he were the next Cowboy Up, Ringo raised his hand and looked at his father, just like he did when he'd won so many rodeos, years before, back in Texas.

"Ringo's got him now," said Doc, slapping hands with the pretty lady to his left, who spun her umbrella. For a second, Doc imagined it was Pomona beside him.

From the center of the corral Ringo swung his foot into the stirrup, grabbing the horn and cantle, and with all his strength, he mounted the beast. Even though they'd bet against the bull rider, in gratitude, Mickey, Tipp, and Conrad cheered when he climbed aboard the black stallion. Three girls stood beside Conrad Cavender, one was his, two were neighbors, stretching high on their tiptoes to see the hands turning on his gold watch. Ringo saw Doc's face and fingers as he'd done on the circuit, smiling, and nodding at what he'd done, wholeheartedly, in the moment, he did it, too.

In the midst of admiration, Conrad Cavender's little girls screamed after he made two rounds in the corral, "Ten, nine, eight, seven," causing Black Rio to jump, and throwing Ringo high off the saddle and into the gate, just like when he was thrown from War Wagon, years earlier.

Rearing wildly, kicking, bucking, the horse jolted out from under Ringo's grip, and it happened, his grip was lost without the stickiness of pine rosin on his hands, the bronc rider lost his hold. Then the horse broke and ran in circles. Spooked.

"Watch out, Ringo!" shouted Bella.

The stallion jumped again when the girls ran to meet Bella, which turned Black Rio in an upheaval, hitting the corral gate and tumbling to the ground, Ringo thumped the rails with his head several times.

Mickey and Tipp danced in the pouring rain.

"Aha, the Georgia boy's won!" sounded Conrad Cavender, handing them the money from his hat.

Ringo was limp. Knocked out. Doc and Bella iced him back to health. Mickey Starr and Conrad Cavender loaded the stallion in a horse trailer, slamming the gate behind the horse in relief as it rained. Later, en route to Georgia were Tipp Starr and Mickey Starr, who'd paid an undisclosed amount in a brown briefcase to Mr. Cavender for Black Rio.

13

The Last Pirate

The storm had passed, the sky widened, clouds opened up, and flags waved, as a gentle breeze made its way across Mandeville. Resting under Bella's care after his crash to earth, Ringo was grateful to accept her nursing talent as satisfactory and refused a hospital visit.

In New Orleans, Doc strolled alone with his hands in his pockets through the alleyway beside St. Louis Cathedral, whistling to the instruments when he was in his hometown. He knew what he'd find and what would be said when he stood face-to-face with his younger brother, who he hoped was a Pope and not the last pirate in the Big Easy.

Making peace with his brother would happen after the Mississippi River and hell froze over and became ice cubes in a tumbler while the world sang "Kum Ba Yah" and meant it. Doc stepped inside retail shops and bookstores, postposing what was on his mind, Chuck, a man he hadn't seen in years, who was most likely to be in his favorite hangout.

Doc noticed how all women were beautiful and how the number of street performers had doubled since his last visit to New Orleans. Other than the painted faces and a juggling act, not much had changed in the French Quarter.

A drunk man pushed a legless Pit bull terrier in a custom-made wheelchair and tried to fight people, only the ones who refused to open their wallet in public, so he could buy dog food and wine. Homeless people slept on benches, blues singers and horns sounded, and in some way, the world blended together on the streets, rich and poor. Timeless canvas paintings of historic places were being sold at Jackson Square in front of candy stores and retro soda shops, all of it lured in tourists and made the town more memorable. Doc Greenway overlooked nothing and appreciated the culture of such a unique city, overrun with heritage and rich culture, nonetheless, it was his hometown; alive and traditional.

Naive and restless, the past occupied Doc's memory, with Frank as the war hero; Le Joie, the wanderer; and Chuck the drunk. He expected his youngest brother to be dead, but if he was alive, his dream was to become the last pirate in New Orleans. Recognized as the wisest one of the four Greenway kids, Doc admired the courage of Chuck, known as the craziest one of the bunch. Turning over unresolved issues in his head, at any rate, Doc needed to see him before he moved to Barringer. Dead or alive.

Imagining a street preacher had knocked on his brother's door, pulling his head out of a glass of whiskey and told him, 'Listen, you need to make amends with your brothers and sister, half drunk or sober, do it, Charles Greenway, and make it right, got it?' but he knew that it was only in his head.

Years of disagreement divided him and Chuck, curling his fist tight to his side, Doc intended to defend himself if anyone crowded him, or if a stranger tapped his pockets for money. Walking by a line of artists, Chuck wanted a dark pirate ship painting as a kid, so Doc spotted one from a local painter, wrapping it in brown paper with a note under his arm. Brilliant gold and black colors were splashed on a smokey, gray canvas, and Doc, being a kind man, purchased it for his baby brother. All of it reminded him of Chuck and how they roamed the streets as kids together, riding bikes and hanging off balconies with beads around their neck. The good doctor kept walking and rushing behind a man driving a rickshaw, while Doc steadied himself inside a pirate bar, grim and dark, a light flickered on the wall.

The place appeared to be closed, so he left the painting in a chair, for another time. Then a big man walked out from the back room. "We're open, painter! What can I pour you, friend?"

With dark eyes and a few teeth missing, broad as a doorway, Doc had found his baby brother. "My brother wanted to buy this bar when he turned eighteen, and Chuck was my best friend, a long time ago." Doc felt like he was imposing, faintly and unsettled, he waited. "His last name is on the door." Doc sat at the bar. "Same as mine and I don't drink, Captain Greenway."

Examining his brother through his red eyes, Chuck cleaned the top of the bar, like he was serving one of his regular patrons. Then all the sudden, he realized who was in his bar, chiseled jaw and clean shaven, he smiled at the man.

"What the hell are you doing here, Gilbert?" The man locked his face in a definite thread of dislike, inside the dark tavern, moving from the cooler to the bar, working to avoid his brother. "Sweet Jesus, did the earth stop spinning last night?"

The Greenway Brothers didn't shake hands or offer the common gesture of a giant manly hug between them, remaining as distant as Union and Confederate soldiers at the Capture of New Orleans.

"Glad to see you, Big Brother."

"Are you?" Doc was stern. "I see you've changed your name from Chuck to Pirate Terrick Greenway."

"It's much cooler than Chuckie or Charles." Laughing, he wrapped his arms around Doc's neck. "I heard you changed your name from Gilbert to Doctor Tattoo, smartass."

His younger brother had a long black goatee, dried, and braided, black beads tied to his chin, like a real pirate dressed on International Pirate Day. Chuck's dark, jet black hair matched his black eyeliner and boots, too. His clothes were a medieval pattern, wrapping himself in a silver belt, sporting a black shirt strongly connected to his vest, roped from his neck to his midsection, he was an authentic pirate.

"It's me in the flesh from Texas."

"I should've grabbed your identification just to see where you were living now. Damn, you look good brother, but why doesn't it surprise me? It's criminal that you have no tattoos after twenty years." He was checking his brother's neck and arms for ink. Chuck flipped his brother's forearms over to find nothing, but pale skin and dark hair on his arms.

All of a sudden, the door swung open.

"Doc, you good?"

"Get over here, Ringo," ordered Doc, flipping his hand in peace. "Meet my little brother, Chuck Greenway."

In hesitation, Ringo reached his hand toward him. Chuck was thick shouldered, at least six and a half feet tall with heeled boots, adding to his large frame, a giant of a man compared to Doc, who looked odd beside the pirate, such a quarterback in a huddle.

"This is Ringo Bare, he's my adopted Texas son, and the bull rider might as well be in my bloodline." Doc hit Ringo's shoulder. "He's a good young man, too. We are proud of him as a bull rider."

"Good to meet you, Chuck," said Ringo, standing beside him. "Doc has told me nothing but good things about you."

Chuck looked at Doc and glanced back at Ringo's shocked face, pulling the beads on his chin, and cleaning an already polished bar, forming a thought.

Chuck poured Doc a drink.

"That's a damn lie! My brother has never said a good word about me in his life!"

Feeling the tension, Ringo stood beside Doc, watching as his father slid a shot glass back toward his little brother's hand, spilling the drink. Redness covered Chuck's face as he became pissed, emptying the warm Kentucky Bourbon in one turn.

"Did Doctor Gilbert coach you to say that crap?"

Chuck poured another one, pushing the glass in Ringo's direction, and stared at Doc, gloating in contempt.

"Chuck!" said Doc, clearing his throat. "My younger brother has the manners of a talking parrot. Until you get to know him and then he turns into a bigger ass each day. The boy doesn't need a shot, he had enough last night with Brandi to hold him for a while, right Ringo?"

He nodded.

"The Carousel Bar?" asked Chuck, beaming at the duo with deep wrinkles in his face, grabbing the shot glass and emptying the bourbon for a second round. The shot glass slammed the table when Chuck finished it.

"You want to take back up where we left off when "Fat Daddy" died, you controlling smartass, you?"

"You heard me!" shouted Doc, who was locked in a stare down with the pirate.

"When life gets tough, Gilbert, here, he runs off to North Carolina, like he did when dad smacked him, years ago when we needed him at home." His brother eyed him. "You were a big drunk back then, though, weren't you, Gilbert?"

"Dad was going to die, anyway," said Doc, rubbing his lip. "His liver was gone from drinking too much, and you are following in his footsteps, I see."

"Let's go, Doc!" said Ringo, pushing him toward the swinging bar doors. "This bar sucks, anyway. Let's go."

"He's the last Big Easy Pirate all right." sounded Doc, walking backwards. "And a damn big thief, that's right, who stole my father's stuff and pawned it for weed!"

Reaching for Doc's throat, Chuck's dark eyes bulged, and his face turned red, "Get the hell out of my bar!"

Hitting Chuck's chin with a right cross, knocking him off balance, Doc reached for him. Rising up with the butt of a pistol from under the bar, Chuck beaded down on Doc.

"Hey, put the damn gun down, Chuck!" said Doc. "You're not Jean Lafitte!" releasing the door from his grip and stepping backwards, Doc eased outside.

"Ringo!" shouted Chuck. "You better get Gilbert out of my face before we settle something from a long, long time ago." With his hands shaking in a rage to fight, Chuck walked around the end of the bar, rolling up his sleeves, and yelled, "And he better leave before I kill him!"

"Don't ever talk to me again." Doc told him.

"You always had something to prove, didn't ya, Little Brother?"

"No. Not always, but I'll start with you."

Doc stood in the light of the doorway, with Ringo tugging on his arm. "Don't call me the next time you need a lawyer or bail bond, Charley."

"Come back, fight me, Gilbert!" He yelled, waving the gun. "Please do!"

Exiting the doorway, Doc eased into the street with Ringo. In a rage, Chuck took long steps, pacing with his gun, and clamping his bottom lip with his teeth.

"Take that crippled boy with ya!" he shouted. "Before I put him down like a wounded horse!"

"You'd be the last pirate, if I hadn't pulled Doc off your dumb ass, Chuck!"

"Hey, Ringo, come back! I'll wreck you worse than War Wagon did." He stood beating the doors with his fist as a mounted policeman rounded the corner and stared at the men. Making their way down Pirate Alley, Doc and Ringo strolled the French Quarter together and cooled off.

"What's your brother up to?"

"Chuck stole it all when my father died. My brother knows what he did was wrong, too."

"Maybe you and him can find common ground."

"It's not going to happen. Look at us now and we're much different as grown men; we'd just kill each other and piss off the mediator."

***

Waking up a year earlier sweating and gasping for air, Doc yelled in his sleep, and that moment crossed Ringo's mind once they left the Pirate Bar. He asked Doc if demons chased him in his sleep. Doc told him the demon was his younger brother, who threatened his life with some Voodoo spell. They didn't talk about it again.

***

"Hey, let's find some Cajun shrimp, Doc?"

"Lead the way."

They walked a mile before Doc cooled down. Like a bloodhound, Ringo smelled shrimp cooking on a fiery grill, pointing the way to a small restaurant.

Standing outside the door, "Oysters, beer, red beans and rice, it's our specialty," sounded a friendly young lady. "Come in, eat with us, gentlemen?"

"Sure will, thank you." Ringo told the lady.

They ordered grilled shrimp and Po' Boy sandwiches before they sat down. Talking until they were as round as a Tennessee Whiskey barrel, Doc kept eating Cajun cooking, told stories about him and Chuck growing up in the city, even laughing about it.

"What was that all about, fighting with your brother?"

Wiping Cajun sauce and bread crumbs from his lips, Ringo finished his plate and listened. Doc dropped his fork and clasped his hands.

"Chuck and my father didn't get along and yet he got everything he owned, Hmmm? It doesn't make sense to me." Doc finished his water, chewing the last bite of his shrimp sandwich. Then he swiftly snatched a shrimp from Ringo's plate, and he slapped his belly and smiled.

"Good place to eat." Ringo splashed hot sauce on a cracker and chased it with a beer. "I favor the red beans and rice myself." He tried to change the subject.

"I never knew my brother to share a kind word regarding my father. I remember calling home from the Army, he'd say, how "Fat Daddy" caused another big fight. But he wouldn't go into details about it until I was stationed in Texas, three years into my tour."

"What started it?"

"Chuck defended my sister."

Ringo leaned back against the wall as Doc stared at his drink in silence. The server was in the back and the bartender watched the server, who had a sweet Cajun accent, and perfumed herself in fruity spray, lingering with her when she walked by the tables. The waitress was more Ringo's age, so Doc didn't speak any more about the waitress or his brother.

"Hey, I got an idea, hmmm?" snapping his fingers and touching his chin. "Let's get the air conditioner fixed in the motorhome and drive to Barringer in the morning? We are finished in the Big Easy."

"Yeah," said Doc. "Outstanding, that's a great idea."

Flagging down the waitress, Ringo asked to borrow a phone book.

"Yeah, of course. Here's your check. I'm Macy if you need anything else. I'll be back with the phone book."

"I'm Ringo Bare. In the restroom, that's Doctor Greenway from New Orleans."

Ringo handed Macy the money and flirted.

"Macy, you have beautiful brown eyes."

"You're a true gentleman and I bet you have a hundred one liners for ladies, don't ya, cowboy? Did you memorize that one liner, or will you just make up another one to get me in bed?"

"Nope. I'm sincere, Macy."

"I'll get you that phone book, Cowboy Ringo." She stopped and faced Ringo, pushing his hat down on his face.

"Pardon me, cowboy, but I overheard how you needed work done on your air conditioner?"

"That's right. We need it to be ice cold, for a long trip."

"Don't leave," she said. "Let me make a phone call."

The bull rider sat and found her eyes to be as appealing as any lady he'd ever seen in the Lone Star State. Graceful. Seductive. Her light brown hair complimented her hazel eyes, and she was considerate of others. Doc returned, crossing his arms and then cleared his throat with some water when he saw Ringo admiring the lady as if he were waiting on a green light to change.

"Where's the phone book, Loverboy?" Doc looked at Ringo, who watched Macy work. In a short time, the waitress returned to the table with two cups of soda.

"You won't need a phone book, gentlemen. My father or brother can fix your air conditioner for you."

The cute college-aged lady jotted something on a notepad, said, "Meet me here after work, say four hours from now. They'll fix it or buy it from you, either way. I live in St. Tammany Parish."

"We will be here at five o'clock," said Doc. "I know where St. Tammany Parish is located." He smiled and nodded.

"That's a deal," said Ringo, shaking her hand.

The lady left.

"I need $100," said Ringo.

Without asking why, Doc handed him the money. Placing the money in a leather pad, Ringo was thankful for her kindness. "This money might get our air conditioner fixed, so we can ride to Barringer, much sooner than later."

"Looks like she may like you, Bull Rider."

"How can you tell?"

"She could have handed you the phone book and walked back to the kitchen, unattended to your needs," said Doc, who brightened his eyes. "Plus, young man, she invited you to her home, Sherlock." He tapped his heart. "Think about her choices and what she did to find a way to get you to her house." They walked out.

"I got a surprise for you," said Doc.

"Your last surprise nearly got us killed."

14

Picture of Paradise

The more Ringo watched Doc play cards at the casino on the river for three hours, the more he thought about Texas and his Uncle Dale Bare, a betting man himself since he was in kindergarten. Weighing his thoughts, Ringo rested his head in his hands and debated. Not sure if he wanted to stay with Doc or catch a bus to Abilene, Texas, wrangling steer on his uncle's cattle ranch seemed to be a much easier road than making saddles in Barringer for a living.

Abilene was a big picture of life on a good sized spread, well established and paying big dollars, where Ringo could start in management, take over for his uncle; work his way into a $100,00 salary in a couple of years, too. Restless inside the casino, he noticed stars hanging overhead the size of baseballs. Ringo imagined the sky in Texas, sinking his boots into the Texas soil again, riding horses on a ranch that seemed endless; a good picture of paradise, it seemed.

The unknown was what he feared the most, even as an adult. Walking around until he found a seat at the ice bar, the bull rider saw a waitress serving drinks in a silver cocktail shaker and became impressed. Sparkling glitter highlighted her sky blue eyes and dark eyeliner caught his attention right away. She talked about the big, fat palm trees in Florida, and how she couldn't wait to move to Key West, drinking and blowing smoke in the Bar at the End of the World was her piece of paradise. Listening to her story, Ringo scanned the red carpeted isles, more modern than drinking watermelon wine on his tailgate and much cooler than his motorhome, he was content. In that moment, Ringo thought of Selena, back in Temple, washing away his memory with a pint of beer wasn't enough to kill the past, nor was it enough to uncloud his future.

The waitress broke his trance speaking about a million words a minute and he listened to a dozen things she wanted to do before she died. The bull rider remembered each one, which reminded him of his own dreams. Surrounding him were a hundred empty leatherback chairs, imprinted with the Saints logo, crafted for comfort and style, but they were vacant at that hour. Lights above the bar turned from blue to purple to pink, in that order, too, and cameras scanned tables and snapped mugshots.

Trendy paintings of a famed blue dog with dark glasses stood out as the primary decor, along with pictures of jazz instruments and well-known musicians were on display. A drunken couple found liberation in the chorus of a rock song from Detroit, swaying behind Ringo, and waving to him, in hopes he'd cut in on the next slow song.

The bull rider wanted to rake in his chips and cash in plans of his own, hoping the hands on his watch turned a little faster, so he could see Macy again. The young Texan tipped the bartender and surprisingly, she kissed his hands and lips, wishing him the best of luck in Barringer. He did the same for her.

Later, Ringo found a chair beside Doc, sporting his traditional dark aviator sunglasses and was seated by a glamorous red-headed lady, who pressed his leg for good luck perhaps. His white collared shirt turned upward, Doc favored style, game-by-game, and like a movie star, he won every hand. The dealer's face was red, and he shuffled his feet when he lost.

"Hey, Doc," Ringo nudged his shoulder. "You got a minute?"

"Yeah. Let me finish this game." He flipped his last card.

"21 wins!" said the dealer.

"Let's go, Doc. We need to meet Macy."

"I'll cash in and we'll go. Hold on, Bull Rider."

Raking in his chips from a green felt table, Doc handed them to Ringo as a gift. Black. Red. Green. Yellow. They left the casino with $3300.

"I'm impressed, but we need to go," said Ringo. "We only have twenty minutes before Macy's shift is over."

"You tapped my shoulder back there, what was that all about?" Doc stopped to listen to Ringo.

"Nothing. Never mind," said Ringo, looking away from Doc.

"You got something on your mind?"

"Nope." Ringo pulled on his hat in the evening sun. "And I don't need a strip club or a massage parlor, like you do to hash out my problems," said Ringo, shrugging his shoulders. The bull rider tried to flag a cab but failed. "I'm heading back to Texas, Doc."

"What the hell for?" His face and eyes surveyed Ringo in disappointment.

"Made up my mind."

"Is Selena having a baby?"

"I'm not sure about that yet? But I'm not going to Barringer."

"We have a damn deal." Doc bobbed his head with a tight face.

"Since our home burned and I lost my girl, I've been depressed." His face was long, Ringo said, "I've decided to take a bus to Uncle Dale's ranch in Abilene."

"You haven't seen Uncle Dale twice in your life. What makes you think he likes you enough to just take your ass in, housing you like some homeless nephew?" Crossing the street, Doc pleaded his case.

"In a Christmas card, Uncle Dale wrote that I should visit him more often and that's reason enough."

Doc checked his watch, turning and waiting for Ringo at the crosswalk. He thought about the fun he had at his Uncle Kenneth's farm and understood his eagerness as a young man.

"You're not going to Abilene!" yelled Doc, shouting over traffic. "Let's grab that cab." Doc flagged his hand. "We're not going to make it to Macy's restaurant in time, walking and talking and stopping in the street to debate."

Whistling and shouting, Ringo jumped in front of the next yellow cab and stopped the car on Canal Street.

"Are you crazy, man?" The cab driver stuck his head out and yelled at Ringo.

Leaning to the cab drivers' ear, Doc uttered, "He just got out of an insane asylum and needs you to take him to 204 Decatur for his medication."

"You guys are nuts, but that's the best grub in town," said the cabby. "I'll have you there in five minutes."

Doc dropped the armrest, turning to Ringo, "Uncle Dale didn't mean for you to stay a lifetime, he meant for you to stay for a long weekend."

Ringo gazed out the window as the cabby turned on Decatur. "I've made up my mind, Doc."

Pressing his fingers together, Doc nodded, speaking in a low voice. "Let me make a deal with you."

"I thought making saddles in Barringer was our deal?"

"Yeah, it still is. Then why are you headed to Texas? You have a problem with making your own mind up." Doc was face-to-face with Ringo, waving his finger in a rational manner.

With a sullen face, Ringo squinted and frowned his suntanned face, weighing his choices and choking on his own inability to make a big decision. The young man from Temple felt a sudden discontentment when he heard Doc's loud voice, ringing in his ears. Being co-dependent, Ringo didn't want to travel alone, the only time he was by himself was on the circuit and with his babysitter, years ago. Up until that point, Doc and Ringo were partners, but in that moment, things changed.

Adjusting his body when the cabby jerked the wheel, Ringo crossed his legs and arms. "Living with my uncle is easier than starting a business from the ground up with you."

Doc gripped the back of the driver's seat, pulling himself around and shaking his head. "The greatest moment you ever had was on the back of a deadly bull, making a damn good living for yourself, and busting your ass to be the best in the world."

"I was a happy man, back then, for sure," said Ringo. "But I'm not a happy camper any longer."

"Is that Ringo Bare in the back of my cab?" The cabbie looked over his shoulder. "Yeah, heck, yes, it is. I saw you ride Devil's Slingshot in Houston about four years ago. Hell of a ride, too!"

"That was a brute of a bull, sir." Ringo told him.

"Listen, I sure hope you get back on the circuit soon, you're the best bull rider I've ever seen."

"Ringo Bare wants to be a rancher in Abilene, though," said Doc, leaning his head back and rolling his eyes.

"Livestock?" asked the cab driver.

"Yeah," said Doc. "He's given up on one dream after the other."

"No way!" said the driver. "He's livin' the dream as a bull rider and a lady's man, I bet?"

"You got one of them right." Ringo told him.

"Mr. Ringo, here, doesn't challenge himself anymore, just chases women, gets drunk and loses my money."

"Ringo was my favorite bull rider on the circuit and I bet you were a proud Poppa, though. I wish my son would get off his ass and get his crap together in college."

"He's not my father," said Ringo, chewing on his lip and looking out the window.

"That might be so. But when he needs something, it's Doc Greenway who sells his favorite horse or climbs a fifty foot windmill to make sure Ringo Bare has what he needs, isn't that right, Bull Rider?"

Lifting his head, "Of course. Listen, Mr. Cab Driver, everything I am and have, is because of this man in the backseat. There's none better than Doctor Gilbert Greenway. I can never repay him, either, and he reminds me too damn often, just don't do that to your son." With a red face, Ringo continued, "Doc could have walked out on me when I was twelve, just like both my parents did, but he didn't. I drink to find my next picture of paradise, so I don't have to look back on the dirty deeds I was dealt."

"But I'm still right beside you, son."

"Count your blessings, Bull Rider," said the cabbie, parking the car at the curb. "Count every one of them, and one day you can repay him, in due time, but first, you pay me."

"He can start tomorrow morning at six o'clock." Doc looked at Ringo, reaching for his wallet. "I'm headed to Barringer with or without, Ringo Bare." Doc uncoupled his hand from the back of the seat. "You make the trip to Barringer, stay for a year and if you don't like it, just leave and paint that picture of paradise for yourself. Give it a year and then decide."

"We'll see." Ringo opened the door.

"I'll buy you outright," said Doc, closing his door. "Take your money, go live with your Uncle Dale, start your life the easy way, Bull Rider. That's my last deal with you. Ha-Ha-Ha."

With a strong Cajun accent, the cab driver said, "I'll volunteer to live in Barringer with the best bull rider in the country." The driver raked his hand through his hair, "When the Saints lose a game, my wife beats me, anyway."

The three men laughed at their own issues.

Stepping out of the car, "That's half the damn season, right?" said Ringo.

Doc flipped out a handful of money, for supporting him.

"Here's for the cab ride and the comedy show, mister. Go buy your wife some roses and pawn that damn television before football season starts. Maybe flowers will buy your way out of a beating on Sundays."

The men kept laughing as the driver landed Ringo's autograph for his son before he pulled away. Turning toward Doc, Ringo walked proudly beside him and smiled, which was in some gratitude, for what was spoken in the cab about him.

"Hey, guys," said Macy, walking toward her car. "I thought I'd lost my new Texas friends."

"We made it," said Ringo. "Thanks for waiting."

Macy placed her hand on the back of Ringo's head. "How's that bump you were talking about at lunch?" rubbing his injury in a circle.

"That $5,000 knot, you mean?" said Doc, examining Ringo with some disappointment.

The bull rider whispered to Macy, "It's better since you touched it."

"She's a concerned citizen." Doc scoffed, placing his hand over his heart. "If it had been up to me, I'd left him under Black Rio, using him as a tackling dummy on Cavender's ranch."

Macy took them to where their motorhome was parked. "We're having a birthday party; I'd love to have you as my special Texas guests tonight."

"Does your father chat with Texans, though?" asked Doc.

"They're divorced, but my mother does. Follow me."

***

Doc and Ringo followed Macy to her mother's house in St. Tammany Parish, a short drive, outside of New Orleans, just north of Lake Pontchartrain. Macy's mother owned a large property, fenced on three sides, with a newly paved concrete driveway and a steady flowing canal that divided the community behind their home. Garage lights were on as her mother stepped down from the back porch to greet Macy and her new friends.

"Hello, gentlemen," said the lady, who was thin with gorgeous long, sandy blonde hair and a bright smile. The smell of apple pie made its way from the kitchen to the foyer, slices of tomatoes and leaves of lettuce were stacked high alongside sandwiches on the kitchen table beside chips and soda for the men.

"Momma?" turning to the hungry men in the doorway. "This is the famous Doctor Gilbert Greenway."

"Gilbert." He told her, kissing her hands.

"I'm Raleigh."

"Good to meet you."

Macy pulled Ringo up to the front of the room.

"This young man is the famed Texas bull rider, Ringo Bare."

Her mother examined his chiseled jaw and muscles, nodding at Macy, adding her approval, and walking around the table in an elegant stroll.

"Ringo, hey, it looks like you could use a haircut or a dog collar from a local veterinarian," said Raleigh, making a ponytail of his thick blonde hair. "I have dog clippers in the garage, young man."

"Mother, be nice."

"I've been telling him to cut that mess since the fourth of July." Doc raised a brow. "Looks like Bigfoot has mixed with a shepherd hound."

Raleigh leaned on Doc and laughed. Dodging furniture and twisting her lively frame, Macy walked through the living room humming, hanging her handbag, and scanning the lake for an occasional osprey perched on a backyard post where their boat was tied.

Turning to her mother, touching her dimples and hair, Macy said, "Where's all the party-people at tonight?"

"Aunt Polly and Uncle Mark couldn't make it. Barbara Jean and Sammy Joe are down with the flu and haven't left the house in three days."

"We are the party-people," said Macy, hugging her mother. "I'm glad I brought these gentlemen, or no one would be here to celebrate your 47th birthday. They're a couple of horsemen heading to North Carolina," whispering and winking at her mother.

"Are you going to Carolina for stud service, gentlemen?" asked Raleigh, humoring Doc, pushing his arm.

The men burst out in laughter. Then Doc examined the modern feel of the stucco walls and admired the white marble floor, pacing around the great room while he flirted with Raleigh.

"These two stallions will be staying with us for a few days, while their motorhome gets repaired." She told her mother in a confident voice.

"Horsemen, huh?" Her mother whinnied and laughed in front of the men, pouring herself another pina colada. A laugh escaped from Macy as she grabbed plates from the cupboard.

"Good sense of humor," laughed Doc.

"Ringo, let's walk outside, see the backyard," said Macy, opening the sliding glass door. "You can help me with the firepit and tiki torches, cowboy."

"I'll follow you, Macy."

Walking across her backyard, she stood at a tall four tier, pineapple shaped fountain and felt the water and splashed Ringo. "I teach riding lessons on Saturday mornings," said Macy, stepping inside the fountain and watching him make a fire.

Fanning the flames and turning, Ringo asked, "You ride horses, too, huh?"

"Been riding since I was in first grade, had Shetlands, Quarter Horses, and bought Mustangs when I was seventeen. Our neighbors have stables and trails ten miles from here and we meet on weekends for trail riding."

Walking over to Ringo, carrying beverages and chips, placing the items between them. "Beer, cowboy?"

Flipping the lid, Ringo noticed the logo landed face down when he caught it. "Tails." For him, it meant a bad sign.

"Good beer. Do you have more wood?"

"One step ahead of you, I stacked the wood between cinder blocks this morning, in hopes of a good party and a bonfire, now look." She dropped her head.

"Wait! I see this as a good sign that we can get to know each other better." Ringo winded her neckline. "Your perfume smells good."

"Vanilla." She turned to him with appreciation. "Doc said, you handled Black Rio with ease this morning," darting her eyes and tucking her hair behind her ear.

"So, you've heard of Black Rio?"

"Yeah. That would've been a great moment to watch a real cowboy ride that stallion." Macy circled the fire. "I'd like to see you ride him again and I'd like to ride anything."

"He'd make a good bucking bronc," said Ringo, rubbing the knot on his head.

She stared at him with an interesting grin. "Are you taking a bus to Texas?" She poked the fire, dusting her hands on her jeans. "Or are you headed to Barringer? That town is growing, I've read about it in a few horse magazines."

"I am not sure. My uncle has a large ranch and a herd of Texas Longhorns in Abilene, I could help him manage the herd of cattle or I could move to North Carolina, help Doc."

Ringo told her about the wide open range of land without big city lights in Barringer, and how Doc said the sun drops behind the rolling hills, causing the town to glow more than any other place in North Carolina.

"There's good money in managing cattle in Texas, too," said Macy. "Long days and nights, branding calves and breeding prize beef cattle; tough life, though."

Rolling a stick in her hand, she impressed him so much he hummed and whistled in a low breath, admiring her as she gazed across the wide canal and lake, adding her silhouette to the landscape.

"Doctor Greenway is headed to Barringer, isn't he, with or without you?" She pitched a small chuck of wood the size of two coffee cans into the fire pit and lit the torches.

"Card games and saddles, that's what he likes," offered Ringo, nodding. "Yeah, I guess he is." He turned up the bottle. "His deal for me is starting a saddlery shop. Doc has the money, and he has a big, dreamy plan for a grand scale barn, and he's ordering leather next week." In a moment of uncertainty, he scraped the paper label off the bottle, tossing it in the fire. "We'll sell Barringer saddles to rodeos and western stores, handmade in North Carolina, shipped to points across the country, I guess."

"If your name is on the saddle, I'll buy one." Macy checked the knot on his head again and relieved the tension from his shoulders with her soft touch and smooth lips.

"You are a saint," closing his eyes. "I'll give you a saddle as a gift of my appreciation, for helping us with the air conditioner and especially this massage."

"I think it's a great idea to make saddles," encouraging him. "I like Doc's idea, honing your talent. Although I've only seen pictures of Abilene and Barringer in horse magazines, I hope you and Doc can work together, seems like a good man."

Her mother opened the sliding door. "Dinner is served. Hurry, come and eat," waving with a glass of wine in her hand. "I know you like a good meal, young man."

"Yes, ma'am." Ringo flexed the hand he cut in the motorhome.

"I can look at your knuckles," said Raleigh. "With a few more beers, you'll have enough courage to let me do surgery, I bet."

"It's fine." said Ringo. "There's no glass embedded into my knuckles."

"Mom's a nurse. Let her see your hand, cowboy."

"We didn't bring a gift, Ringo?" said Doc, taking a drink of tea and standing in the kitchen. "I have the perfect gift in the motorhome. I'll be back in a minute."

The phone rang.

"Here, Macy, it's your father."

"Hello." Macy answered, her dimpled cheeks rounded. "Well, I'll have Reggie fix it since you're too busy with your new girlfriend to help. Okay, I'll tell her, love you, too," chewing gum and winking at Ringo.

Touching Ringo's shoulder, Macy kissed him when her mother wasn't looking, a little peck on the cheek and she hung up the phone.

"Mom, your ex-husband said to tell you, 'Love you, Honeybun.'"

"That man loves all women," wheeling her head around. "After he slipped off to Gulfport with that thirty-five year old blonde *do-anything* of a nurse, I've hated him ever since." She stood and handled her glass, pouring herself one more. "Think I need another drink, how 'bout you, Gilbert?" she asked while reaching for the pitcher.

"Nope. I appreciate the offer, though." Doc walked over to where Raleigh was leaning against the bar. "It's rough finding the right person, isn't it?"

Taking a drink, Raleigh wiped her lip, "Heck, yes, it's rough. To me, there's no such thing as Mr. Right."

"Ringo, let's go check on the fire again." Macy suggested, signaling him to follow her, twisting her hips and dancing to the music her mother switched on through the house speakers.

"Looks like the sun has officially disappeared," said Ringo.

Macy stopped at the doorway. "Mom, would you ice the champagne?"

Raleigh held the birthday cake, twisting and dancing, "Already taken care of it, babe."

"Before you run outside, let's blow out the candles," said Raleigh. "We're in good company to make a wish."

They sang "Happy Birthday" and cut the cake.

"What did you wish for?" Macy asked while handing out plates.

"I wished these men would never leave."

They stood and laughed, looking around the room.

"Don't tempt us," said Doc. "We're having a good time."

***

The brick home had four tall windows on the second floor, but a wood door led to the living room on the first floor, and two garage doors were open for a wide view. Doc and Raleigh made their way around to each room and back to the bar to talk. By the water, Macy and Ringo reclined in Adirondack chairs, flirting and enjoying each other's company.

"You have a beautiful home," said Ringo, twisting to see the second floor, and admiring his new friend.

"Let's go," offered Macy. "I'll give you the grand tour and show you my art collection and some pictures of when I was riding trails in Mississippi and Arkansas.

The stairwell was painted yellow with skylights pointing at the moon and a black telescope stood tall in the corner, which was found angled toward the canal at a row of fine homes, the same style and value as her mother's home.

"We have lived on Legendre Drive since I was in first grade." She stood looking out the big window. "We moved from San Marcos, Texas to Mandeville, in 1986, but we love it here."

"Texas? Really?" He tilted his head at her.

"Yeah."

"So, that's why you didn't mind helping two fellow Texans, down on their luck, in dire straits, limbing a broken air conditioning across the Big Easy, huh?"

"Whose room is across from yours?"

"That's my younger brother, Reggie, who rarely goes outside, or talks to anyone. He's a nutcase."

"Your brother stays in his room all day?"

"He refers to his room as a Yeti Cave built for a one man show." She took a drink and laughed. "Most of the time, he looks at car magazines and half-naked women, the ones who live across the canal."

"He's a telescope man."

"Well, my brother can fix the motorhome since my father is busy with his *lady* friend. Let me ask him." Macy closed the door behind her and returned after a short disagreement.

"He said, he'll look at your air conditioner tonight since the people across the way have their lights off."

"Tell him the caveman, the keys are in the ignition and I hope he can fix it."

"He wants to go to some mechanic school in Nashville," she added, taking a seat at her desk. "I hope he leaves soon."

***

Most of the home had hardwood floors and the top level had gray carpet, lined throughout the rest of the home. After a short tour, Macy grabbed Ringo's hand and pulled him down the stairs.

"Babe?" said her mother. "Doc and I are going out for ice cream; we won't be gone long."

"We're looking for a root beer float," said Doc.

Ringo spoke up, "You kids, don't stay out too late."

Spirited and friendly, Raleigh kept up a beautiful place on the water, a mother proud of her house, raising two kids by herself, she had her moments. Her lake house at Christmas was admired by hundreds of people and each room had a story to tell, framed pictures, a grand view of the easy flowing canal, where birds perched, and Macy photographed gators. Occasionally, Reggie adjusted carburetors and changed out his mother's breaks and drums, handling breakdowns in the neighborhood, a hobby turned into some extra money for him.

"Did you hear that?"

"I did."

"My brother started the motorhome. Dad thinks he's the second best mechanic on the water."

"How is Reggie with air conditioning compressors and belts, though?"

"Reggie can fix anything when my father isn't available."

Looking out the window, Ringo asked, "Does he have the parts to do the job?"

"We'll soon find out."

Ringo sat, spinning in a leather chair. "We may have to spend the night here, if that's okay with your mother?"

"It's fine." She winked and wiggled her toes. "We have plenty of room for good company."

Staring deep in her eyes, Ringo was lost, touching her face and neck, a lady refined and seductive, he thought. They were attracted to each other, hearts racing and hands touching, Ringo walked to where she was standing by the window, Macy was close enough to kiss him, leaning in, she kissed him again.

Macy opened her eyes.

"More please? And that's just one step closer to getting to know each other."

"I have one more. What was that look for?"

She walked across the room. "We shouldn't have kissed each other."

"I thought you wanted to kiss me. You gave me the sign, winking and flirting with me."

"The sign?" She scoffed. "What?"

"You looked me up and down, checking me out since lunchtime." He reached for her. "Doc even noticed how you undressed me with your eyes."

"No way!" Macy scowled, pushing him away. "Let's not speak of this anymore. I'm not fast, Ringo Bare. This gal," tapping her chest, "she's not one of your rodeo queens."

Several minutes went by before she spoke to him again. The thought crossed his mind that she may be a nutcase like Reggie, with a few bolts loose, or she was playing some game with him. Ringo wasn't sure.

He smiled. "You certainly kissed me back, a few minutes ago."

"You rushed across the room and kissed me when I turned to you."

Her golden earrings and red lipstick just added to her looks. Thin. Seductive. A thought crossed Ringo's mind, but he was confused and didn't know what was next.

"I don't care if Reggie ever finds the parts, I'm fine with you here, even though you have mixed signals." Something caught Ringo's eye on the wall, he grabbed the picture. "Who's the guy in the picture with you?"

Her finger touched the glass picture frame.

"Well, that's my boyfriend. Make that my ex-boyfriend. We have broken up a few times, it's an on and off relationship."

"Boyfriend?" holding the picture and chuckling. "No way, he dresses like a seventh grade skater kid."

"That's why we're not together, well, one reason."

"Who's the guy in the other photograph? You have seven pictures, here. Are all of these guys your ex-boyfriends?"

"I haven't found my groove yet," she admitted. "I go through men like Elizabeth Taylor did. I tell them, '*Honey, I won't keep you too long.*' So, don't you get too comfortable in the saddle, Mr. Ringo Bare."

He took a deep breath, shaking his head in amazement, trying to figure the lady out, wondering what game she was playing with him, too. *Thank God, I'm not staying too long,* he thought.

"My last guy, he's working on an oil rig in the Gulf of Mexico," breathing a deep sigh, moving her hand to his chest. "Haven't removed his picture yet, happened last month and we're still on the fence, working things out."

"In this picture, he proposed, right?" Ringo spoke in a gentle voice. "Did you accept?"

"Yeah. I guess, I did accept..." She said softly, applying lip balm and puckering her lips at a small, envelope sized mirror. "Then the thought of marriage caused a huge argument, so we broke it off. He'll be home in a few days after you leave, and we'll talk it out again."

"A big congratulations to your engagement is in order, I think?" Touching his chin, "Lady, it looks like you found your groove, collecting a few men in the process, with pictures to prove your trail ride happened." Realizing he was just a number; she snapped his photo and they kissed again.

"My father doesn't like the guy in the fourth picture," she explained, walking over to her trophy case.

"The big question is," he grinned, "are you in love with any of these guys?"

"Heck No! I'm looking for a rich man with one foot in the grave and a big house in Maui. Hmmm, I mean, a man with kindness and a good soul in his big heart, one who cares for his wife, young or old, the endless love type, ...the bull rider type."

"Maybe you don't date, you just interview men." He laughed, grabbing his chin. "Sorry, I didn't bring a typed resumé with me for the interview."

Belting out a laugh, Ringo sat and fell back on her bed, cracking a rib as she kept talking about what it took to please her. Macy tilted upward and the certainty in her eyes offered him some hope and when she finished talking twenty minutes later, he concluded his thoughts. *Wild as a panther.* Ringo told himself. *She's not for me, but I have learned something from her.*

"I'm not ready to settle down or be anyone's widow when the oil rig blows sky high or a hurricane hits the Gulf of Mexico, making me live on edge each weekend." She jumped around.

"If you want my opinion, you're not ready for marriage because you're not in love. And don't pick a husband because of his career path. Make love because you love him, and you see yourself with no one else. Make him your soulmate."

"I need to tell him how I feel, don't I?"

He nodded along with her.

"I didn't realize it was that obvious. Anyways, my mother says that marriage sucks eggs."

Ringo held a trophy in his hand. "He won't take *no* for an answer, Macy. He's not going to let his little trophy wife-to-be get away from him, I'm sure of that. I wish you the best."

She rested on the edge of the bed.

"But when I want a wedding....," howling. "I'll have one and with the right man or men, too." She held two pictures in her hand. "He's not the one to spend my life with, though."

"What does the "Almighty, Mister Right" look like to you?"

She laughed. "I need to make my own way in life, my mother said, 'Don't depend on a man all the time to...' putting her hand over her mouth, peering at the lights that glowed atop the dark water. "Let me show you where I hang out."

Headed downstairs to the living room, passing the half dozen succulents, wreaths hung on a rock fireplace leading to the grand living room, the place she read and painted her pictures, it was amazing. Her home was breath-taking for all the young men who toured it. Macy's favorite room in the house, the one where she could kick off her shoes and be herself, without twenty questions about the wedding and if her father was going to help, was beside the grand living room.

Reaching in the refrigerator, she asked, "Do you want some kombucha?"

Nearly spitting his beer across the room, he said,

"Kom-whatcha?" doubling over him. "Is that what they call *it*, down in Bayou?" He asked, grinning from ear-to-ear.

"Did you think I was referring to sex, Tex?"

"Well, I wasn't sure if my picture was going up on your wall of shame or not?" Ringo examined her while he looked at rodeo pictures on the refrigerator door. "Were you?"

"No, no, and no way." She laughed. "We don't have pet names in Mandeville," walking toward him fluttering her eyes in low light, showing off her flat stomach. "Love, it is just plain, hot and spicy love, here, in Louisiana, with me, that is."

"Either way, I'll try some kombucha then," widening his eyes and looking at her flat waistline with the silver belly ring shining in the glare of the kitchen light. She hid the bottle behind her, moving close to his face, pressing the bottle against his waist. "Here's some kombucha."

"Hey!" He jumped back. "That's like ice. What's this stuff?" taking the bottle and reading the label.

"It's fermented tea." She responded.

"I'll stick to beer," holding his amber bottle and speaking Chinese, "Do you hear tiny Chinese voices telling you to submit to the kombucha when you drink this stuff?"

"You could do an Asian commercial."

With a serious face, he said, "You were saying upstairs, not to depend on a guy all the time to do what?"

"I mean, I'm not anyone's second fiddle."

Leaning forward, he said, "You need to be lifted on a tall pedestal and praised, little lady."

He hobbled over to where the kombucha was sitting, handing it to her, and she noticed his considerate gesture, and kissed his cheek for his good deed.

"Take a drink, you might like it."

"You've made me curious," said Ringo, popping open the lid and sipping the bottle. "This is different. And I like the taste."

"Good, though, right?"

"I like it." He said, wiping his mouth.

"You don't really like it, do you?"

"Nope."

"I'm glad you tried it. That means, you are accepting of change. It's a good sign to have, at least, that's what one of my friends in the Wolf Howling Club said to me."

He heard what she said, but didn't comment, in fear of hurting her feelings.

"This drink is awful. Is it out of date?" Ringo closed his eyes. "Yuck! This must be ancient; you need to send this bottle back to China."

She took the bottle from his hand, laughing. He leaned over, pressing his lips to hers and holding her soft face. Then the lady turned her head and stood.

"Remember, you don't like my kombucha," walking backwards to the kitchen, then twisting her rear, she howled.

"Let's see if you like my apple pie."

"Good idea," said Ringo, rubbing his thin beard. The bull rider followed her through the side door to the garage, where she had a spare refrigerator stocked with homemade pies.

"How's the air conditioning?" Macy shouted to her brother.

He signaled; good thumbs up.

"Reggie just fixed the air conditioner!" said Macy, who was pointing at a dark haired boy about seventeen, listening to the radio with the engine running. Ringo felt the cold air with his hand and knew Doc would be ready to drive to Barringer at sunup. After meeting her, Ringo was ready to leave.

"Cold and frigid," said Reggie. "Like when Macy dumps one of her many boyfriends for a new guy in town." Her brother turned, squinting his beady little eyes at Ringo. Opening up the motorhome door and aggressively nailing Ringo in the head as he walked close to the vehicle, Reggie laughed.

"Watch it!" shouted Ringo.

"Looks like my mother and Doctor Texas just pulled up," said Reggie. "Guess you two love birds lost your play time," howling at the moon and walking by Macy. "Enjoy the cold air, knot head." Reggie threw a rag at Ringo, slamming the hood and hatch of the motorhome.

Standing beside Ringo, Macy asked, "So, will you and Doc have breakfast with us in the morning? After breakfast, that's when I usually go jump in the hot tub nude."

"I'm afraid we will be leaving early for Barringer."

"Leaving for good? I thought you might stay a few more days, and... and.... learn to love my Kombucha."

Raleigh and Doc walked in the large garage, showing off their ice cream and milkshakes to Macy and Ringo.

"We are headed to North Carolina," said Doc, checking the cold air from the passenger's seat. "If the bull rider decides to go to Carolina, that is, we'll make western saddles soon."

"It sounds like you're running from something, old man," teased Raleigh, gripping Doc's shoulder and pinching his rear.

"He's chasing a dream," said Macy. "We all have dreams to chase. Some ladies watch them ride off into the sunset and want to be where they are, right, Momma Raleigh?"

"You got it."

Ringo stared into Macy's soft eyes, just like he did all the others he had known that summer. Uncertain. Confused. Interested. He howled and laughed and had no idea why. They walked inside to the kitchen and Raleigh opened the cabinet.

"I've always wanted a farm." Raleigh told Doc. "Anyone want a nightcap?"

Doc shook his head. "None for me."

"Can you grab Ringo another beer?" asked Macy. "I'll take a glass of Chardonnay. That's my nightcap, it keeps me from twisting and turning in my dreams."

Walking over to her mother with the wine bottle, Macy whispered, "Could you say something to convince these two cowboys to stay a few days, please?"

"We hope to have horses to train by autumn and saddles on their backs by winter," said Doc.

"Horses, for what purpose?" asked Macy.

"Quarter horses for barrel racing," said Doc, putting his arm around Ringo's neck and shaking him. "Ringo makes the best damn saddles in the country. So, our saddles and horses will be a good combination for training bronc riders for some extra cash."

"Busy fall," said Ringo.

"Bull Rider, get some rest because the motorhome must leave before sunup to make Barringer by sundown."

"Do something, mother," Macy whispered a second time.

"Macy and I have the next few days off," explained Raleigh, who stood between Doc and Ringo, hugging the men. "We'd be offended if you left so soon, how 'bout it? Can you stay, gentlemen? You wouldn't leave two attractive, half-naked Mandeville ladies behind for an empty house in Barringer, now would you?"

Macy winked at Ringo while Raleigh kissed Doc's cheek, smiling in anticipation.

The guys looked at each other's indecisive faces.

"We have extra sleeping bags or beds made for kings and queens," said Macy, howling.

Doc's eyes got big. "Ringo, can we stay?"

"We have to stay."

They all four howled.

"Two days, that's it," said Doc. "We have custom Bordeaux saddles to make in Barringer and a Teddy Roosevelt saddle to find."

"It's going to be fun!" Raleigh hooked arms with Doc, rubbing the top of her wine glass with her long fingernail.

"Macy, we've got to treat these men to the best brick pizza this side of Chicago," hugging her daughter. "For our gratitude, we'll need to plan a road trip to Barringer in the fall."

"Ladies!" said Ringo, with his arms open wide. "That's a deal we can't pass up." Standing beside Doc, Ringo replied, "We will wait in North Carolina."

"So, you're joining your old man, Bull Rider?"

Ringo gripped hands with Doc, pulling him close. "Macy convinced me; I need to make saddles."

Macy hugged and kissed her mother. Then kissed Ringo. "We are good friends now."

"Barringer knows how to draw a crowd," said Ringo.

"And if they don't, we'll show them how, Macy." Her mother sipped a milkshake and then her wine, calling it "Cream of Chardonnay" on a stem.

"That sounds like a road trip to North Carolina," said Macy, hugging Ringo. "I heard the fall of the year in Barringer is so beautiful, gold drips from sugar maple trees, and you can catch it before it hits the ground."

"It's true," said Doc, winking at Raleigh. "You will have to visit Barringer to find out the truth. I'll be waiting on you under a sugar maple tree, it may be a dreamy-illusion, who knows?"

"Dream until it becomes a reality," urged Ringo, pulling on his goatee.

A giant smile curled on Doc's face as if he would have been the man who enjoyed a good nightcap with Raleigh, but he stayed sober. The two men may have taken up homestead in Mandeville, if the timing was right and saddles didn't have to be made for Mickey Starr. They had obligations. Doc had always met his deadlines, determined to stay on track, and lead by example.

Raleigh turned up the radio.

"We'll have an extra night to entertain these ladies, make it count, Bull Rider," said Doc, turning to Ringo.

"Yes! Yes! Yes! said Macy. "It will be a wonderful night in Mandeville."

Well, the ladies danced around the men and the night was still young. "Lionel Richie couldn't have sung it any better himself." Ringo told Doc.

The four of them told stories and laughed late into the night. They talked about ideas and the many places they'd like to see in North Carolina, planning for it to happen on a sunny autumn day.

15

Baggage Claim

Two brick fired pepperoni pizzas, tons of soda, and a pitcher Abita Turbo Dog were shared, while Doc and his new friends told heart wrenching and funny stories, hurting from hours of laughter in the living room of Raleigh and Macy's home. Surprisingly, after a bit of small talk and hesitation, the men learned the Mandeville Howl, a cool teachable moment for a couple of fun loving cowboys. Something that started as a communal effort, to mimic sounds of the Old West, kept happening from porches and balconies each night at the same time, even Reggie joined in on the global movement. Bigger towns, especially out in the Wild West, such as Billings, Boulder, Denver, and now Mandeville, Louisiana howled when the clock struck eight, too. While Doc and Raleigh stayed outside releasing their inner wolf howl, Macy and Ringo split the last box of cheesy breadsticks, then Macy dug deep into the cabinet for a hidden, dusty bottle from Tennessee.

"Let me top you off, Ringo," said Macy, nodding, lips tight, eyes painted blue, and her movements and style started to impress Ringo. "Since it's your last night in town, would you like to remember it with a special treat, close and personal, something behind closed doors?"

"I think so, of course."

Placing her chin on his shoulder, she fell into his lap, and whispered seductively in his ear several thoughts, as a heavy silence fell on the room. Her words made his blue eyes bug and find the ceiling, then they found each other. He heard her word for word, and for whatever reason, what she suggested formed a frog in his throat and his heart became alert. He repeated it, but only to himself.

When Doc and her mother walked through the room, having their own conversation about religion and sex before marriage. Perhaps, with a bit of conviction, Macy finished the kiss and touched his chin.

"What's that again?" Ringo asked, changing the subject, lifting his bottle to meet her crystal tumbler.

"Tennessee Whiskey," said Macy. "Made from corn, filtered in charcoal, and stored for a few years inside oak barrels."

"Hmm. I'm impressed." Ringo felt the warmth of the drink on his tongue, a different flavor than an Old Fashioned and homemade watermelon wine.

"Good. It might loosen your Texas butt up for a sweet slow dance later and we can turn down the lights."

"Okay. You're serious, aren't you?"

Swirling her whiskey with her little finger, she kissed him, soft and subtle, tempted and followed by a low howl. "You heard what I said, right? I invited you to my home, fixed your air conditioner, and now what do we do?"

"Will we? That's the whiskey talking, and you don't mean it."

"I meant every word." She waltzed her way across the room, stood on his tip toes, something unusual in his eyes, and proudly laughing, she took a bow. Ringo stood and applauded. "Are you afraid this lady can out drink you, make you stay in Louisiana? Perhaps, fall in love again, Mister Ringo Bare?"

"I'm not much for being seduced from whiskey, but the ballet was an attractive rendition, and you really impress me."

"You wanted to kiss earlier," said Macy, touching his smooth face. "Take a drink, then kiss me," running her fingers down his face, humming a George Strait song, "You look so good in love."

Ringo and Macy whispered to each other for a while, and he was content holding her. Out like a light, Doc dozed off in a large grandfather recliner. Raleigh woke him and stumbled to bed, begging Doc to follow her and then they just kissed and decided on another night when she was without whiskey. Doc's eyes were heavy, and she was flat on his back in her bed asleep in a few short minutes, so he kissed her and he returned to his recliner. Laughing at Doc for talking in his sleep around midnight, the cuckoo clock sounded in the corner, Doc snored and howled.

Ringo walked over to Doc, "Hey, wake up, sleepyhead! Go get in bed, Wolfman Jack Greenway, you're waking the dead with that damn snoring and Mandeville Howling bit."

With the help of more whiskey, Macy choked a laugh back, doubling over in the kitchen witnessing Doc's strange howling episode and comedy show.

"Okay. Yeah. I'm up, Cowboy Ringo." He struggled to open and widen his eyes, making his way across the room. "I can make it upstairs, Macy. You kids have fun. Don't stay up too darn late, cowboy."

Climbing the stairs, Doc was tired, but made it.

"I'll have a pot of coffee brewing for you in the morning, sir," Macy sounded.

"No need for an early coffee, we'll grab something on the road," said Doc, winking and pointing at Macy and Ringo. "We need to roll into Barringer before sundown. You're a sweet lady, Macy, and much too good for that guy you are seeing on the oil rig. Dump him, and date Ringo. The bull ride isn't Coyote Ugly yet if you grade on a curve."

"Bless your little heart, Doc," said Ringo.

"Tell your sweet awesome mother in the morning, she's a peach of a woman and how much we have appreciated the hospitality," waved Doc. "Goodnight, lovers."

"I'll tell her, Doctor Greenway."

"See you in the morning, old man," said Ringo.

"Mom wants you two men to stay a few weeks, move in with us ladies and keep us company, and fall in love. She likes you. Do you know what your father did for mom's birthday?"

"Nope. Knowing Doc, I'm afraid to ask."

"He bought her a case of Andy Oliver wine and a gold necklace."

"He's a regular Midnight Romeo," said Ringo. "That's the best wine on the market, shipped from Virginia, I believe."

Macy pulled Ringo close enough to kiss him. "I'd like you to stay here, and we could get closer. Fate has it right, we are destined to become lovers, start a big family together."

Echoing in Ringo's head was Doc's voice, '*Keep your pants buckled, Bull Rider. Don't get any crazy ideas about staying longer than we have to, either.*'" Dimming the lights, Macy wrapped her arms around his waistline, yanking their hips together, and for the first time she let her hair fall beyond her shoulders and it was radiant flowing when she moved.

"Do you like me this way?"

"I love it." Taking a deep breath, "I'll be gone when you wake up in the morning." His face was sober. "I think we need to stay in contact, though, don't you?"

"Doc said that you need to go to bed."

"Let's go." He smiled, reaching for her.

"Stay a few more days, take the bus to Barringer, if you like me? Pretty please, Ringo, for me?"

"Doc will kill me and feed me to the gators in your canal. I've given him my word and made a deal, too. I know we are just getting started as lovers, but I'll be gone in the morning." Ringo kissed her forehead. "I can't stay, doll. Soon as I get this big order finished for Mickey Starr, then we'll meet in the mountains of Asheville, I promise."

"You're missing out, Mister Ringo," swirling her finger inside his palm and kissing him.

"We'd make a good couple, don't you think?"

She brushed his cheeks. "Maybe we'd be the best couple since Cleopatra and Mark Anthony. It would be a film, "Beauty and the Bull Rider," something of a mad love story.

Being an adorable Teddy Bare cowboy, ladies fell in love with Ringo Bare, right away, and it was no different for Macy, either, who was a love story herself. Her only problem, one that

Doc pointed out the day before, was she fell in love with a man's image, not his true character and it was something that was only temporary and superficial. That's what Doc told him to avoid in a relationship, a true sign of something short lived, turned in his mind. Admittingly, they became good friends on the trip, building a renewed confidence in the bull rider. Too much like his mother, Ringo was positive she wasn't the lady for him.

"We'd be a darling couple," Macy said, as a whiskey tear fell from her eye: one of hope and desire, genuine and true, perhaps; she kept crying when he spoke of leaving, brushing her cheeks. "I'd be pregnant by Labor Day, if you stayed." She cried more. The one thing that made her cry was rejection and she wasn't used to it.

They both laughed about it, too. Then he poured more whiskey and toasted one of the coolest ladies he'd ever met. Indeed, she was serious about being a mother, sooner than later.

"I'm just kidding you, Ringo. How about twins by Christmas? We could ride horses together, give lessons and make good money off your good name."

"We should get started then," said Ringo, laughing and unbuttoning his shirt. "My motto is, 'Don't put off until morning, what we can do tonight and now what?"

She whispered in his ear, which became her signature move when they kissed, wanting more than his attention. Her hands were on his chest, something he favored, too. Twirling her long hair, she whispered, "Can you stick around, see what happens? I have never been with a guy."

"Save it for a special time." He buttoned his shirt.

Becoming curious, he asked, "Does Tennessee whiskey make you whisper in a low voice and howl?"

"Maybe. Yeah. I'll be back," walking down the hall with a yellow night light to guard her steps into her room, she had something on her mind.

While she was gone, her brother walked out of his room, standing tall and round, then Reggie stared at Ringo, like an armed guard, angling his head at anyone around.

"Hey, strange guy," said Ringo, offering his hand for fixing the air conditioning. Ignoring him, Reggie turned and stood in the doorway and burped.

"Hmmm. Baggage Claim Cowboy, I heard you were the type of guy who'd give me the shirt off your back, huh? Thank you for caring so much for your fellow man."

"Hey, "Reggie the Jackass," what are you talking about?"

Her brother didn't even turn his head or see his hand extended, Reggie kept walking through the kitchen and into the garage. Macy scooted down the hallway in a pink nightgown, wearing fluffy pink socks, dancing, spinning, and laughing for her date.

"Did you miss me?"

"Yeah." He sat up tall and pointed to the garage. "Reggie just called me the "Baggage Claim Cowboy," and kept walking to the garage. What's wrong with him?"

"He has harassed every guy I've brought home. My brother is an inconsiderate ass when I have company."

"Where's he going this late at night?"

"He's a bit of a perv, watches the neighbors through his telescope and binoculars at night. There's a couple who makes strange love across the canal in that big three story house and Reggie enjoys the Late Night Show with Deva Let a Man."

"What?" Ringo stood. "Do you want me to stop him?"

"Leave him alone, he's a thoughtless pervert." She grabbed her nose. "Couples make love in big houses around here all the time, so what?"

The whiskey added fire to Ringo's bloodstream, he didn't mind fighting men or bulls after whiskey ran through his veins, but disrespect pissed him off. Rage crawled over his skin and into his face, dying to talk to Reggie about being a jerk to his sister and mother, too. Macy finished her glass, poured more, and belched.

"Do you want to watch a movie, Ringo?" Placing his hands back on her hips and slow dancing, she waited for an answer.

"No. I'm fine," he replied, holding her face with his hand. "I just want to be with you, not worry about distractions or the long trip to Barringer."

Walking over to get the Tulane football schedule, she said, "If we meet October 18th, like we planned.... Wow! O' Lordy!" She covered her mouth.

"What is it?"

"That was the weekend I was supposed to be married."

"Looks like you got a lot of breaking up to do, Lucy."

They moved to the sofa, grabbing her stomach, she groaned, moaned, and fell backwards.

"Ringo let's make a toast?"

"What's the special occasion, doll?"

Ringo held her hand from spilling her drink.

"Let's make a toast to Barringer, then make mad love."

Touching her chin, he kissed her, and suddenly, the door swung open.

"Macy!" yelled Reggie. "Where did our darling Mother Raleigh hide my telescope?"

"I have a shirt like that," said Ringo.

Reggie brushed cracker crumbs off the shirt.

"I have good taste in men's clothes, don't I, Ringo?"

"Fine taste." Ringo smiled and offered a thumbs up.

With a flush red face, Macy asked, "Did you look in the garage, pervert? The telescope is on the table in front of the big, white refrigerator or it is upstairs? I don't know."

"Hey, Teddy Bare, I fixed your junkie air conditioner, assman. Thanks for noticing my wardrobe and it's cool, too."

"Reggie, go do whatever it is you do for entertainment and leave us alone. Get out!"

"I'll be in my Yeti Man Cave if you need me, doing manly things," said her brother. "It's a member's only cave, Ringo. No Texans allowed." Flipping his chin, Reggie waved and walked away. "See you in the morning, Sister Macy, my love child, sister. Have a blessed night, War Wagon, wherever you are?"

"Get out!" yelled Macy.

Ducking his head into the room, "Hey, Ringo the Rodeo Clown, hope you get carjacked in Barringer." Reggie stood in the doorway. "I saw War Wagon on the internet, he sure took out your lucky rabbit's foot. Ouch, man! Tough blow, Rodeo Quitter! I bet that hurt your pride and career, didn't it?"

"Watch your mouth!" shouted Ringo.

Reggie belched and slammed the door.

"My brother makes me sick. Loser!"

Reggie walked down the hall, hanging his arms low like Bigfoot, when he was last seen in the Louisiana swamp, carrying two gators on each shoulder.

"Heck of a paisley shirt Reggie had on, though," said Ringo.

"Shhhh. This is our time, lover." Macy kissed him and unsnapped her bra. "Do you have to drive tomorrow?"

"I usually drive halfway." Ringo nodded when she opened her gown in the nude and stared at him, hair over her shoulders, smiling.

"Maybe we should call it a night and go to bed then."

Unbuttoning his shirt and showing his abs, Ringo asked, "Is this our unforgettable night of making love?"

Rubbing ice on her neckline, she whispered, "You have that cozy recreational vehicle now, and it's private, something of a memory," leaning over his body with her long brown hair, covering him as he kissed her body and face. "But I can't make love tonight, you'll have to wait." With a sincere voice, she continued and sat. "My cousin has a cabin in the high mountains of North Carolina, the town is called Leicester, near Asheville, the view on a clear day is twenty miles or more. I need to visit her in the fall, know what I mean?" She wrapped herself up.

Rubbing his chin in a curious manner, Ringo said, "We could meet at the cabin, fall in love all over again?"

He met her in the room she'd picked out for him to spend the night in, turning her in a circle and slowly lifting her off the hardwood floor. Once her feet returned to the floor, she ran into her bathroom.

"Are you sick?" Ringo held her hair again.

She started crying, "I'm bad sick. I can't make love. Can I have your bed and you sleep on the sofa, please?"

"Yeah, it's a fair trade." He hugged her.

Tucking her in the bed, she closed her eyes and fell asleep. Kissing her forehead and turning out the lights, the party was over. Later, Ringo finally dozed off and the big clock sucked in air and bellowed, "Cuckoo! Cuckoo! Cuckoo!"

He jumped up and laughed and fell asleep.

***

The next day, Ringo and Doc had lunch in Atlanta, where they howled, laughed, and listened to a man shouting, "Whatta ya gonna have? Whatta ya gonna have? Whatta ya gonna have?"

Hotdogs and fries from The Varsity satisfied their hunger for a while. Doc walked around the motorhome, noticing his map was missing and his Big Bailey fedora was gone, too. Ringo opened all the compartments in the motorhome and shouted, "Where the hell is our damn luggage?"

Looking inside all the compartments, and crawling under the beds, Ringo walked outside and looked inside the motorhome compartments again.

"That piece of work has stolen our bags! He had my damn shirt on last night, too." The bull rider stood in the middle of the motorhome, and told Doc, "Reggie is a dirty, lowdown Louisiana dog?"

Crawling out from under the motorhome with a wide grin, covered in grease and road dust, Doc belted out, "Ha-Ha-Ha-Ha. He's smart, but the good doctor planned ahead, cowboy."

Ringo raised his hand and stepped forward, "This ain't funny. My new cowboy boots are gone. That was the pair I bought in San Saba, for you and then decided they fit my feet better. Worked my ass off for those boots on the pecan farm. And who steals another man's underwear? Now, I'm out of underwear and boots."

"Listen, my Uncle Kenneth taught me a few things in my life and Clem Cline did as well."

"Like what?"

"Make sure you have a decoy, and if you have nice things, don't show all your cards in the first round." Doc laughed. "Reggie laughed when he told us that his new underwear was kinda tight in the crutch, too. He's a damn thief."

Following Doc around the vehicle, he watched him tote an old leather sack with an apple painted on both sides, sporting four apple tags on the handle. He looked over his shoulder as they entered the motorhome, pouring out the contents on the table, watching the bull rider's eyes widened, Doc and Ringo sat in silence for a moment.

"Where'd you get all that money, Doc?"

"I hide things in saddle bags and saddles, motorhomes, and boots. I stash stuff in totes and pouches until I need them." The good doctor held things of value close to his person and only he knew where they were kept. "When I die, check all my saddles, saddle bags, boots, and you might find a few items, you didn't know I had or we had."

Ringo flipped through the stacks, lost in amazement, and counted how much money was before him, and moaned.

"That's a heck of a lot of loot," said Ringo. "You need to get that money to the bank, before this motorhome catches fire or we get robbed."

"It's fine with me, laughing, as long as you don't cook."

"I'm not cooking when you have lobster money."

"This money reminds me of where I came from, in New Orleans, I mean, my upbringing, and how hard I've worked," a knot formed in Doc's throat. "As a teenager, I climbed fruit trees, and shook Anna apples and Molly delicious down to the ground, until I had enough food to make my mother proud of me."

"Did she make apple butter for you?"

"She fed Chuck, Le Joie, and Frank. My mother and I made applesauce and apple juice together. We were hungry." Slow tears fell from the corners of Doc's face. "When my two brothers and sister were babies and toddlers, I helped." Doc's eyes watered more with each sentence. "Deep down, inside, I helped as best I could when I was a teenager. My dad was out of work and my brothers and sister were hungry, Ringo. So, when Pomona left you with me, I told myself you'd never go without a meal, even if it was an apple, long as I could feed you."

"You never told me the applesauce story. You're a heck of a man, Doc Greenway, and your siblings will always remember you, for the apples and love you stood for, in tough times."

"When I see this big red apple painted on my bag, I think of Frank and Chuck, and see Le Joie's face, small and full of hope, too. I hope they do the same."

Doc neatly stacked the money back in his apple bag, Ringo noticed how much he had in the motorhome, or that was all he cared to reveal to the bull rider. More was in the bank; he just knew it.

"Doc, Reggie stole all of our luggage, too!"

Ringo was in despair, clutching his face, and pacing around the motorhome.

"Here, I wanted to see you sweat and hoped you'd cry over your damn cowboy boots." Doc opened a tiny compartment.

"You hid my favorite cowboy boots inside the stove?" Ringo laughed and hugged his father.

"I knew Reggie was a damn thief when he walked through the house; caught him taking money from his mother's purse and I warned him about it, too. So, when I went outside to get Raleigh's birthday gift, I hid a few things from that no good perv kid."

"When you came back inside with mud on your back, I thought you'd tripped over the dozen pink flamingos in the front yard."

Ringo grabbed his boots, trading his top-sider shoes for his San Saba cowboy boots, and stomped his heels in some relief.

"You don't think your *old man* is a fool, do you?" Doc asked while walking back through the rear of the vehicle, where he hid the money in another secret compartment he'd made.

Doc handed him a small plastic bag.

"Here, I got this for you."

"What the heck?" yelled Ringo. "You bought me Texas Longhorns bikini underwear?" The bull rider fell back against the seat when he saw the orange and white shorts.

"No. I didn't." Doc brushed his mustache. "Clem Cline told me to give the bikini underwear as a gift from him and he didn't want you to be without your Texas drawers."

Throwing his only pair of underwear across the motorhome, he jumped in the driver's seat. "You wait until Clem Cline's birthday, I'll get him a pink leg lamp, with fishnet stocking and a sign that says, "Turn me on, Clem."

"Those leg lamps are in style again."

"You know, Reggie stole my saxophone, don't ya?"

"Look under my polyester sport coat. I knew he wouldn't steal my jazz sport coat and blue slacks."

"You are something else, you know that?"

Doc told Ringo how Clem Cline cried like a baby the night before they left Temple. "Clem Cline wants you to know something, Ringo."

"What's that?"

"That you're the best bull rider he's seen since he watched his father ride in 1944. He's not the only one that thinks that, either."

"I dreamed about being on a bull again."

"I can see you waving to the crowd in those Longhorn boots and bloomers," said Doc, grabbing his belly. "That's a fashion statement in Austin, right there."

"Let's go to Barringer, Doc." Cranking the vehicle, "Sit back and enjoy the scenery."

16

Like an Old West Painting

Barringer was a welcoming place, nestled in the midst of rolling hills, was well-kept, coveted farmland, where hundreds of horses and cattle were scattered across the austere landscape, like an Old West painting. North Carolina had winding country roads that led folks off the beaten path to small farms and larger tracts of land, just the same as Central Texas did. The grass was green and lush, a prime spot where two men could rough up their hands on new leather and raise a herd of horses, starting a spread of cattle, if they so desired. In Barringer, folks gathered on weekends for car shows and lake cookouts, and without a doubt, the town was a place where relationships blossomed under a starry, moonlit night.

What occupied Ringo's time was more thought provoking, he recalled a woman and sometimes more friendships crossed his mind each day, tumbling inside the bull rider's broken heart, too. He was a curious young man who believed in truth and consequences, who'd been taught well by Doc Greenway and Clem Cline. The truth was, he had thoughts about being in a relationship again. Curious about Macy, Bella, and Brandi, while pushing Selena as far west as he could out of his heart, to start a new world in Barringer.

His time apart from Macy turned into a long drive in a motorhome with Doc. Every time Doc dozed off in the passenger's seat, Ringo howled, and Doc slowly lifted his hat over his eyes, "You'll fall asleep soon, big boy." The doctor grinned. "That was a good one, though."

Right off, Doc could tell Ringo was bitten, deep in the heart, by the Love Bug of Louisiana, or some strange Voodoo spell, that he should've left in Mandeville. His father didn't know which one of the "Honey Bees" stung Ringo the worst, but he was preoccupied, talked less, and pondered more than ever. The ladies tried their best to gain the attention of the bull rider, and they did, too; he did the same.

Reminiscing about his own 'Trail of Love' in the Bayou, Doc thought of the pleasurable nights he'd spent with Mary and Pomona over the years in New Awlins and wanted that same love for himself again. Something about the Big Easy, the act of winning and losing and even trying, was discussed, or was it just love sliding through the open Carolina air?

"Sometimes a lady is like a river, Ringo," explained Doc, watching the bull rider ease the bulky motorhome off the exit ramp in Troutman. "And you're just left standing on the riverbank, watching her travel right through your eager and hopeless hands. Then you decide to jump right in, half-heartedly at first, then wholeheartedly, yet without regret, taking a chance that you're not over your head in love. The union of shared feelings, it's a wonderful bond, a bit of euphoria and elation happens, time and time again."

"I seem to go underwater, though, in my own emotional whirlpool, drowning in only a spoonful of kisses." Ringo turned off Interstate 77 onto Highway 21, headed into Troutman. Then it was a short drive to Barringer, a strange land for Ringo and a homecoming for Doc.

"Ringo, it's hard to lasso the wind and make a memory come to life again, until you get serious about any woman and stop playing around, sowing wild oats."

"The worst part, dreaming and not doing anything about it." Ringo adjusted his hat from the evening glare on the windshield. "That becomes a nightmare of regret and days of soul searching, of what might have been, huh?"

"Hey, how'd you like Louisiana, anyway, Bull Rider?" taking off his seatbelt.

"I'd love to answer that question. Let me see, I had a gun barrel to my head, thrown from a wild stallion and nearly died. Next, I was threatened by "Chuckie the Pirate" and lastly, I got all my luggage stolen by some pervert car mechanic. Oh, yeah, I was seduced and learned the Mandeville Eight o' clock Howl. But I did hold her nude body and kissed her soft skin, though."

"You played King Oliver and rocked that song. Damn, I'm proud of you, playing that set like a professional musician. In just a few days, think of the life experiences you just had; you lived and loved in Sugar State."

"The world's a show, old man. Show 'em whatcha got to offer and be genuine about it, Doc."

The men stood and looked at Uncle Kenneth's home.

"Come on. There's something in the barn I want you to see," said Doc, pacing across the farm. "According to Clem Cline, it's still here."

"What is it?"

Doc walked ahead of Ringo, "You can have it, he said." With his hands in his pockets, he kept walking to the big red barn.

"Can you tell me?" Ringo insisted.

"It's Uncle Kenneth's old farm truck. Clem Cline loved his half-brother and told me about it."

"Is it for farm use only or can we drive it?"

"You made the trip to Barringer, didn't ya? We have saddles that need made and old trucks that need fixed. Plus, you might need wheels, and ...it beats walking or riding a horse three miles for an ice cream sandwich."

Doc removed his hat.

"I can fix this Ford truck," said Ringo, popping the hood. "It isn't that bad, a little rust around the fenders, the floor is solid, but does it crank?"

"Man look at this place," said Doc, walking under a sugar maple tree. "Pastureland to the right, the barn to the left and good neighbors are nearby. At least that's what Uncle Kenneth told me a few years ago about our neighbors."

Ringo sat on a straw trailer and soaked up the long view.

"Holy cow!" shouted the young man, grasping the tailgate and scanning the fields. "Uncle Kenneth let this place grow up, didn't he?"

Doc stood against a post and looked across the land he once roamed as a teenager. "Yeah, he did. I believe we need a farm tractor and sharp bush hog to clean this mess up. Kicking the clay dirt after a fresh rain. "We need two farm tractors for this job."

"We could make this place look as good as the one we left behind in Texas, but I doubt it." Ringo rubbed his head with both hands, melting in frustration, at the work ahead of him.

"He got sick and too old to work the land," said Doc, who stood at the fence. "Uncle Kenneth let the place go downhill. It's officially the worst farm I've ever seen in my life."

Walking to where the grass and field met with the help of a stream, the bull rider said, "Who has time to make saddles and work this land?"

"Hey, we're strong grizzly bears." Doc stood beside him with his hand on his shoulder. His legs were like noodles from driving. "It'll take time to bend this place back into shape again, but we can do the work."

"You left a well-respected Texas horse ranch for this overgrown North Carolina briar patch, Doc?" Ringo hammered the barn door with his fist. "This place sucks eggs."

"Little bit of sweat and we'll have the fields ploughed and planted soon." He stood beside Ringo, rocking back and forth on the heels of his boots. "We are a couple strong backs and tough hands, we can do it, can't we, Bull Rider?"

"No way." He sighed and rolled his eyes. "This place will send me on a bender." Ringo trailed behind Doc through the tall grass and weeds to a second barn with a bigger loft, half wide as a football field.

"In the early 60s, I helped Uncle Kenneth build this barn," resting his arms on a swinging stall door. "We worked daylight until dark, sweatin' all summer until we got it done. We could hardly move after we'd finished up. My back ached for a week. Looking back, it must have been the grace of God, who gave Uncle Kenneth the power and energy to build this place. Some of the best days of my life were spent on this farm."

"What made you move to Barringer?"

"I saw a chance to get out of New Orleans, escape the dirty hands of my father, and rode a bus to Paradise, North Carolina. That's what I called it the 60s. Hopped on a bus with a blackeye and a busted lip, too, and got the hell out of town. That's why Chuck was pissed at me a few days ago. When I mention Barringer, Chuck goes nuts, but he's never been here."

"You got into a fight before you left New Orleans?"

Slow to tell his story, Doc began, "My father wasn't a good man, Ringo." He stared at the ground. "Chuck turned out to be just like him, rotten to the damn core, inside and outside, and still today, bad blood drips through Chuck's dirty veins and my father was no different."

"I didn't get a black eye from my father," said Doc, dropping his sullen face and moving his mustache. "He wasn't around. I didn't get a baseball glove or a birthday card. Not one freakin' time did he care to call me once I lived in Barringer." His boot hit the barn. "I won't forgive him for cheating on my mother, either. Worst man I have ever met."

Ringo held his balance with a pitchfork, standing in the doorway of the barn, Ringo nodded and understood his resentment.

"Some men think loving your family is a weakness, I guess, but it's not. Love is a bond of strength and character. Being a father to the fatherless will make you a different kind of man and the world needs that kind of man, more than they need macho men. Bullies like Calvin Coolidge Cartwright, they get theirs in the end."

Closing the stable door, Doc locked the latch and remembered how Uncle Kenneth tapped the door three times for luck. Something that wasn't in the almanac, but he did it.

"Yeah, it's easy to find something else to do and not take on the responsibility of being a parent. I'm not a parent, but I'll be there for my kids through thick or thin. Try my best to be a better man than my biological father was to me, you can bet on that."

In the twilight, Doc remembered something significant to him, snapping his fingers and walking to the broad side of the barn. "I remember something else. Let's go take a look at the truck I learned to drive in, cowboy."

"Behind this big barn, I bet?"

Doc took a sharp left outside the barn and underneath a blue tarp was the shape of a truck, buried in dust and dry straw, parked with four bald tires. The evidence of heavy rust was shone on the driver's rear bed panel and on the tailgate.

"Holy cow!" said Ringo. "This was your first truck, a 1956 Apache?" pulling a second tarp from atop the truck bed. "Are you kidding me? This is a Big Window Apache."

"Yeah, that's my truck." Doc smiled, popping the hood. "And with a little work, we can get it running again." He opened the door for Ringo, "Hey, jump in, cowboy." Looking at the silver gauges and the black hood, Doc said, "Uncle Kenneth drove the truck for the last time two years before he passed. He told Clem Cline the title and the keys are at the bank, in a safety deposit box in Troutman."

"How much?" asked the bull rider, wiping the dust from the dashboard and turning the knob on the radio. The battery was dead. "Couple thousand, I bet?"

"Are you crazy?" said Doc, grinning. "I can't sell this truck to you, buddy. No money can buy this truck."

"Why not?" working the visor and adjusting the rear view mirror. "You don't need it." Pressing the clutch, Ringo ran through the gears once or twice, checking the transmission, and it wasn't locked up, the gears worked.

"No. Ringo, I couldn't sell my truck to you." Doc shook his head. "But I can surely give it to my son. Can you get it running in a week or two?"

Ringo twisted his head around to see if Doc was joking and he wasn't, looking at him from under his ball cap, he said,

"Are you serious about giving up your truck?"

"I've taken care of you, so far, haven't I?"

"You haven't killed me yet."

"It's still early evening." Doc looked inside the glovebox for anything of value. "There's a diner in Troutman, let's check out the house and find some food."

"I love hometown diners."

Preserved in the barn, the bull rider felt the interior bench seats, dusty and rusty, the dash didn't even have a ripple or crack in the surface. The Apache Chevy was waiting on Doc and Ringo, like a talented horse that needed a rider, and the land needed a couple of good hands, turning the good earth.

For a few minutes, Ringo spoke about upgrades and new tires, and how he could have the engine humming again. The truck needed a new timing belt, Doc told him.

"I'll have it running in seven days. Does Troutman have an auto parts store?"

Reaching in his pocket, Doc eased a smile on his face. "Sure does, see Blankenship and Melson. Let's flip a coin for it. Heads, I drive first."

Walking around to the hood, Ringo handled a quarter inside his palm, rolling the coin over his fingers.

"Tails. I'm the man chosen by the coin to drive this Apache into town."

"Would your Uncle in Abilene give you an Apache Truck?"

"I don't think so," flexing his shoulder. "When can I get the keys?"

"I'll have them for you in the morning after I open an account and make a big deposit. Hope you like that classic Chevy over your normal Ford," said Doc, laughing.

"That may be why you gave it away."

Later, Ringo nosed around the barn with a flashlight and looked for wood to build saddle racks, so they could start making saddles and marketing the brand sooner than later. Doc, on the other hand, wanted to see the inside of the home where he spent several years of his young adulthood before joining the Army.

Walking in his uncle's two story farmhouse singing and whistling, Doc suddenly stopped cold in his tracks, shaking and chill bumps ran down his neck. Making his way to the green telephone mounted on the wall, he heard the ringing in his head, a dreadful reminder of how he got the blackeye and a bloody lip in the first place.

Doc sat at the kitchen table holding the green phone, pushing it across the table, line dead, but he could hear voices from his past ringing, afresh. He recalled his last morning at home in New Orleans. The dark day had crossed his mind only a few times in twenty years or more, but not until he held the phone in his hand and squeezed it as tight as he could was reminded of the day he bought the bus ticket to North Carolina. Then he remembered when he was sixteen, in 1964.

***

Running down the stairs of his New Orleans home as a teenager, yelling, "Dad? Dad. Uncle Kenneth just called from Barringer, North Carolina," catching his breath as ideas rolled through his head, humming like a fast train on an open track about what he wanted to do that summer.

"What does my rich ass brother want this time, Gilbert?" said his father, picking food from his teeth and sucking on his lips, making a tsk, tsk, tsk... noise.

"He wants me to stay with him in Barringer and help him build a barn." He sat down at a small kitchen table. "Can I go, dad, please, please, please?" He examined his father's smirk. "What do you say?"

"Build him a barn, is that right?" His father kept his big arms crossed most of his life, and that day was no different. "He wants you to work on his farm, make him even wealthier, huh?"

"Uncle Kenneth wants to teach me how to make western saddles, too." Gilbert sat at the table, shuffling his feet in excitement, and ringing his hands, "And he'll teach me about horses on his big farm in Barringer."

"What the hell is that good for? Horses smell." His father crushed the newspaper and threw it against the wall with a wild look on his face and leaned back in his chair.

In a low voice Gilbert added, "You brother said, he'd teach me how to drive his 1956 Chevy Apache truck, too." The boy placed his hand on his lap. "Can I go, Daddy Luke?"

His big, round father raised up over top of Gilbert, and flipped the table across the kitchen, food and beer splashed on the floor. Young Gilbert impacted the hardwood before he had a chance to draw his next breath, and stars circled the boy's head, not being thrashed that badly since Calvin Coolidge Cartwright jumped him in a back alley fight.

"You want to spend my damn money on a freakin' vacation in Barringer, learn to drive his Chevy truck, and play around with horses, huh, boy?" Standing over him, shouting and spitting in Gilbert's face.

The force of the heavy table dazed Gilbert. In a rage of jealousy, Daddy Luke hit him repeatedly in the face and kicked him several times in the ribs before he satisfied his anger. Weighing less than two sacks of potatoes and a few coffee cans, back in those days, Gilbert remembered blood on his mouth and how red the blood was on his lips and hand. His good school clothes were stained, too. The best thing he had was ruined, he thought.

"Use my damn money for a bus ticket, so Gilbert Greenway can have a big-eyed time and party in North Carolina. I don't think so, boy."

Crawling backwards across the floor and with all the strength he could muster, Gilbert lunged and kicked his father's fat legs out from under him. He watched as the big man hit the floor. Unable to gain his balance, Daddy Luke crashed onto the hardwood floor and his head bounced.

"So, you think you are going to kick my ass, Fat Daddy Luke!" rolling around on the floor, drawing back with a block of wood, Gilbert pulled from underneath the door, clubbing his father in the head several times. The old man was out cold. Senseless. Motionless. Eyes closed. At that point, Gilbert didn't care if he was alive or dead.

Standing above him, he yelled at his father, "What a piece of crap, you are! You'll never touch me again!" Dusting his hands, Gilbert slammed the bloody block of wood on the floor and kicked it.

His father didn't move a muscle, thick and heavy, like he'd passed out drunk every weekend since Gilbert was born. Barely sixteen, Gilbert ran to the nearest pawn shop with the only items he owned, a guitar and a saxophone, where the man at the counter was generous in his offer. In the early 60s, it was just enough money for a bus ticket and a sandwich, that's all.

On June 6th, skinny Gilbert Greenway caught the bus in New Orleans and never looked back at his home. With only water between bus stops and the kindness of an elderly lady from Montgomery, who'd sat beside Gilbert for most of the trip, he wouldn't have eaten a morsel of food. After explaining his busted lip and telling his story, she gave him part of her tomato sandwich, three salty crackers and some goat cheese, for his aspirations of wanting to become a doctor. Gilbert gladly accepted it. He wolfed it down, like a stray starving dog. She tucked ten dollars into a book she was reading, handed it to him and stepped off the bus in Atlanta. He never saw her again. With a full belly, he traveled from Georgia to North Carolina, having great expectations about living in Barringer, North Carolina.

***

Walking up the staircase to his old bedroom, down the hall, Doc stopped at the end of the long hallway, where some of his uncle's belongings were packed away in a leather bag he'd made and didn't sell. More good leather was thrown over a cedar chest and some was placed on a bench, long before he became ill. Out the window, majestic puffy cotton clouds and bright stars made him feel at home again, standing as if he'd never left the room. The pink and blue sky seemed endless over Barringer; the picturesque landscape burned an image in his memory of a town, deep in his heart that never left him. What was a dot on the map for most people, was home to Doc Greenway, a place he'd missed, and wondered about was his new residence.

The fight in his father's kitchen, was a memory no different as an adult, tumbling in his mind, real to life, which was marked as the last conversation he had with his father. Months later, his father died of heart complications, leading to a stroke and a heart attack while fishing. Gilbert never attended his funeral but called his mother and told her how sorry he was for leaving her behind, restless and free, a man yet to prove himself. His move to North Carolina divided his friendship with his siblings, and sadly, few words were spoken after he left his hometown of New Orleans.

His uncle was the most honest man he'd ever met and spoke frankly to his nephew. "Don't blame yourself, Gilbert.

Not being able to make this right, well, that's Luke's fault not yours."

Those were the words his Uncle Kenneth told him when he handed him the keys to the Chevy Apache. Next, Gilbert turned the steering wheel as he pulled into Barringer, "I'll do better than he did as a father, you can count on it."

***

The words rolled inside Doc's head over and over, as he found himself in his Uncle Kenneth's room handling leather that would be useful for Mickey Starr's saddle bags, at least some of it was still in good condition, rubbed with a little mink oil and elbow grease.

***

In January of 1965, only six months after he'd moved in with his Uncle Kenneth, his Aunt Sandy suddenly died, just a month before their anniversary, too. It was a sad time for Uncle Kenneth and Gilbert in Barringer. Over time, he discovered he'd become a shoulder to lean on and an ear for his uncle, referred to as "A good someone to talk to," he told his nephew.

A year into his stay, loud voices came from Gilbert's room as he screamed, "Leave me alone, Fat Daddy Luke, get away from me!" fighting his father underneath his covers, freeing himself from the raging nightmares, a gloomy and lonely stretch of his life; one he got through.

"Gilbert? Gilbert," said his uncle. "It's okay, wake up!" nudging him after midnight. "It's a bad dream, you live here now. Your father is miles away. Relax. I'm your father, Gilbert, from here on out."

A dozen times Gilbert remembered his shirt being ripped off of his back by the hands of Fat Daddy when his mother was at the laundromat, lying to her about how his clothes were torn from his body when he raged against his kids. "Fighting the neighbors off, Ma," he told her, lying, in fear of another beating.

To keep that restless boy busy, Uncle Kenneth taught him to cut leather and make prize saddles for local shops to sell, and in time, Gilbert became fairly talented. He loved the craft of making raw leather into something of the Old West style, and useful for farmers and cattlemen, alike. He stayed with his Uncle Kenneth until the day he shipped out to Vietnam. Then Gilbert observed how different his uncle was from his father, a stout gentleman, thoughtful and caring, and the kind of man he modeled his life after.

In line with other recruits, Gilbert stood worried, headed for Vietnam, unlocking flooded eyes, when Uncle Kenneth clung to him in the drizzling rain. Then Gilbert hugged him and stood ready for war, witnessing the difference between love and hatred and how a good man was the example of fatherhood, not the exception. For Kenneth, to be a man of authority meant being purposeful and thoughtful, he said,

"*'If a man wants to make a genuine difference, he can do it, with character, too, for himself and for others.'*"

"You may be my nephew," touching his shoulders, "but if you fight the Vietnamese, like you have taken care of me since Sandy died," speaking with a broken voice, "you'll be home for my birthday, having won the war in a few months."

Hugging his gray-haired uncle, Gilbert saluted him at the bus station in Barringer, and told him, "If I die at war, please don't tell anyone that you are my uncle from Barringer." Kenneth stood confused. Yelling from the bus window, Gilbert said, "Tell them you're my father, you tell them that much, Dad, okay!" Uncle Kenneth cried like a baby and his uncle saluted him in honor, watching his nephew's hand hang out the bus window, disappearing in the distance, off to war.

Cupping his hands and trailing behind the bus at a slower pace than he'd imagined, Kenneth's voice, still broken, said, "Give 'em hell, Gilbert! Come home soon, my boy."

That's why Barringer felt like home to him, more than any other place he'd been in the world, the town was his homeplace. His uncle washed and shined that Apache Chevy truck once a week, prepping the vehicle, for when Gilbert returned home from war. Polished and shined. His uncle had that vehicle ready to drive once his army boots slapped the clay soil of Barringer. Gilbert returned.

Hugging his nephew until their hands made an impression, Uncle Kenneth was thankful to have him by his side again, home at least.

"Glad to be home."

"Missed you, son."

After the barns were built and the fields were planted, Gilbert received a letter of acceptance from Tulane University. Uncle Kenneth proudly made the trip to Tulane with Gilbert, where they had a drink together at the Carousel Bar in New Orleans. Having only a few hours to spare, Gilbert's family wasn't at home when they stopped by in the fall of 1970. Unknowingly, Kenneth Greenway has adopted Gilbert in high school and became his father. Gilbert called the man "Dad" until the day he died, thirty some years later.

17

Busted Flat

With a sense of accomplishment Ringo stood on the middle rung of Kenneth's old wooden ladder, bending, and swaying under his own weight. What was scratched on napkins, three weeks prior at Hotel Monteleone was finished, the saddlery shop was done. Accepting Doc's suggestion Ringo took the formal liberty of hammering all seven nails into the metal branches of a new lucky horseshoe, turned "heels up so his luck would never run out in Barringer," he said, marking the last task before more leather was ordered. Doc ran his fingernail over his jawbone, and pondered, "I just realized something."

Ringo made his way down to the hardwood floor in a state of confusion, turning and facing the horseshoe as if there was an unlevel feature, or something more was wrong with his lucky horseshoe.

"What?" arching his head behind Doc. "I don't see the error," said the young man, who stood behind one of the finished saddles, and watched Doc rest his hand on the horn of the first saddle.

"The horseshoe is tacked perfectly, and all the letters are correct," said Doc, laughing. "It's the acronym we didn't consider." The men had a good laugh because they now understood.

"Saddles of Barringer," folding his hands until he hunched over laughing in reach of Doc's shoulder, who raked his short hair and curled an easy grin.

What Doc had promised Ringo about a saddlery shop and what they had discussed on the road from New Orleans to Montgomery, had the capacity to store more leather from Luray, Virginia than they'd first anticipated. However, the next trip was written on a second napkin by Doc, an old-fashioned style was adopted, drawing with some humor, they'd accepted it to be the beginning of something great between them.

"Hats and boots, too." Doc shared his idea.

Ignoring Doc, Ringo laughed, "The last pasture is ready for horses," said Ringo, resting his arms on the fence post and kicking his foot on the wooden rail. "Let's stick to saddles for now, see what happens, huh?"

"I'll call this place Hermosa Lugar," announced Doc.

"Explain that in English, please," said Ringo, who watched wild turkeys fly from the field to the woodland in grace and peace. "So, what does that mean?"

"The Caballos would call this farm "a beautiful place," widening his thumb and pointer finger across his salt and pepper mustache. "The shop is ready for saddles, too. Sealed from the elements, Uncle Kenneth is looking down from heaven and he's proud of us, right now, Ringo. We did it."

In a low voice, "I'm supposed to fly to New Orleans this weekend to watch East Carolina play Tulane," said Ringo, staring at his father. "Macy planned this months ago."

"What are you saying, Ringo? We have four weeks left to make saddles for Mickey Starr, and that's a tight schedule," throwing his hammer against the wall. "There's no time for a long weekend of football and partying in New Orleans." Doc stood with his arms folded. "You can watch the damn game on television, eat popcorn and yell at the dang referees from Barringer, just like I do, partner!"

"I promised Macy."

"Has she called you since you moved here, huh?"

"I haven't heard from her." Looking out the same window, he looked at her in the picture on his desk.

"Seems she's made up her mind not to call you." Doc goaded, picking up his hammer. "There's no evidence that she's in love with you, buddy. Let me tell you, she's in love with herself and loves whoever pleases her on that particular day. Let her go and go your own way."

"If I would've been a rich bull rider, she would have chased me to Barringer, and we'd be a hot couple by now."

"There's something I've planned tonight; you are a big part of it. I'm having a welcoming bonfire and a little cookout for our neighbors, right here." Doc stood in the doorway with his back to Ringo.

"What's the big occasion?"

"To be friendly, meet the neighbors, of course," narrowing his eyes with a smile.

"That doesn't sound cool at all."

"We're cooking some of their beef cattle for supper and I promised them your Texas Cowboy Stew, too. I told them it was so hot the fire department had to water down the last bowl you made in Temple." He laughed at Ringo, and started singing, "Hot stew in the city, cooking wild and lookin' pretty."

"That's not funny." Ringo shook his head.

"Maybe you can give the young girl a tour of the place since you don't have to pack for Louisiana now?"

"What do you need me to do?" Ringo shrugged and wiped sweat from his forehead. "I'll just say a few words and leave, if that works for you?"

Doc took off his cowboy hat. "It's not. I'm going to buy a few parts for your truck in Troutman, the least you could do is be cordial in return and gather some good wood for the fire."

"Yeah, I'll have the wood stacked by the fire, limbs from the last storm will work."

"Make sure you take a shower, you stink like a dead animal," said Doc, laughing. "Use some French cologne, some soap on a rope, and wash off that dang skunk smell from your hands, too."

Ringo sniffed himself, shrugging his shoulders as Doc closed the door on the truck. The place looked great, the truck still needed a few things, but it was running well. Doc stood outside the grocery store when a sharp dressed man pulled up in a new Ford truck with more teeth in his smile than anyone should ever have in public.

"Showman Wagoner!" shouted Doc, who walked over to his truck. "How have you been?"

"You know me?" rubbing his beard. "Who are you?" asked the gentlemen in a western vest and flashy blue cowboy boots, hair slicked back like he'd flown in from Beverly Hills. Snubbing an old acquaintance intentionally.

"Doctor Greenway from Temple, Texas," said Showman, offering his hand and standing to the side with his hand on his elbow.

"Are you the golfer who made the hole in one at the Temple Shootout, won a million dollars, back in '88?"

"No way." Blocking the sun with his hat, Doc said, "I don't play golf," standing the same height as the card champ. "But I bet on the golfer to eagle or better, and I won $30,000 from the club president."

"You're a betting man?" Showman asked. "Did we play cards once or twice?" rolling his gold watch around his wrist, and wiggling his fingers, covered in diamond rings.

"Yeah, we did play poker several times, Showman."

"Well, Doctor Greenway, welcome to Barringer."

Offering a Creole accent, "Glad I found you, Wag-O_Ner."

Showman tucked his hands in his vest pockets. "Did we play poker in Waco about five years ago?"

"We did play downtown, and I recall, having a buffet and playing for big money, too."

"I do remember winning against you, Doc. It was on a Saturday night, the next week, I took a Cancun vacation with a sweet little honey blonde on your dime." Showman's eyes blinked. "My cards won $25,000 from you that weekend. I'd love to play you if you have any money left?"

Red ran across Doc's neck, "I still have a few bucks to spare." Both men crossed their arms, locked their eyes, arming themselves in curiosity.

"I've retired from losing, but here's my card. Track me down, five of us play at my mansion in Barringer on occasion, and bring some cash, play with the big boys, or are you a kibitzer now?"

"I'll see what I can do, Wagoner."

"What's your name again, Gilbert Something?" The man walked away and didn't care what his name was.

"Doctor Greenway!"

"I'm glad you moved here." The poker champ laughed out the side of his mouth and rubbed his bottom lip. "Are you the guy who has the new leather shop in Barringer?"

"Yeah," squinting his eyes. "Why?"

Showman pressed his hand on his chin, and shouted,

"Could you make me a leather wallet? I'll need something to hold your money in." Showman stepped inside the bank and waved through the large front window, tall as a spruce pine.

Soaking up the evening sun, Doc's blood simmered, having a great desire to kick the fly off his head that had landed while they were talking. Instead, he was one step closer to a card game with Showman Wagoner, the one he'd traveled halfway across the country to play, even dreaming about it. Later, in a fit of rage Doc smashed a bag of ice into a million pieces, remembering how Showman taunted him after winning in the last poker game, years earlier.

Back at home, Doc strolled through the living room and found the magazine with Showman's face on the cover, the seventy plus pages would help light the fire alongside the kindling for his big party.

Ringo had the oak wood cut and stacked for the bonfire but didn't plan to stay long enough for a bowl of stew to cool down. Doc iced drinks in an old metal cola cooler, staging it on the back deck while Ringo prepared dinner, slicing and chopping vegetables for a small crowd. He placed food on a traditional red and white cloth and glanced out the door to check on the arrival of their visitors. No guests. Doc turned the radio to a country music station from Charlotte, while he flipped steaks and burgers and sang along to the music. Without burning the house down, Ringo prepared his famous Texas Cowboy Stew and a surprise dessert.

***

As the blazing orange sun faded like someone had lowered a distant sheet of soft clouds to earth, falling behind a row of tall cedars at the end of Doc's property, he noticed a short man with no hair and a well-built woman walking toward his home.

"Good evening, neighbors!" said Doc.

"Good to see you again," a tall lady with gray hair replied.

"Wonderful to see you again, Reid and Martha. Ringo will be glad you made it, too." Doc hugged Martha and shook Reid's hand, sporting a neighborly smile.

"We wouldn't miss a delicious meal," said Reid.

"It's a beautiful place." Martha stood on the deck. "My daughter, Sarah Ann, is supposed to join us tonight."

"She is still getting ready." Reid glanced back at his home. "Sarah will bring marshmallows and some bamboo sticks, one of her favorite things to do."

"Great to have you folks over." Doc pulled chairs from the dinner table for Martha and Reid, who admired the bull riding pictures of Ringo that hung on the wall and spoke about the sport for a few minutes before the meal.

"You have done a lot of work to the place, tan tile and sage paint," said Martha. "You have made the place home again, Doc."

"We've been busy making saddles as well," said Ringo, walking through the farmhouse nodding in confidence. "I'll be outside if you need me, Doc. Good to meet you folks."

"It will be dark soon," said Doc. "You may want to do something with that firepit, but don't set the yard ablaze, or I'll call Smokey Bear on you."

"We can't stay too long," said Reid. "Martha's sister is in Silver Wings Hospice Care in Statesville."

"Is Mary Ellen your oldest sister?" asked Doc, with a long face.

"Yeah, it won't be too long." Martha caught tears with a tissue.

"If you don't mind, I'd like to see her." Doc rubbed his thin beard. "Mary Ellen used to make the best spaghetti and meatballs when I lived here, back in the 60s and 70s. I thought she was a beautiful lady."

Martha held Doc's hand. "We'll eat quickly, then ride to Statesville, and you can see her."

"You can ride in our new Caddy, Doc," said Reid, pointing to the driveway. "Burgundy in color and right off the showroom floor in Mooresville. She'd love to see you."

Reid, Martha, and Doc finished dinner, but skipped dessert, and said goodnight to Ringo. The bull rider listened to an owl hooting on the branch of a sugar maple for over an hour, while he finished a bowl of stew.

Hearing a young lady's voice talking to the cows in the neighbor's barn, Ringo became curious as any man would in his boots. The bull rider walked toward the barn and rang the cowbell in the doorway of the barn, recognizing the beauty of her long golden hair, who stood in a jean jacket at the water trough. Cows mooed and the herd moved to the barn when the bell sounded.

With her back to the bull rider, "Not another prank, bad deal, Daddy. The cows will think it's time to eat again," said the lady.

"Though, I have a great appreciation for pet names, you can call me, Ringo, until we get to know each other better."

He lifted up his head and their faces met for the first time, knitting his brow, and then grinning when she stepped from behind a wooden wall, an unfamiliar voice alerted her.

"Sorry for yelling, I thought you were my father."

Hobbling through the barn, Ringo followed her to the other end, to where she brushed her prize Hereford cows. He noticed her elegant egg-shaped face and her bright smile pulled him even closer to where she stood.

"If I was your father, I'd make you come and have dinner with me, how about it?"

"Were you the one burning the ribeye steaks earlier? I thought Kenneth's home was on fire." She laughed.

"They call that style of cooking charred steak in Texas."

Turning her eyes to him, she walked to where he was standing and dropped the bucket, dusting her hands. "Well, here, in Barringer, we call that overdone beef and if I were Doc, I'd teach you the difference between well done and overcooked steak. You'll enjoy a juicier steak, not a dry and burnt one, by adopting my advice, Ringo."

Walking back to where the bell hung, he tugged on the rope, "Maybe you can show me how things heat up in Barringer." He rang the bell again.

"Let's go," she said, washing her hands in the spicket. "I'll show you how to turn the steak and sear diamond grill marks that a lady likes to see." Sarah Ann walked, shaking water from her hands. "Folks in this part of the country, they prefer to see meat on a plate, not walking or being burnt to a crisp."

Her sassy attitude impressed him right away. Sarah Ann added dedication to her work, strutting in tight blue jeans and making tracks to the grill. Adjusting his cowboy hat, Ringo followed as she walked ahead.

"Do you know how to Texas Two-Step, Alabama Clog, or possibly you could teach me how to do the Carolina Shag?"

"There's a place in town to dance, and I've been there a few times, with guys who can dance better than they cook, that's for sure."

She turned, watching him limp across part of the broom grass, where he crossed a small stream and then made a trail through the lush green grass until they reached the hot grill, still smoking.

"I'll stay long enough to teach you how to make diamonds on steaks. Then I'm gone."

A few minutes later, Sarah Ann had diamonds on the beef and returned home. It wasn't long before the glow of a flashlight brightened as Ringo crossed her farm in the distance, heading toward her back steps.

"Oh, how are the steaks?" asked Sarah Ann, flipping the switch to the back porch. Ringo surprised her with a covered plate, he'd hidden behind his back. "I thought you might be hungry."

He spoke with a deep voice and his eyes shined sky blue as he stood in the doorway with a stout pose, making sure she noticed the cologne he'd splashed on his neck.

"O' mercy bless your little heart for crossing the yard behind a skunk. What's that smell?" angling her head outside, closing the door. "It's strong, too, really strong on the back steps."

"There's no skunk." He sniffed his shirt and questioned his choice of cologne, at that point.

His thick blonde hair covered his ears and his bangs partially blocked his blue eyes when he stepped into the light. She hooked the latch, and darted her eyes at his sharp look, a bit different than before, pressed slacks and a tucked denim blue shirt. His silhouette framed part of the doorway causing her to take a second glance at his sleek and polished style.

"That was kind of you to drop by, before the giant Carolina mosquitoes carry you off."

Handing her a hot plate, the proud bull rider waited for her reaction. Then she winded the restaurant style food he'd prepared for her, placing her nose gently over the plate and turning the tin up, her mouth watered after working in the barn.

"Oh, this looks delicious." She folded back the tin. "I'll leave it for my father, he doesn't mind a burnt, dry steak."

"What?"

"The corn on the cob looks buttered for heart surgery and I'll eat the sweet potato and green beans, though, if that makes you happy?"

"Sorry, I didn't know you were a vegan."

"I'm not. I'm a prime rib girl, with a splash of Au Jus on the side. Now that makes my day, Cowboy Ringo."

"I'll grill a prime rib for you next time."

She nearly spit her soda across the room.

"The beans are a bit salty. Ummm, Chef Ringo, you roast a prime rib, you don't slap it on the hot grill as if it were a ham slice. It's a lot like a friendship, seasoned in marination, and it takes time."

"Two hours, I heard, before a Carolina lady crosses the state line into Virginia, and rushes for the nearest chapel." He grinned with a deep smirk, tapping his boots.

"When does the buzzer sound in bull riding again?"

"To score points in Texas, it's an eight second ride, like the movie, starring Luke Perry." Ringo tipped his hat.

"That's how long a Texas guy lasts in bed, I've heard."

"Wow!" He covered his face with his hat.

"Don't mess with a Carolina gal, Tex, you won't win."

"Mostly nuns live out this way, I have heard."

She walked around the kitchen. "No nuns. We're just rough and tough and don't take a lot of crap from arrogant guys, who think they need to be on the cover of Gentleman's Quarterly."

He walked around the kitchen admiring the pictures and pristine decor, wondering how to best approach her. They stared at each other, back and forth, and then she blinked and turned away, grinning.

"Oh, hey," snapping his fingers with a serious face, "Sarah Ann, do you have any bread pudding in your fridge?"

"No. But I *love, love, love* bread pudding." She sat on the bar stool. "I'd kill for bread pudding."

"Good." He opened the door to leave. "I have heard it is a tasty treat and I happen to have some bread pudding in my fridge." Walking down the steps, and shouting, "I'll have an extra plate by the firepit for you. Do you want to share bread pudding later?"

She rushed over to the door, hanging outside barefooted, "Stop talking to my parents. They know I love bread pudding and you better not be lying about having bread pudding, either."

He kept walking and whistling and was happy he had a beautiful stunning neighbor. Then he turned and waved like every bull rider did in Waco after a good ride on the circuit, flapping both hands above his head as if he'd won, or better yet had her favorite dessert inside his fridge.

"Your parents seem to like my bread pudding as much as Doc does." He cupped his hands. "There's a fire burning bright, and I'll have bread pudding tonight."

Sarah Ann fixed her hair and makeup, slipping on her turquoise leather vest and gray cowboy boots, made her way to where two chairs were placed by the firepit. He saw her coming from a distance and stood for the lady, reaching out his hand like Doc taught him to do. Ringo gazed at his bread pudding and then at her plate, clearing his throat. "Here you go," handing her a fork. "You clean-up well for bread pudding, don't ya, Sarah Ann?"

"This looks delicious. I *never miss* bread pudding, but I can't stay too long."

"Why not?"

"I have a big date tonight in Barringer. Bread pudding might mess up my lipstick and it might be a long kiss and cuddle kinda night, you know what I mean, don't ya, cowboy?"

"Big date, hanging out at the convent."

"No. His truck bed." She joked with him and tasted a tiny bit of bread pudding, anyway. "He's a hot race car driver, though."

In great anticipation of a wonderful evening Ringo positioned himself in his favorite Adirondack chair beside the warm fire, in sudden disappointment, three bites was all it took to make the dessert in his plate vanish. Later, six beer bottles were empty by midnight, a long night of watching the stars alone, he thought. When a sports car pulled in Sarah Ann's driveway, Ringo focused on the young man kissing her goodnight and walking her to her doorway. They stood for several minutes and kissed. Ringo counted twenty kisses before he finally left.

Adjusting the fire, Ringo noticed Sarah Ann's bedroom light was on for a short time, then the room faded to black. On the eve of a Hunter's full moon, the firepit burned until the last amber turned dark as the side walls on his new truck tires. Ringo collected his empty bottles and hoped Sarah Ann's date bombed.

Questions rolled through his mind about the lady with long wavy golden hair, who occupied his thoughts and because of her, Ringo was thrilled to be in Barringer. Striking out, the bull rider called it a night and was proud of his awesome bread pudding.

18

The Unexpected Kismet

After Ringo's heart had been shaken to the core in a handful of unraveled relationships, being hit harder than a rough rider on a bucking bronc in Mandeville, was when he realized Barringer had endless possibilities in the romance department. Something brewed inside him, genuine possibilities, and for the first time in a long while his heart hummed. From that night on he wondered what burned inside Sarah Ann's heart, focusing on tomorrow and the next week with her and months ahead. Not adopting any poor practices from his mother concerning courtship and without crediting a point of merit from his pseudo father, Doc encouraged Ringo to journey on his own romantic path, who said,

"Even vulnerability is better than being alone, make an effort to crash and burn every once in a while, the embers will keep you warmer than clutching your own hands on Friday night."

The classic Apache truck was tuned up with a new four barrel carburetor and raised white letter tires, but the vehicle was plagued with considerable rust, planning to restore the automobile as soon as he sold a few saddles. Ringo washed and shined the painted places, dodging the rust, until it was accepted as a road ready classic again.

Mannerly and curious was Ringo's platform for the night. His Southern charm worked in his favor in Texas and even in the Bayou, he thought Carolina ladies were no different, a bit more difficult perhaps. Proud of what he'd done to restore life into Doc's Apache, it was time to speak with his elegant neighbor, sincere and intimate, hoping she'd be impressed by him enough to spend some time together. So, with a new spicy brand of cologne and some overdue courage, Ringo crossed Doc's property unsettled and full of questions for Sarah Ann. At midday, she could be found in her barn, brushing her horse in the cool autumn breeze and she was even prettier when she worked with livestock, too.

"Hey, Sarah Ann, I brought you a glass of lemonade," covering his heart with his hand, to convey his unfeigned style, stepping inside the barn to offer her a break from her chores.

"Are you trying to seduce me with some Voodoo potion that Doc taught you how to make, hidden inside some lemon pulp?" She unbridled her prize horse, feeding the gelding a handful of grain, then walked over beside Ringo, smiling. "You are a sweet guy, you know that. Bread pudding. Lemonade."

"No seduction yet. But it would be an honor to take you out tonight in Troutman. We could catch a movie, dinner and dessert." Adjusting his cowboy hat, Ringo gracefully handed her a silken flower that was hidden in his back pocket.

"I love dark velvet-red roses and lemonade. You are too kind and stop getting secrets from my mother."

"Are you busy tonight?" He turned a grin. "Your mother, she said you weren't doing anything, and I-I-I found out from your father that you're not committed to that guy you were kissing for twenty minutes last night."

"What about Selena in Texas, and Macy and Bella, your Louisiana lovers? You have a list of ex-girlfriends along your trail, Cowboy Ringo. I have done my research on you as well." She hung the bridle up in her supply room and leaned in the doorway.

"Hmmm."

"Yeah, hmmm. And who was the other pretty little show horse you spent the night with at the Hotel Monteleone? Was her name, Brandi McGregor, the hot as heck model from Savannah, who has been on magazine covers since she was old enough to wear a two piece bikini on Tybee Island. She's pretty, right? And "Hot as the Arizona Sun," or at least that's what was printed in one of the newspapers."

Pulling her long hair back, she watched him look inside his cowboy hat for a quick comeback line or some guilt free rebuttal, but she knew them all herself. Sarah Ann had the "goods" on that bull rider, just the same and right out of the bucket chute, too, she showed no mercy.

"Brandi and I went out once, and she's pretty proud of herself. The lady has little modesty left in the world."

He sat and took in her beauty and the way she worked the horses impressed him. To Ringo, dedication meant as much as beauty and class in a relationship, more in Doc's book.

"Those ladies have no place in my life. I've moved from one relationship to the next, trying to find someone I can't live without."

"Don't you mean, you're trying to find another one night stand to notch your saddle bags with on Friday night?"

"How did you find out about them?"

"I heard Doc speaking to Brandi and Mickey on the phone when Doc borrowed my father's electric apple peeler."

Lifting his head, "That man takes pride in my mishaps."

"Your glorious Savannah pop tart will be here soon, little Miss Brandi. Wasn't she the one who attempted to burn down The Famous Tobacco Barn, years ago?"

"I'm sure it was an accident. She's a nice lady."

Raising her voice, "Mickey Starr and the police caught Brandi in the act! She had the barn in flames when authorities arrived. They were smart enough to capture it on film, too. Whatcha going to do when they come for you, Bad Girl, Bad Girl?"

"So they say, you can't believe everything you find on the internet. Her and Mickey Starr hugged and reconciled their differences, and she's a good girl now. All of that stuff is behind her."

Placing her hand on her hips, Sarah Ann asked, "Are you defending her?"

Brushing his chin with his hand, "Well, we just don't have all the facts, now do we?"

"She went to jail! I have enough information to know you might be in love with that Georgia peach, just like all the other guys who follow bright lights and big images."

Ringo waved his arms, "It was just a phone call. And she's not coming to Barringer, anyway, is she?"

"When she stops by to see you, Ringo, don't let her near my hay barn or anything flammable, please. I know her type, she's a barn wrecker and a homewrecker and a slut, for sure."

Moving beside her, he said, "She called to check on the progress of the saddles for Mickey Starr." He brushed the horse beside her. "That's all, I bet?"

"Brandi?" She touched her lips. "Wasn't she the one you had drinks with at The Carousel Bar and slept with in New Orleans? How'd that workout for ya? Catch anything?"

Ringo's face turned blood red and he stopped what he was doing, glancing at her stern face and knew Doc must have spilled the beans about the Hotel Monteleone, meeting the "Son of the South, the hot model, and the millionaire, Tipp Starr.

"We never slept together." He continued brushing and checked the horse's teeth to see if they needed to be floated or not, but they didn't. "I slept on the cold hard floor."

"Come on, Ringo?" pulling her golden hair over to one side and twirling it, round and round. "No man sleeps on the floor with Brandi in the nude. Listen, if you ever want to mean anything to a lady, make it meaningful from the beginning. My father gets on his soapbox, day in and day out, but he makes perfect sense sometimes about the intentions of men."

"You seem mighty jealous of Brandi."

"No. Nah, no way." She continued to water the horse, scoffing. "I don't think so. It's not my style to go downtown, to be an uptown girl, anyway, like your Southern Comfort lady from Georgia."

He pointed at her feet.

"Whose bed have your boots been under, Little Darling?" touching the back of her neck.

Respecting her more each day, Ringo followed her from the barn to her house and wanted to know more about her. She bothered him, flirting more each day, and she checked his dating background with Doctor Greenway, which impressed him.

"You have a great mind. Your father said you wanted to be a veterinarian, a large animal doctor. That's cool. It pays well, too. I know Doc must have spent $20,000 on his horses last year and our friend Clem Cline spent twice that much."

She swung her long hair from shoulder-to-shoulder as she walked. Her answers were brief and to the point when she decided not to respond in detail, but seldom did she unfold her dreams to him. The lady bottled up her emotions and he respected her silence as much as her conversations, too.

"I see you got Kenneth's truck started."

"Did you see me working on the truck yesterday?"

"Yeah."

Ringo wiped his forehead, "I thought you were watching me work with my shirt off." He stared as she turned away. "A little owl told me that you were nearby."

"What will you do, now that bull riding is over?"

"Craft custom-made saddles and work on trucks, I guess." Tilting his head, "I bet you can't drive a stick, can you?"

Stopping in her tracks, he knew that would get her attention. "I'm not afraid to shift gears and turn the tires on your truck, Ringo."

Grinning, "Well, that's good." He stood tall and confident, getting lost in her soft, brown eyes, "How about dinner tonight at Drew's Texas Cattlemen? They have prime rib and bread pudding on special. And I don't use a coupon like your other cheap dates do on weekends."

"Wow! Bull rider, you're some big spender with the ladies, aren't ya?"

"Only when I want to spend more time with someone."

He admired the eyes of a pumpkin she'd carved the day before, preparing for Halloween, and talked about the trunk or treat events and corn mazes in the local area, promising to tour him around to a few of her favorite places.

Taking off his hat, he asked, "How about a candlelight meal together and some dancing, you game?"

"I will regret this, but I'm going to say *yes* to dinner."

"Well, good. We'll have a blast." Turning his eyes wide, "I'm not surprised," he answered. Ringo held out his hand and she gripped his fingers. "I reserved a table for two this morning for us."

Pulling her soft hand away, "You're one cocky Texan. I think I may have a headache from all the arrogance drifting in the air and I could cancel, you know?"

His grin ran away from his face, "Please, please, don't cancel. I was totally joking, somewhat."

"Well, pick me up at seven o'clock," closing the door behind her and waving through the glass.

Days and months had passed since he'd been that happy about being with a lady or even dating someone with as much class and drive as Sarah Ann, which made him feel better about North Carolina. Doc would be proud of him for not picking up a lady like his mother, too.

***

A spark of hope lifted his attitude, dropping his long face as he pressed his white shirt, and hobbled through the house in a sublime state instead of tacking saddles like he'd promised Doc he'd do. The bull rider found the mirror to be his friend. Being a diehard Bears fan, Ringo watched Texas beat Baylor in college football. Then he nervously pressed his tan slacks and tidied up his house since Doc was shopping for a used truck in Asheville, one that would satisfy his needs for hauling saddles to rodeos and other events. His father planned to return by Sunday, with or without a truck.

Ringo took a short nap with his cowboy hat on his face, like he did in Texas before each big date. Afterwards, he tried on his outfit in front of a standing mirror, failing at his attempt with a navy tie, and opting for a blue sport coat instead.

Sarah Ann spent an hour in the garden tub with the jets spraying her back from riding horses and practicing her barrel racing, having a small amount of pain in her left hip. Then she curled her long hair, outlined her eyes with a dark pencil, added light brown eyeshadow and snapped on the silver necklace, the one her late grandmother had given her as a lucky charm. She smiled and promised herself, "it's only one date" and still a bit skeptical about Ringo's long line of questionable ladies. Her heart was especially concerned with the night he spent in New Orleans with Brandi, crossing her mind a dozen times, and something about Brandi didn't sit well with her.

Ringo knocked on the door. Her parents planned an overnight trip to Blowing Rock, like they had done each fall since she was old enough to stay alone. When Sarah Ann opened the door, Ringo removed his hat, and noticed her silken hair was curled. Glowing with a contagious smile, he adored her ever more each time he saw her.

"You look radiant, Sarah Ann." He stood examining how different she was when she worked the stables, compared to the way she dressed in her evening wear.

"I just threw on a few things." She checked him out. "I like your Texas boots and don't you look handsome in a western sport coat."

"You look beautiful, Sarah Ann, as pretty as a picture."

They checked each other out as he kindly opened the truck door for her, imagining Doc had done the same when he was his age, dating in the city limits of Barringer. She continued to stare at him when he was courteous and attentive to her needs.

"Here, take my coat. Autumn nights are a little chilly in North Carolina, and I don't want you to get cold."

Her guard dropped a little and she became comfortable with him, settled and relaxed, more each day. At the restaurant Sarah Ann locked arms with him, snuggling him close as they walked past western cattle photographs, mounted longhorns, and long rifles racked atop old horseshoes. Amid one of the finest establishments east of the Brazos River, Ringo was proud of what he'd done to have her on his side, and they looked good together. An elderly couple told them the same thing, as the place reminded Ringo of Temple, Texas, too. Not having to wait less than two minutes, Ringo and Sarah Ann were guided to a candle light dinner at eight o'clock, right on time.

At the end of the room was a linen covered table, a small clear vase filled with a single red velvet-rose, a formal place setting, and between the utensils was a stamped leather menu. Ringo pulled out her chair and couldn't help but smell the sweet bouquet of perfumes on her neckline that awakened his senses each time he was close enough to dance with her.

"Right by the fireplace," said Sarah Ann, leaning forward and touching his hand, smiling. "My parents and I have eaten here dozens of times; I've never been fortunate enough to feel the warmth of the fire on my legs. Played well, a special treat, Mr. Ringo."

"Bull rider's luck, I guess."

"No. This is what happens when you plan something nice for someone else." Winking at him, she acknowledged what he had done over and over.

"It's an incredible place to eat and an authentic steakhouse," said Ringo. "I'm glad you're with me."

Clearing her throat and whispering, "Aren't you going to flip your coin, check your odds on your date tonight, like you do before football games and bull riding events?"

Feeling embarrassed that she'd figured his method of advancement with his coin, a slight superstition, he sipped his drink and snickered, wanting to check the read worse than anything. He peacefully declined.

"You've been talking to Doctor Greenway too much."

She laughed at him, "I'm curious to know if you think your coin will give you some luck tonight, covered in the sack, that's all? I'm a curious gal."

"Being with you, that's winning either way."

"We'll see, cowboy." She turned to flag the waitress.

***

They'd finished a mouth-watering prime rib and their sweet potatoes were drizzled lightly in a stream of melted butter, paired with fried okra and carrots. "Divine." She told him. As common as it may have been to order, they halved the ranch dressing and talked about their sweet tooth for a good dessert. Out of bread pudding, she frowned. However, a petite waitress lit a vanilla scented candle in the center of the table, recommending the dark roast coffee, one set aside for couples, and for those who enjoyed good company.

"Could I interest you in our house dessert?" handing Sarah Ann a small, leather covered book with a dozen pages of pictured treats, ranging from Mochi to Pavlova to Nanaimo bars. They both declined the wine list.

"Yes, please," said Sarah Ann. "My mother brags about the Creme Bruleé, do you have it?"

With her hands clutched, the lady nodded and smiled.

"I will have the same dish, please," said Ringo, pointing at the picture.

"Our Creme Bruleé has received several awards, from Orlando to that elegant place in the Shenandoah Valley, Andy Oliver Vineyards." The waitress stood with her hands behind her back. "You'll be extremely pleased in the rich flavor."

With permission, the first bite of Creme Bruleé was served from the fork of Ringo to Sarah Ann, rubbing the caramelized sugar on the tip of her nose as they flirted back and forth and drank coffee. The attraction was too obvious. He left a generous tip for the lady's hospitality.

Taking the keys from his hand in the parking lot, Sarah Ann insisted on driving his classic truck for the first time, zooming past the pumpkin fields and horse farms and past Lake Norman, she was having fun. Then Barringer. Ringo knew if she could handle a farm tractor in the tight turns of a hayfield, his truck would be second nature, shifting gears and pressing paddles with ease. She handled the vehicle without a hint of hesitation, a credit to her gender, he told her.

For the first time on a date, he became a sightseer, pointing at a motorcycle shop, located between a tanning salon and a tattoo shop on the edge of Barringer. Under a moonlit sky, Sarah Ann parked the truck and killed the lights at the top of her cousin's hay field and kissed him. When the porch lights flickered at the nearest farmhouse and the mosquitoes buzzed too close to their heads, he took over the wheel and drove slowly through the winding country roads to her home.

"That was a wonderful night." He held her hand.

Ringo had lost twenty pounds since leaving Texas, cutting his waistline to the size of a bull rider or bullfighter.

"It's not over." She wrapped her hands around his waist and kissed him for planning a wonderful dinner and treating her as if she was royalty, a queen, no less. The way she squeezed his hands and tugged on his coat made her consider what he'd said as she turned to her house and then turned back to his place. He was jovial.

"Can you come in for a while?"

Sarah Ann was a sweet lady, who worked at a soup kitchen when she wasn't barrel riding or training for regional competitions at Iredell County Fairgrounds. Once a month she supervised a small reading club of special needs children at the Troutman Library and ran laps with a small group of girls on weekends. Ringo knew her heart was in the right place, the kind of lady Doc would approve of, that is, if he had the courage to consider an engagement ring. Her character and reputation was without blemish in the local community. Taking a deep breath, Ringo realized his trip to Barringer was more than he'd planned. Better. Much better, especially when her soft eyes sparkled under pale moonlight.

"Yeah. Sure." She stepped inside. "I've always loved Kenneth's farmhouse."

Opening the refrigerator, Ringo replied, "I don't mind good company."

"That's to be determined."

They laughed.

Walking through the home, she admired the modern style living room, and from her parents was where Doc bought a long, cozy sofa, replacing the unlevel bargains Uncle Kenneth had left behind for Clem Cline to deal with. The dreadful, outdated 60s watermelon green, mismatched furniture, had to go, he told her. Doc eagerly donated the relics as quickly as he could, a better fit for an antique store in Statesville, and not cool enough furniture for a couple bachelors to own.

The storekeeper told Doc "It's a rare collection, for sure, but it might bring a fair price to a blind man."

Doc wasn't offended.

"What did he say about the watermelon style?" asked Sarah Ann.

"That's the ugliest living room suit I've ever seen, but I will take it for my blind brother, he's not picky. I'll tell him it's back in style again, and he might believe me."

They shared stories and laughed for an hour.

In consequence, Ringo picked out a deep cushioned tan sofa, three days before his date with Sarah Ann, hoping she'd have a drink with him and feel the warmth on her legs beside him at the fireplace. They enjoyed telling rodeo stories and shared jokes which made them cramp up from laughing. Then she buckled over in laughter when he told her about Black Rio and being knocked out for ten minutes. To her knowledge, it was the first time she remembered stepping foot inside the house since high school, except for when she volunteered to walk Kenneth's beagle until he felt better. After a few hours they made their way to the kitchen, where he brought out a chilled bottle of Moscato in one hand and mocha coffee in the other.

"Hot coffee or wine?" he asked, stepping behind the wall to see her face.

"I'll have a glass of wine tonight." She stood, walking up close to him. "I'll make coffee for us in the morning, Bull Rider."

The cork popped.

"When will we get up?" An image flashed in his head as he tended to wine on the counter top.

"Where would I sleep, though?" Sarah Ann asked, covering her grin, speaking loudly as he poured her glass. "Tonight, I might as well save my parents the worry of being grandparents too late in life and lasso you up."

"Let me get my boots off and I'll grab my rope." Ringo declared in all seriousness, smiling, and hopping through the kitchen on one foot, tugging on his cowboy boots and hoping she was for real, unbuckling his rodeo belt.

"Keep your pants on your hips, Ringo. I'm joking with you about the rope."

"Do you know how I can tell if a mad bull is going to take me down or not?"

"Nope."

"It's all in the eyes, lady. It's all in the eyes, naturally."

"What do you see in my eyes, Ringo?" She touched his face and gripped his hand, wrapping her up close.

"I see a woman who has been lonely, but for some odd reason," moving within arm's reach, "tonight, she turns her hips like she's happy and loneliness doesn't exist any longer."

"I see in your eyes, a cocky guy who is better with horses than ladies," smiling, "and better at bull riding than he thinks he is. He watches the crowd too much, for who's watching him. And let's not forget how he flirts, and he better not miss what's right in front of him, for flirting with Brandi, either."

He let out a laugh he couldn't hold back any longer. Ringo saw what she was doing, using the ice maker, and filling a cup while he rested on a tall stool, flirting with him.

"Ice lasts longer for a lady's hot flashes, I've heard."

"You are full of yourself tonight, Mister."

"Nope. Here's a bucket of ice for your neckline."

"Well, I've seen the way you look at me."

"I was just wondering why you dress like an old lady when you work in the barn, that's all."

"Dress like an old lady?" dropping her jaw. "We are good friends, and can speak freely without hurting each other's feelings, right, hmmm?"

"Yeah, of course," buttoning up his shirt and pulling his boots above his calf. The bull rider became curious about what was on her chest.

"I believe you would have more confidence as a bull rider again if you and your foot climbed back on a bull and tried it again. I mean, you are able and fit again, aren't ya?"

Taking a seat beside her, he said, "Wow! I didn't see that coming, doll."

Sipping another drink and handing him an empty glass, she said, "I'm going to need more, just bring the bottle since we're friends, and can speak freely to each other."

Ringo rubbed his chin as War Wagon flashed in his head, hooking him, bucking him, and being trampled had haunted his life for years. That night in Texas crossed his mind when he thought of riding again.

"You heard about my injury in Waco, didn't ya?"

Rolling her eyes with flushed red cheeks, she answered, with what was on her mind, "It was the bull that hurt your pride. That's all."

"I see it's going to be a long night in Barringer." His face turned rosy-red as he poured her a second and a third glass, moving from the kitchen to the sofa. "What's your point, anyway?"

She stood and clutched her wine glass, walking around.

"You have more capability than you practice. I've seen you work my horses and handle bags of grain on this farm, standing all day with custom saddles in your hands, so why not ride bulls again?"

"So, you think I'm lazy and faking my injury?" He slammed the bottle on the oak coffee table, making a thumping sound. "I'm not a man looking to gain sympathy because I failed at riding a bull on television. This pain, it's real. I don't look to lessen the blame for what I do." He pulled off his boot. "Surgery after surgery, cut after cut," pointing at his ankle, "and this ain't something I can fake, dear!"

"Maybe not, but you could push yourself more."

Rubbing his nose and sniffing, "Are you freaking kidding me?" pointing his hand and pacing around the living room. "Did you see War Wagon crush my foot three years ago? That bull could've killed me!"

"How long are you going to milk that Jersey cow injury, Ringo? How long? I saw it online. Overcome the injury, be the exception to the rule, I say ride the circuit."

"You've had too much to drink and said too much already."

"I've been here too long." She stood. "I'm leaving, good night!" She finished her glass on the way to the door. "That's my two cents, though."

"Damn it, Sarah Ann!" He slapped the cork into the bottle. "You're drunk. We were having a great night before you got drunk. That's my two cents."

She held the door. "Do you think I was being too brass, a bit salty, perhaps, and too forward for you?"

"Nope." He touched his lip. "You are an insensitive ass, little lady."

"You can start with my *little* Shetland pony and work your way up to bigger bulls again."

Ringo bit his tongue, locking his chiseled jaw as he watched Sarah Ann slam the back door behind her, stomping the ground and balling up her fists, ready to fight. The lady marched herself across the backyard under the glow of a streetlamp and he watched her go. Every so often in the dark shadows she turned back to see if he was watching her and knew the mind of that stubborn Texas bull rider. In spite, he tipped his cowboy hat, with his shirt unbuttoned, and pleasantly waved as if everything was alright home.

Around midnight his eyes were heavy as he reclined in peace on the sofa, then the doorbell rang. Half asleep, turning a cocky smile, Ringo stood, glowing with a bit of overconfidence jumping in his mind.

"I knew she'd come crawling back to me." He told himself, whispering and pulling back the window curtains as a thin female knocked on the front door.

"Baby, I missed you." She wrapped herself around his neck and kissed him.

"Brandi?"

Two more truck doors slammed in the distance.

"Tipp and Mickey Starr." Ringo held the door.

Lowering Brandi to the hardwood floor, in a bit of midnight shock, he asked, "What are you doing in Barringer?"

"Brandi had a modeling party in Charlotte with her agency," said Mickey. "Tipp, here, he wanted to see your saddle company since we were in the area."

"Congratulations on the new modeling job," said Ringo.

"Hmmm, thanks," said Brandi." Pressing her hands against his chest as if they were back at the Carousel Bar again. "Mr. Bull Rider, Ringo Bare," speaking in a Lowcountry *Gone With The Wind* accent, "Would you be my handsome date?"

Ignoring her, he shook Tipp's hand first. Then Mickey hugged his neck and slapped his shoulders, sporting a big grin.

"It's a long way from Savannah to Charlotte and up the road to Barringer," said Mickey. "I'm sleepy. Tired as heck, too."

With a bottle of beer in his hand, Ringo grabbed what his guests might need for their stay. Pillows. Blankets. Towels. "Make yourselves at home."

"It's so good to see you," said Brandi, smacking her red lips.

Mickey pushed his luggage and brushed his hand through his short gray hair, hanging up his hat on the wall.

"Doc said, we couldn't see the saddles. But he wanted us to stay a few days while he's out buying more Bordeaux leather in West Virginia and Virginia."

"Sure. Yeah. Stay as long as your travel will allow." Ringo explained where the food and drinks were in the kitchen and cupboard. "Bedrooms are upstairs and downstairs; showers for the men are upstairs. Bubble bath for the lady, it's right through those doors. I serve breakfast after the first rooster crows."

"Appreciate the hospitality, Ringo." Mickey climbed the stairs to his room. "I'm tired, see you in the morning for coffee."

"I'm wiped out." Tipp shook Ringo's hand again and followed his grandfather. "See you in the morning, Ringo and Brandi."

"We'll have a good time in Barringer," said Ringo, hanging his hat on the rack beside Mickey's.

Speaking in a sexy voice, "Hey, how does your cowboy hat look on my head, Ringo?" She ran her hand across the brim and down his nose with her long finger nail touching his lips. "We are together again; it must be fate."

The back door opened swiftly.

"I'm so, so, so sorry, Ringo. Please forget what I said, can you?"

"Sarah Ann!" shouted Ringo, who looked at Sarah Ann and then Brandi, pulling his hand away from Brandi.

"Ringo?" said Sarah Ann, in a shocked voice. "I didn't know you had company and I should have called first."

"Is she your late night cleaning crew?" asked Brandi, handing her a broom from the corner.

"I'm Miss Brandi McGregor from Savannah. This bull rider has invited me to stay with him for a few days, see his saddle collection and tour his home. You can clean in the morning, right?"

"I'm not the cleaning crew."

Squinting her eyes and netting her brow, Sarah Ann shot daggers at Brandi, whipping her head toward Ringo, and suddenly did an about face, to hide the pain in her eyes. Embarrassed and broken-hearted, she ran back home, brushing tears from her cheeks as they rolled down her face, like a trickle of rain had started to fall from heaven. Far from her image in the mirror, her heart felt crushed, crying more than she had in a long while.

In bed, she covered her eyes beneath a fluffy pillow and replayed the best date of her life. Remembering how they joked and laughed, her hope, deep down, was that he felt the same way. Her desires were sincere, kissing him goodnight and good thoughts crossed her mind about them dating, not just on weekends. With Brandi in the picture, Sarah Ann didn't have a chance to unfold her true feelings to him, or to talk more about seeing each other again. Thus, she curled up and fell asleep, broken into a thousand pieces, hoping for something more.

***

Brandi crossed her long, smooth legs, and watched Ringo pour her a tall glass of wine and plated wheat crackers and some cheese at the bar.

Ringo heard Brandi's voice, but all he thought of was what a wonderful lady Sarah Ann was, and how much she meant to him. Ringo needed time with her alone, a moment under the moon, where she felt comfortable again. To hear him out, if for only a moment, to walk and talk things out, would mean the world to him.

Pulling her long hair behind her ear, Brandi asked, "Who was that witch?"

"My neighbor and good friend." He nodded. "She's my best friend."

Finishing half her glass, Brandi smirked, "I believe someone is in love with the maid."

"Shampoo and a hairdryer are in the closet, down the hallway. Help yourself, and I'll see you in the morning."

He started up the staircase.

"Hey, Ringo, one more thing, I've been wanting you to do for me. Never mind, though."

Stopping in his tracks, he turned, "Yeah?"

"I have one question for you."

"There's a long pillow on the bed," said Ringo. "Make due, it's not the Hotel Monteleone, it's Barringer."

In a sincere voice, she asked, "Could you help me with this dress?"

He knew he shouldn't get too close as the words to a song rushed through his mind, *Fire is the devil's only friend.* He knew he needed to march upstairs and fall asleep; walk away; say goodnight and get out of Dodge.

"Sure."

She adjusted her tight fitted midnight blue dress, with lines of whispering silver and sparkling indigo, undulating, and uncovering her shoulders, squaring herself and whipping her hair around her neck, far from the zipper. All of a sudden, her sweet perfume and hairspray woke him up and with little effort, he was close to the fire, real close to the heat. Her eyes bubbled as she winked over her shoulder and her heart responded to his touch.

"Go on." She pushed her dress down, snug to her hips.

He took a deep breath, and the brim of his hat popped her shoulder and fell to the floor, bending back up, he tried to concentrate on the zipper.

"There you go." He was proud that he'd controlled himself.

Turning around to face him, she pressed his tight stomach, moving upward and holding his hand, she said, "Can you honestly walk away from a night with this brickhouse?"

"You are one voluptuous woman. Everything is working, so I better go. You are a sexy brickhouse, for sure."

Brandi dropped her dress to her skinny waistline and heard someone walking around upstairs. Tipp dimmed the lights accidently, Ringo cleared the lump in his throat and admired her body, while Brandi clothed herself.

"Hey, don't mind me," covering his eyes, "just grabbing some water." Tipp saw everything she had and so did Ringo.

"Here you go, Tipp," said Ringo.

The dark kitchen was quiet as a mouse until Tipp finished his water. Brandi stared at Ringo, nodding at the bull rider, and in a moment of awkward silence, Tipp knew something was up.

"Just like Hotel Monteleone all over again. I've interrupted you two, having a private dance, Ringo. I'll see you two lovebirds in the morning. Goodnight."

Tipp climbed the stairs.

"Well, it's an amazing brickhouse." Ringo walked over to her. "Wow! I can't take a tour of your house, right now."

She poured her own wine and emptied it in one turn, smacking her lips, and blowing a kiss off her hand.

Walking over to him, "Yeah. I was afraid you'd say that, and you can't *Cowboy Up* anymore, either" raking her nails down his chest. "Well, not like you once did before you became limp in your…in your foot, not riding bulls. You may not be man enough to peel this Georgia Peach, anyway."

Ringo tapped his buckle, turning his head, "Could you spin around once more for me, doll."

"How was that?" She placed her hands on her hips.

Grinning and touching his thin beard, he said, "Wait! Have you added an extra room to that brickhouse?" pointing at her rear. "Put on a few pounds since, I mean, since you left New Orleans, and it's hardly noticeable, to the naked eye, that is."

"You're an ass, Ringo. Seven pounds and everyone notices my figure."

"This cowboy, he's *up* to bed."

"I'm here for a week. You'll give in to this brickhouse, I bet money on it, cowboy?" turning her rear to him.

19

Brother Nature

After a week in the autumnal color of the Blue Ridge Mountains, Doc left Asheville and traveled northeast along the parkway in a late model truck he'd bought. Hitched to the bumper was a used horse trailer, he'd picked up for a grand, from a man who wanted out of the horse business, so he could spend the winter in Naples, Florida. In search of high quality leather, Doc was out of his element, a certified wanderlust.

While latching the trailer gate, another man walked up behind him in a green shirt and blue jeans, rounded specs, and wore a red, white, and blue ball cap that had seen better days. The curious gentlemen needed a conversation perhaps, speaking of his time in the Army, and what he'd seen while delivering horses in New Mexico and Texas. Thus, Doc became his friend. Outside a general store in Buncombe County, the veteran sat on his tailgate telling his life story, and questioned Doc about his journey. He unfolded his map; the men connected the line to Doc's next destination for him.

"What are you doing in these parts, anyway?" he asked, brushing his beard with his hand, and blowing smoke out his nose. "There's no horses in this trailer. Are you runnin' shine, mister?"

"No, sir. I'm lost."

"Chester Billingsley," holding out his non-smoking hand toward Doc.

"Gilbert Greenway. Ches, I'm trying to meet a deadline and find leather to make saddles."

"Greenway, you seem shaken up."

"I don't think you can help me, though."

Doc kept his eyes on the grid.

"I wouldn't be so sure of that, 'cause of my age and eyesight. My memory is the best thing I have left."

"Okay, then soldier, let's test your wits." Doc removed his dark glasses. "I'm in the market for leather hides."

"Cow hides, huh?"

"If you would have said that ten minutes ago.... I'd be in my rocking chair, picking my banjo; you'd be gone by now."

"I did. Well, point me to fine leather, old timer."

Using a magnifying glass, Billingsley thumbed the paper. "I don't need a map. I've got a mind like an elephant. Asheville Hides, that's where you need to be shopping."

"Just left there and they're sold out," said Doc, watching the old man move his mustache, angled his head, popping his ear with his thumb for a better thought. Ches pulled his ear and hummed, as if it was a lever to a magic chamber, unloading at a laundromat, for coins and answers.

"Write this down, young man."

"Good. We are getting somewhere, Chester."

After a half dozen suggestions from the wizardly man, he spoke, "Here's where I'd go to find hides, Greenway."

After some note taking and ear popping, which was in Doc's favor, pointing him to a string of good tanneries and leather masters, some better than others, he told him. The second leatherman turned him north to the rugged terrain of West Virginia, from there, a third man turned Doc to Virginia. All scholarly and unrepentant to what Doc needed to locate, was not exactly what he desired, though. The fourth man was aged, held himself up with a cane, routing him to a rolled leather tannery in the Shenandoah Valley, where Doc gassed the truck, and made it to where he needed to be, by close of business. Then after a long day, he stayed the night in a nearby hotel, filling his belly with shepherd's pie and Southern sweet tea.

Doc finally returned to Barringer about midday on a Tuesday. He assumed Ringo had gone into town for lunch with Sarah Ann, but he had other plans. One truck was parked in his driveway with Louisiana tags, so Doc walked through the house, and didn't see movement. Then he heard someone in the barn singing a Johnny Cash hit, easing up behind the man, pressing a gun to his back, Doc said, "What in the hell are you doing in Barringer?"

Doc gritted his teeth and clinched his fist.

"Now Gilbert, is that a cordial way to greet your favorite brother?"

Dropping his gun, Doc checked to see if anything was stolen or damaged, but it was fine, the shop was okay.

"Chuck, what's your mission on my property?" Doc locked eyes with his brother. "By the way, my favorite brother is Frank, until you change and move up the chart, then you'd still be tied for second brother."

The smell of leather and cow hides were strong from where Ringo had worked on Mickey Starr's saddles and saddle bags for almost a week, making progress, some, at least.

"I got bad news, Gilbert."

His brother pulled up a stool at a tall desk, and Doc replied, "It's always bad news when you're around."

Doc sat across from him in the corner and leaned forward, with a great desire to know why he rolled into Barringer.

"Ringo's mother is dead."

"Are you serious? Pomona passed away. Are you sure it wasn't Romona, her sick twin sister?"

"Yeah, that's what I heard; Pomona is gone."

"Pomona called the bar searching for you and Ringo, needing someone to talk to last month and she needed money."

"Of course, she did."

"I was able to help her, somewhat."

"Damn it! I've loved that woman my whole life." Heartbroken, Doc slapped the leather until an imprint presented itself beneath his hand.

"Three or four weeks ago, she died, I guess. One of my friends told me in the bar on Labor Day weekend, I think."

"Another pirate told you or were you talking to a drunk parrot, Chuck?"

"Don't be an ass, Gilbert."

Taking a deep breath, Doc shook his head and remembered her as a princess, young and radiant, a knockout blonde, turning heads wherever she went.

"She wasn't around much for Ringo growing up." Doc's eyes watered. "I wonder how he'll take the news."

"She was a heck of a lady," said Chuck, pulling on his goatee.

"You could have called me." Doc twisted the chair. "How'd she die?"

"I'm not sure. My friend didn't say." Chuck dropped his head. "Yeah, I should've called you. Sorry, bud."

"What else are you here for?"

"Got out of the bar business and wanted to see you. Plus, New Year's Eve will be my last day in the bar and I want you in New Orleans to celebrate with me. I will receive a big check from the new owner, and it would be my pleasure to take you out on the town."

"We haven't been that close, not enough to share a drink in years."

"Thought I'd find you, make amends." He sniffed. "Hang out with you. Had a vision about what Uncle's Kenneth's place would look like since you were the lucky one to catch a bus, stay here while we were all stuck with our wonderful "Fat Daddy" in New Orleans."

"You got another brother in Denver, go see him." Doc fell against the wall in disbelief. "Go check on our sister in South Dakota, talk to her and buy her a cool ape hanger chopper."

Chuck stood tall and broad in the doorway, moving around in a nervous manner, and reached in his pocket to light up a smoke, flipping his lighter and grinned, as if there was more to talk about.

"You can't smoke in here with the leather and the saddles," stabbing a knife into the wooden table. "Let's go outside by the firepit, before you blow us up."

Doc and Chuck stacked old boards from the barn, downed timber, racked pine needles, even started a fire together for the first time since they were teenagers. The Greenway Brothers talked about old times, how they ran the streets of New Orleans as kids and how they missed seeing each other on holidays. Doc grilled chicken and topped it with Cajun beans and fresh corn from his neighbors garden, still curious about Chuck. Under normal circumstances he would have chased his brother off, but felt he had something he wanted to say, so he planned to listen. Smoke covered the sky of Barringer, rolling like black cotton clouds into heaven as they cleaned up the place and talked.

"You want a beer, Chuck?" asked Doc, dragging the cooler between them.

"Make it two beers. Where's Ringo?" Chuck scanned the horse trails and fields.

"I'm not sure. His truck is gone, too. No one is at the neighbor's house, either. I just drove from Virginia myself. Been gone a week, picking up new leather for Mickey Starr."

Chuck rolled up the sleeves of his black shirt, the name Terrick was tattooed on his arm. Doc noticed things like that. Then Chuck pulled something from his pocket and lit it up.

"This is good stuff. Hit, Gilbert?"

"Is that your last one?"

"Yeah. Fresh from New Orleans and somewhere else before that, trucked in from Mexico, maybe?" Chuck couldn't stop laughing and grinning.

Doc took the joint between his thumb and pointer finger, then flipped his wrist as hard as he could.

Raising up like he'd been stung by a wasp, "Why in hell did you throw my grass in the fire?"

"Don't bring weed around me! You got that? Do you hear me?"

Laughing and taking a drink of beer, Chuck said, "Yeah. You got soft over the years, Doctor Tattoo."

"Nope." Doc rubbed his face. "I've gotten real about life. Come to think of it, just get the hell out and grab a hotel in Barringer!"

They stood ready to slam each other.

"Take it easy! Don't push me, Gilbert. I'm gone." Chuck raised his hands, not wanting to start a fight. "I'll be back when you cool off and we'll talk more, Doctor G."

"Get off my property!"

20

By the Light of a Lantern

Two days later, Chuck returned drunk as a skunk, staggering around the fire and kept his balance with a stick, raising his hands differently with each story he told. Doc allowed him to stay for the night and gave him an encore for his impersonations and enjoyed his company. Both men doubled over laughing at all the stories Chuck had collected in his bar since they'd last met for coffee last, which had been a decade or more. Tall tales were told by lawyers and truckers and teachers, Chuck remembered them all. They told Chuck everything after a shot of whiskey at his Pirate Bar. Then after a few hours, Doc and Chuck were caught up on their stories. They knew better than to speak on politics, Bill Clinton, Ronald Reagan, or religion. Surprisingly, Doc knew there was something else Chuck had on his mind, so he waited patiently and handed him beer and whiskey, to speed up the process with his brother.

To have a conversation without disagreement with Chuck, was unknown since he was highly strung since birth, and loved to fight and was known to start most of them. Then all of a sudden, Chuck became silent and sobered up his voice and eyes, opening the next to last beer in the cooler and looked at his brother who was sawing limbs off a cedar tree when he realized Chuck had closed his eyes. Doc waved his hand in front of his face and went back to cutting the limp, dropping cubes of ice down his open shirt, which elevated Chuck's character again.

"What's up, Chuck?"

"What the hell was that all about?"

Doc hoped he'd reveal what in God's name he was doing in Barringer. The truth. Then it happened. Chuck's dark, glossy pirate eyes beamed, and he tapped the seat beside him, wiping sweat from his brow and burned a handful of paper rolls from his wallet.

"Did I tell you about the last time me and Fat Daddy went fishing together?" Chuck cleared his throat.

"Nope." Doc sat. "I don't believe you did."

"Back in the late 60's, you were in service or out at Tulane, I forget, and Frank was in the Air Force. That left me, mom, and Le Joie at home with Fat Daddy."

Sitting up straight, Doc tuned in and listened as Chuck, handled beads in his beard, grinning, and he hesitated, slowing his speech down. Then he stood, and shouted, "I had to do it, Gilbert!" His eyes were full of memories. "I just had to do it!"

"Do what?" Doc asked, raising his hands. "What in hell did you do, Chuck?"

Anyone within a quarter mile heard them yelling. For thirty years, Chuck had bottled up his last fishing story. Doc dropped the tailgate, walking between the fire and his truck and he listened, pacing, and waiting on his brother. Finally, Doc sat again.

"Calm down and relax, Chuck. You are making me crazy, here."

"That son of a bitch shouldn't have done it, Gilbert. And I wouldn't have done what I had to do, either."

In a calm voice, Doc asked, "Brother, what happened?"

Chuck stood tall and recalled the dark night like it happened a week earlier.

"Le Joie walked over to me, her eyes were full of tears and she whispered in my ear, 'Fat Daddy did it again.' She hugged me, crying on my shoulder for ten minutes. She said it again, 'The bastard has been doing this to me for years.' Kissing her forehead, I suspected it, but I wasn't sure until she said it with her own mouth."

"Was he messing with her?" Doc gripped his knuckles.

"Yeah, for sure." Chuck nodded. "She tried to fight him off, for years and years. She was too small. He'd gotten bigger each year since I was in high school."

Rubbing his eyes, deep in a rage, Chuck busted the truck bed with his fist and cursed for five minutes.

"Calm down, Chuck. Finish the damn story." Doc handed him a bottle of whiskey, red faced and flushed. "Finish the story, tell me."

"Gotta be drunk before I can talk about her, Gilbert. The truth hurts too bad when I'm sober." He pounded his chest in anger. "Damn him to hell!" coughing. "I gotta have a strong drink."

"Here, here, drink this bourbon." Doc slapped his shoulder. "What happened?"

"Our father, Luke "Fat Daddy" Greenway jumped in the truck, hammered on some cherry moonshine, he'd bought at a good deal. Our Daddy made his big money reselling the liquor, making him happy as hell and his pockets even fatter."

Mad tears rolled from the corners of Chuck's eyes.

"Son of a bitch!" said Doc. "I never knew him to be sober. Not one damn day was Fat Daddy ever sober."

"So, I, I, uh uh,.." he laughed, "I beat the hell out of the truck hood and eyed him through the windshield the whole damn time. Then I hitched up the Jon boat and told him some Cajun men were claiming they could out fish a Creole on any given night 'Dad, they're catching 100 lb catfish in Sugar Lake.' That's what got him pissed, too."

"The old green Jon boat?" asked Doc. "I can hear him shouting 'Who dat catchin' my catfish?' running his dang trap."

"Who dat catchin' my catfish," said Chuck, his speech slurred at the end of each sentence. "I remember driving as far as I could to the end of Louisiana, for all the pain he'd caused our sweet mother and Le Joie. He beat on us since we were old enough to walk and talk."

Whittling a stick, cutting the wood in anger, Doc turned his head toward Chuck, who hung his head and snored.

"Damn it! Wake up, Chuck, finish your story."

Chuck's eyes rolled and his head bobbed.

"What? Hey, yeah, yeah, I'm up. Dad was a fat and mean bastard. We were halfway between New Orleans and Sugar Lake Bayou when I told Fat Daddy 'keep drinking that sweet shine, Pops' and he did just that."

Doc twisted the bark off the stick, scaping the wood and cut his hand by accident. Blood dripped down the stick and his eyes were full of resentment and redness, shaking when he thought about his father and what he'd done wrong.

"I bet he was singing," said Doc, wiping his mad eyes. Memories of hurt were unleashed, and he didn't forget his own pain, something that never escaped him, either.

"Yeah. He was singing and couldn't carry a tune in a fish bucket."

"I can see his fat face with the window down, flapping his mouth and waving his mason jar."

Chuck finished his beer and chased it with Kentucky bourbon. Tears worked their way slowly out of both brothers, an unsettling pain and good trait, in times of recollection.

"He spilled a half jar of moonshine climbing, in and out of the truck, pissing every thirty minutes on Highway 23. Then Fat Daddy shouted, 'Take me to Sugar, take me to Sugar, take me to Sugar, Chuckie.' He nearly broke my shoulder with a punch. 'Let's go, Pirate Boy!' I was a pissed off teenager and he kept beating my arm, hammering me with his fist."

"He called us pricks and bastards all through school," said Doc, tightly squeezing his cut finger against his jeans. "Always made fun of us, too, didn't he?"

"Yeah. I hated him, Gilbert. I hated that damn man." Chuck stood, staggering, waving his hands, "But I.....I took that big shit to Sugar!" laughing. "The faster I drove the more shine he chugged. I stopped the truck in the town of Davant, he yacked again. But for some reason I can't remember the next town south of Davant, though."

"Phoenix. It's Phoenix, brother."

"Hell yeah, Phoenix," said Chuck, sighing. "Good memory. Phoenix, now that's a town hotter than New Orleans."

Doc walked around the truck, thumping the bed with his fist, and slamming the door, out of control. His brother was usually level headed, listening as a judge on trial until someone mentioned his father. Then he unleashed the inner rage that rarely came out in public. "I hated Fat Daddy!" said Doc, rolling his ball cap in both hands. "I hated him so much, Chuck. There was no peace until he died of a heart attack."

Chuck touched his lip before speaking, "Gilbert, do you know where the gravel turns right on Tidewater Road, down in Venice?"

"Yeah, yeah, at the marina." Doc snapped his fingers and leaned on the truck hood.

Chuck threw his empty beer bottle into the blazing fire and shouted, "I hate Fat Daddy! But I got him good!"

Patting his brother's shoulder, "Hey, calm down, relax. I want to hear this story, take a seat on the tailgate." Doc told him as he handed him another beer from the ice chest. Both gentlemen reclined and caught their breath.

"What do you mean, you got him good, Chuck?"

Tapping his bottle, Chuck cleared his dark eyes, and continued, "At the top of the ramp, Fat Daddy rolled over drunk into the boat. I backed the boat in the Bayou, Fat Daddy dropped his line for a big catfish and about thirty minutes later, a heavy fog covered us like a damn blanket, Gilbert. Then he got crazy on me again and stood, flapping his big, fat belly and arms at me."

"Singing and drinking, I can imagine Fat Daddy drunk again."

"He made fun of my long hair. 'You look like a freakin' hippie who smokes pot, Chuckie Boy. You cut that top mop off or I'll cut it for you, you got that?'" Chuck took a big drink of beer. "I tied my long hair up into a ponytail and without an ounce of regret in my sober veins, I did it. I was calm, too."

"Did you shoot Fat Daddy?"

"Nope. I took the oar in my hands as Fat Daddy stood singing and staggering in the light of the lantern, and at the end of the boat as the heavy fog rolled in, I said, 'Hit me again Fat Daddy, use the oar this time, Carencro.'"

"He liked to beat his boys."

Pointing his chin at Fat Daddy, Chuck said, 'Take a good swing at my face, would ya, and black my eyes again?' Then I handed him the oar."

"What did he do?"

"I said, 'Whatcha goin' do, Fat Daddy?' and I had my hand on the throttle."

"Did he slam or club you?"

"Our old man spat in the water, laughing, and stuck out his famous fat tongue, gripping the oar with both hands like a baseball player would do in the batter's box. He planned to kill me, right there, and dump my body in the water. I just knew it."

"What did Fat Daddy do?"

"He said, 'What'd you call me, Chuckie Boy?' Then he cocked the oar back and swung. I dropped down in the boat and he missed my head by inches and clubbed the gas tank."

Turning toward his younger brother, Doc wanted to see his eyes when he told the rest of the story.

"Did he strike you again?"

"I clicked the motor into reverse, and Fat Daddy lost his balance, when suddenly he fell so sweetly in the water of Sugar Lake Bayou!" Holding up his hands as if he was a title fighter, Chuck, shouted, "He splashed like a baby whale, jerking his arms, bobbing, and flapping. He was in trouble and he knew it, too."

Doc leaned back, "Fat Daddy couldn't swim."

Chuck jumped up and down, moving his arms around, like he was swimming in the dead of night. "I saw Fat Daddy flapping with the oar and in the thick dark of night, I aimed the lantern so he could see my face, and yelled, 'That's for Le Joie and Frank and Gilbert, you dirty sumbitch bastard, and this is courtesy of Captain Chuckie the Pirate!' I sat still that night, gripping the throttle, and watched him struggle and splash like a lost whale."

"I had no idea." Pacing around Chuck, Doc said, "Dad was too fat to swim, wasn't he?"

Doc listened and had no idea what chaos was going on back at home while he was in the war and in college. Chuck, broad as an oak tree, stopped and turned to Doc with his eyes watery and bloodshot red, and then he stared into the dark sky. "He couldn't paddle much, either."

"What did Fat Daddy say or do?"

"He yelled, 'See ya in hell, Pirate Boy!' I eased the boat back and he disappeared into the thick fog of Sugar Lake Bayou.

I heard him scream, cry out. For years, I was haunted by his screams and cries."

"Gator?"

"I cruised the boat by the bubbles and there were two gators." Chuck closed his eyes. "Two of the largest gators I've ever seen were churning on Fat Daddy as he held on to the oar with a death grip."

"He was bad news," said Doc. "Cared more about his dog and money more than he did his family."

"Sorry, we lied to you about his heart attack. Fat Daddy died the way I just told you and it was my idea to make up the story and lie to you, way back then, too."

"You did a good job of it."

"I should've told you the truth, years ago, Gilbert. That's why I am here, brother, the real truth about Fat Daddy."

"If it wasn't that day, there would have been another head to head clash between you and him. That's the truth. I love ya, Chuck."

"I like ya, brother," laughing. Chuck sniffed and laughed again. "No matter how bad things get between us, we're still brothers at the end of the day."

Opening his eyes behind his fingers, which were covered in black onyx rings, Chuck said, "I thought about the time when Fat Daddy busted your lip and mouth at breakfast, the day you wanted to take a bus to Barringer, work this big farm. I have thought about it alot and I was jealous."

"Not long after I got here, Uncle Kenneth had me design a saddle for him, a Teddy Roosevelt saddle, made with diamonds and gems. But it's gone now. Not sure where it is."

"O' heck, big brother, I saw the most incredible Teddy Roosevelt saddle last night." Chuck slapped his shoulder. "It's a hell of a saddle, too."

"Where?" Doc stood.

"McCarthy's Dance Hall! Showman Wagoner has the saddle encased under a box of glass. The saddle and fenders are full of diamonds and gems. It's the bomb, the best damn saddle you've ever seen."

"Uncle Kenneth was a gemologist and traded horses for diamond rings and necklaces and bought hundreds of gems. Some of those diamonds were Aunt Sandy's and he sold the saddle when she became sick."

Chuck nodded. "She was a beautiful woman, blonde hair and her green eyes sparkled when she laughed, with sexy rounded lips. She would have made a good pirate queen."

"In the early 60s, Ken and Sandy drove to see us in New Orleans, she was wonderful and loved us very much, too." Slapping his hands together, Doc said, "We gotta get that damn saddle back in the Greenway family. But how can we do it?"

Doc remembered his uncle's pale skin, working and running his small hands through his short gray hair. Uncle Kenneth was well thought of for being a saddlery master, a little man in his old age who worked day and night. The Teddy Roosevelt saddle was Aunt Sandy's favorite saddle. Her picture still hung inside Doc's house, mounted atop the mantel, and Doc had no plans to remove her photograph.

"He had to sell the Teddy Roosevelt saddle to pay for her medical bills." Doc looked at his brother for a plan.

Showman announced last night, 'Any man who can ride the meanest bull in the world, he wins the Teddy Roosevelt Saddle and a $100,000 grand prize.' I thought of you."

Chills ran down Doc's neck. "I know who can ride that bull. Ringo Bare can ride that damn bull and Clem Cline can be his trainer."

"Hell no, Gilbert. Your son hasn't been on a bull in three or four years. What makes you think Ringo can ride?"

"We have to get that saddle back in my hands, that's the only way we can get it." Chuck shook hands with Gilbert.

"I don't think he can ride, but I'll help ya."

They were brothers again. Chuck talked about when they shared a room together as teenagers, swapping Mickey Mantle baseball cards and eating apples on the bed. Friends. Brothers.

"That's one hell of a saddle," said Doc, turning the pages of the past in his mind. "We'll get that damn saddle."

"I remember Frank's black eye." Chuck held a sour face. "Le Joie's bruised arms and tears. Our sweet mother stressed over which one of us Fat Daddy was going to beat next. Mom cried every day to protect us, stepping in the way to take his punches when she didn't have to."

"Fat Daddy hated Uncle Kenneth." Doc told Chuck. "What did you tell mom when you got home from Sugar Lake Bayou, the day Fat Daddy went in the water?"

A chilly wind blew in, bending trees from a westerly shift, Doc sat by the fire and watched the dark clouds hang over Barringer, while Chuck spit whiskey into the blazing fire and flames shot up. His face turned pale and hung on his chest.

"On the way back home, I stopped in Boomtown, flashed a fake ID, had a few beers at the casino and got a screaming eagle tattoo on my arm with Fat Daddy's shine money. The sun was up when I pulled into our driveway. Mom and Le Joie cried all night, worried about me. Mom told me; they'd smoked all night. Mom let Le Joie have a beer for the first time, for her nerves, I guess. Our mother was a wreck at the kitchen table. Our sister was asleep on the sofa, had prayed so much, she fell asleep like an angel."

"What did you tell mom and Le Joie?"

"I said, 'No more pain, pretty mother. Then Le Joie woke up screaming and thought I was dead. Mom said, 'No more hurt either, Chuckie, I love you for whatever you did,' she cried, without even knowing what had happened to Fat Daddy. She even liked the eagle tattoo."

"She didn't live much longer after that night, did she?" Dropping his head, Doc took off his glasses and cleaned his eyes as if he had been at a funeral. "She was a great woman who never had a chance to live a peaceful life."

"Two months after Fat Daddy disappeared in Sugar Lake Bayou, she died."

Exhaling after his confession and pounding the chair, Chuck was relieved that he'd told his brother everything, the truth, too, word for word, how it happened.

Doc hugged his brother wondering what pain he had bottled up for thirty years, what relief his mother and sister felt when Chuck walked in that rainy morning from hitching back home. Three days later Chuck reported his father missing, telling the police that he'd driven to Venice to fish and that was the last time anyone had seen him. Chuck asked the police to call him if they found him. They never called. Three months later Frank moved out and joined the Air Force.

The next morning Chuck remembered every word of what he told Doc, and just to check his story about Fat Daddy, he had Chuck tell the story a second time. Word for word, not a detail was missing from his original story. Chuck had told the truth.

"You know sometimes I see Fat Daddy," said Chuck, eating a bowl of oatmeal.

"You do?"

"I see him on the back of a milk carton." Chuck pulled his beaded beard, with a big laugh. "Ha-Ha-Ha, swimming to Mexico, Gilbert."

"I'll look for him in the cheese and dairy section next time," said Doc, covering his chest with his hat.

"I see him splashing in the ocean, paddling his way to Cancun." Chuck nodded in confidence.

Doc leaned back in his green chair, the antique leg folded under his weight from laughing, and he ended up on the floor. Chuck helped him up. Two brothers, one in creed, the other in crime, the longest conversation they'd had together since Doc was sixteen. When deer crossed in the front field, they sat on the front porch and finished a pot of coffee.

"When is Ringo going to meet his real-father?" Chuck fired up a cigar and blew smoke rings.

"What do you mean?" Doc stopped the wooden swing from moving.

"That's Mickey Starr's truck in the driveway, got Georgia tags, ain't it?"

"It's his truck. Yeah. He dropped in while I was gone to Virginia. How'd you know? He took off with Ringo, I guess."

"Grandson and grandpa, hanging out in New Orleans and now in Barringer, huh?" rubbing his chin and mouthing the fat cigar, bending a smirk.

"What the hell do you mean?" Doc raised his voice. "Why are you saying all this grandson and grandpa bull crap?"

"Mickey, Tipp, and that hot model, Brandi, stopped by my Pirate Bar in New Orleans, mouthing off and half drunk. They saw my name on the door and asked if I was related to Doc Greenway. I told them you were my brother and you just moved to Barringer, North Carolina."

"What's that have to do with him being Ringo's grandfather?"

Chuck finished his beer and stood looking out across the field. His voice got deep, "He said his son used to date Pomona, back in the early 70's when she was in college at Chapel Hill. They met in anatomy class." Chuck snickered. "I guess Mickey's boy and Pomona must've gotten extra credit for their homework." Laughing and coughing, amused by his own words, Chuck smoked.

"I remember when I first met Pomona, Ringo was twelve at the time, and she'd gotten pregnant while she was a sophomore at North Carolina. Her parents got mad and kicked her out. The next week she moved to New Orleans with her cousin, hoping to make it as a big-time chef."

"She cooks a good meal." Chuck confirmed.

"Pomona once worked at Commander's Palace. We dated for a few weeks and I told her I was moving to Texas. Her eyes lit up, and she said, 'If you don't mind, I'd like to go with you and take Ringo?' So, we moved to Clem Cline's ranch in Temple."

Chuck blew smoke rings and shook his head.

"I remember when you took that little philly to Temple and you were one sucker to let her stab you with her spurs. She took your money, too, I bet?"

"She was the most beautiful woman I knew. I never knew Mickey Starr's son was Ringo's father, though."

"She stopped at the Pirate Bar a few months ago, too."

Doc put his elbows on his knees, groaning and moaning.

"How did you find out Ringo was his grandson?"

Chuck leaned against the porch post.

"Pomona had secretly been in contact with Mickey over the years, but she didn't care if she saw Ringo's father again."

"So, she must've called Clem Cline asking for me. Then Pomona told Mickey I'd be at the Pirate or at the Carousel Bar. You told him I'd be at the Carousel Bar that evening, didn't ya?"

"Hell yes, I did. I knew you'd show Ringo the bar since he was old enough to chase women," rolling a cigar in his fingers. "I know your favorite stops in the Big Easy."

"Ain't that just peachy, Mickey agreed to buy saddles from us to help out his own grandson's saddle business," said Doc, staring at Mickey Starr's truck. "Hmmm, well, that's interesting to bring Brandi along, to make love with Ringo, huh? She might be a midnight special."

Chewing on his cigar, Chuck said, "Use a hot lady to meet his grandson for the first time.

"Your story is true, little brother. Hope he keeps his word, paying the bill for the fancy Bordeaux saddles."

"I'll certainly make sure of it." Chuck crushed his cigar. "He'll pay or find ten dead horses in his bed."

21

Father Time

For several days, Doc and Chuck cut and shaped Bordeaux leather, pouring the sweat and talking about what might become, good or bad, of the likes of Ringo. They suspected Mickey of threading high hopes into the bull rider's ears and telling him how great Brandi was for him. The next day, a strong storm knocked out power in Barringer as they stitched the final saddle bags for Mickey, working by the glow of a flickering candlelight, watching sand fall through an hourglass and trying to meet their deadline.

With far less experience than Ringo, Chuck was powered by whiskey and sweet tea and red beans, favorites he'd acquired a taste for since he was old enough to pet a dog. Nonetheless, Chuck was a good storyteller and caught on to the craft of saddlery faster than most people and marked only twenty days left to complete four saddles. The timekeeper, Doc noticed Ringo was nowhere to be found. Who could blame him, though? The bull rider had made friends with Brandi and Tipp and became the local tour guide of Barringer. Doc anticipated a friendly trap was being set to lure Ringo into the hands of Mickey Starr and maybe stiff him with the bill, he thought.

"There is no way we can get this damn job finished without Ringo," said Doc, wiping his red hand with a towel.

"Where the hell is that boy, anyway? He has missed a bunch of time on these saddles."

Not missing his chance to debut as a comedian, Chuck had an undeniable trait he hadn't left behind in New Orleans.

"Leave that poor boy alone, Gilbert, he's with his Poppy now. What if they're fishing or better yet buying a new truck for Ringo Bare?" Chuck teased in a deep voice, tugging at his goatee, and grinning at Doc, who wasn't amused.

"Grandfather, my ass?"

"Gilbert, I bet you a milkshake Ringo spends Christmas in Savannah. Are you still a bettin' man, brother?"

"I'll take your ice cream money."

The second evening was no better. Sunshine redeemed the day, though. Chuck was the closest to the window and could see anyone who traveled the dirt road or crossed the field by the apple orchard, even if a stray dog or the speedy mailman made movements, he saw it. Having labored for eight hours, the two of them needed a break and some food.

"Here comes a classic '56 Apache Chevy truck," said Chuck, standing at the window. Ringo is the driver, but wait, is that a passenger?"

"Ringo decided to show up, huh?" Doc kept working.

"Looks like the cavalry has come to rescue us from this leather sweatshop made by Doc Greenway." Opening the door to the shop, big Chuck smiled and raised his beer.

Ringo and Mickey waved as they walked inside the house. About that time, Chuck pulled a tack hammer up close to his lips and offered the play by play.

"Ringo Bare is walking to the base, the sign comes from his new coach and grand-poppy, Mickey Starr. The crowd roared as the bull rider raised his hand to the little workers in the leather dugout shop. Mickey gives the signal. Looks like his grandfather is *mighty* thirsty, so it's the seven innings stretch and they're on another lunch break, it's family time."

"Shut up and get to work!"

Chuck danced around the room.

"The lights are on at home, and it's a homerun. Ringo opens a bottle of beer for his grand-poppy. The crowd goes wild. Fans, this is a Kodak moment, for sure. I think we're going to see more of this teamwork in the future, don't you, Doc Greenway?"

"Have you ever been to Sugar Lake Bayou? Wanna go?"

Halfway from the shop to the house Doc walked beside Chuck watching the big guy run around him as if they were kids in the streets of New Orleans again, leaning forward, like he's stealing the bases on a baseball diamond. All the sudden, Chuck jumped on the first step of the back porch with his hands in the air, turning circles and curling a smile above his dark pirate goatee and taunted Doc.

"It's another homerun! Let's celebrate with Mickey "Mantle" Starr and Ringo "Yogi" Bare."

"Hey Chuck!" yelled Doc, still watching his brother celebrate. "Chuck!"

"What?"

"Don't you miss New Orleans?"

Bowing to Doc, Chuck propped open the door to the kitchen.

"I think I'll join the post-game *par-tae*." Chuck adjusted his shirt and fixed his hair in the mirror. "I'll toast champagne with the legendary Mickey Starr, if you don't mind, brother?"

"Good to see you again, Mickey," said Doc, shaking hands with the old man.

"You're sweating, Doc," said Mickey. "Been working on Bordeaux saddles, I bet?"

"They will be finished soon." Taking a seat at the kitchen table, Doc sipped his ice water in curiosity. "I believe you met my younger brother, Chuck, back in New Orleans?"

"Heck, yeah, I did." Mickey slapped his shoulder. "Served us a mean Cliff's Old-Fashioned, too. Hey, and that homemade Absinthe rocked Brandi's world, my friend. She even got romantic with Tipp after the liquid loosened her bones."

"Hey, don't tell anyone about my Absinthe, it's not legal in the U.S. yet," said Chuck, laughing and gripping Mickey's hand. Then Chuck saw the bull rider. "How have you been, Ringo?"

"Chuck, this time, it's peace pipes, my friend," said the bull rider. "No guns, knives or blood and welcome to Barringer."

"Like Chuck has ever done anything illegal," said Doc, chuckling. "Ha-ha-ha. His birth was even questionable."

"Watch it." He smiled at his brother. "I'll drink and explore more of Barringer tonight. I can see better under neon lights, anyway."

Chuck, Mickey, and Ringo sat at the kitchen table, Doc served ham sandwiches and chips for the guys, tapping his boots on the hardwood, deep in thought.

"The vintage Bordeaux saddles are almost finished, Mickey." Doc chugged water.

"What about Tipp's twenty saddle bags?" asked Mickey, looking at Ringo and then he eyed Doc. Ringo had no clue Doc and Chuck had finished the bags.

"Bordeaux bags are done," said Doc. "If I can get Ringo back in the shop, that is, we'd knock the last few saddles out pretty quick, I believe, huh, Ringo?"

"Good. I've been busy as the tour guide and entertainer." Ringo raised his glass. "Since we're ahead of schedule, Mickey invited me to Savannah to see The Famous Tobacco Barn." The bull rider took a bite of his sandwich and nodded with his cheeks full toward Doc.

"Don't talk with your mouth full, Son," said Doc.

"Tipp and Brandi are meeting us here later," said Ringo. "We'll leave in the morning for Savannah."

Turning red as a fire engine, Doc beamed at Ringo, and had to know for himself the truth, why Mickey stopped in town.

"You mean you and your grandfather, here, have gotten closer and now he wants you to meet the rest of your family, down in Savannah, isn't that right Mickey?" Taking a bite of an apple, Doc thought of his own family growing up.

Rolling his eyes and cleaning his glasses, Mickey found a way to keep his hands and eyes busy as Doc crunched the fruit.

"Doc, I meant to talk to you and Ringo about this in a private conversation," said Mickey, sighing. "But I just haven't gotten around to it yet."

"Ringo, your mother knew the whole time but never said anything to you or me. She's known about the Starr Family before you were born, of course."

"Is this all true, Mickey?" locking his hands behind his neck, Ringo waited for an answer. "Who is my real father then?"

"My only son, Danny Starr dated Pomona in college," said Mickey, who was rotating his gold watch. "It's all true."

"Ain't this just the damn Starr family reunion!" shouted Ringo, pushing his plate away. "Hot damn! This is worse than being kicked in the head by a damn bull."

"That makes Tipp your half-brother and the legendary Mickey Starr is your wonderful grandfather." Chucked stood looking around the room, shrugging his shoulders beside Doc.

Feeling like an outcast, Ringo yelled, "Is my father going to jump out from behind the barn in his Barry Allan suit, and give us the news flash, huh, Mickey?"

"It's a lot to handle, Ringo," Mickey admitted. "But your father would like to meet you, three days from now in Savannah." Their eyes connected. "I expect you'll be there, grandson."

"I don't need to see my worthless father!" Ringo shouted at Mickey. "Doc Greenway is my father. I've never seen Danny Starr's ass all my life. He doesn't know me, and I sure don't need his fatherly advice."

Grabbing his hat and keys, Ringo cranked his truck.

"Where are you going?" shouted Doc, standing on the front porch.

Ringo spun out. "I'll be in town!"

Mickey opened the screen door, "I'll send Tipp and Brandi to check on him later. Let him cool off."

"No need to make it worse," Doc told Mickey, looking down the long driveway as dust clouds followed Ringo's truck for a quarter mile. "I wished you would've let him finish the damn saddles before you pissed him off, being some Super-Grandpa."

Mickey lined up in Doc's face.

"Listen, Greenway, I won't pay you a damn dime, if Ringo Bare doesn't finish all my Bordeaux saddles."

"My son will finish his deal with you," rotating a toothpick in his teeth, Doc grinned. "I promise you that."

"Ringo Bare's Saddles are worth a mint. Leather hammered by Chuck Greenway hands ain't worth piss in the pasture."

"Saddles of Barringer is Ringo's brand, not mine." Doc knew he could kick his head off his shoulders if he made a wrong move or scoffed him. "He's the champion bull rider, not me." Doc grinned. "Well, it looks like you need to handle your business with your grandson, send him back to the shop, or you'll be greatly embarrassed on television without Bordeaux under your Georgia butt."

Blood rushed through Mickey's face and a lump formed in his throat, chugging the last of his beer. "I'll get him back in the shop." Mickey wiped his mouth and slammed his fist against the porch post.

"You will do it in an apologetic manner," Doc told him.

Doc cussed Mickey, who lost his temper and took a swing at Doc's head, and when Chuck saw what happened, he rushed outside and divided the men before they killed each other. That's when Doc's linebacker sized brother packed Mickey's bags for him and hauled his butt to the nearest hotel. On the drive to the hotel, Chuck admired a cigar that Mickey pulled from his shirt pocket.

"Do you mind if I have one of your Fuente cigars, Mick?"

"Let's do the math, Pirate, if I smoke one and give you one, I would be without. That would be unwise of me, right?"

Noticing how the cocky man had snubbed him, Chuck said, "Mickey, I'd love to take you catfishing, how about it?"

"Lake Norman?" blowing smoke out the window.

"Nah. I'm talkin' big cats." Chuck grinned and gripped the steering wheel. "I'd love to take you to the water of Sugar Lake Bayou, it's in Southern Louisiana, a real paradise, sir."

Mickey scoffed at him and kept smoking.

22

No Man's Land

Relaxing at the place that offered him the most peace, Doc stared into the flames of a backyard fire, and deep in thought, he wrestled with his own family concerns in a moment of reflection, not being any different than most men his age. Thoughts of his father and mother rolled in his head like Texas tumbleweeds, pictures in his hands of Le Joie and Frank, neither of whom he'd seen in years, rushed through Doc's heart and he had no idea how to resolve his brokenness and talk to his siblings. He concluded that some things, especially the past, could not be resolved, but could only be remembered or coped with each day. Tears of anger formed in Doc's eyes, thumbing through the back of his wallet, where he found Pomona's picture, too. He missed the chance to tell her how much she meant to him, and he often reminisced.

After finding out what took place with Ringo, Tipp and Brandi decided to search for the bull rider after dark and knew he would be soaking up suds. Drafting a small map of two potential places, Doc left directions for Tipp and hoped Brandi might be able to convince him to come back to the saddlery shop. The idea of Ringo finding his biological father had plagued Doc for over a decade, the answer made things worse. Some wounds never healed, no matter how many times Doc patched them up with prayer and good advice, reappearing like a dark storm.

Doc directed Tipp and Brandi toward Barringer from the porch. "Vega, it's a dark tavern near the only red light in town," handing Tipp the napkin. "Rough crowd, too. Might be a cover band playing anything from Willie Nelson to the Eagles on stage, but scan the booths for Ringo, and be sure to ask the guys at the pool table if they've seen him. Most guys on parole with Pitbull's will guard the jukebox. Be careful. Don't take Brandi inside."

"When we do find him, I'll lift Ringo's spirit with my brickhouse," said Brandi, smacking her lips and winking at Doc.

The first stop was a dead end. "He's not at Vega." Tipp told Brandi from the parking lot, while she checked her makeup in the mirror.

Five blocks north of Vega, stood McCarthy's, a large barn converted into a western dance hall, fashioned and modeled from a western movie set in Cody, Wyoming. Walnut tables and booths were filled to capacity, three dance floors were lively with couples, and the search for Ringo continued into dimmer parts of Showman Wagoner's dance hall.

Like a bullet out of a gun, ladies flocked to the jewel of the place, a stunning, one-of-a-kind Roosevelt diamond saddle was on display under clear glass just as Chuck said, causing photographers to bring their cameras to McCarthy's Dance Hall. Far more attention was given to the diamond saddle than the gift shop of Kingman turquoise, silver tone and gold tones, basket weave holsters, or the dozens of other western saddles for sale along the wall.

The town became more famous when McCarthy's Barn was built in 1988, hosting live auctions of World Champion Quarter Horses for Rough Riders to showcase their talents and the best line dancing competitions were found east of Waco. Barringer, North Carolina was the only place in America where a $100,000 custom-made saddle could be seen on display, a coveted Teddy Roosevelt saddle, crafted by legendary local Kenneth Greenway himself.

The diamond saddle was equipped with a mule hide wrap, dark as night leather, brass hardware, saddle strings and a matching flank cinch set. People came from ten states to witness sparkling diamonds from Africa, crafted into handmade leather of the highest value, and the leather was something to see, the Teddy Roosevelt saddle drew large crowds to Barringer on weekends. For obvious reasons, ladies stood beside the Teddy Roosevelt saddle for photographs, comparing their own diamond rings to the sparkling jewels once worn by Sandy Greenway.

No one had seen or heard of a saddle of such caliber in the United States. The last Rough Rider saddle crafted by Kenneth Greenway, was finished in the summer of 1994, just seven months before he passed away.

"Chuck, you know why I left Texas?"

"The Teddy Roosevelt saddle, of course."

"Aunt Sandy's diamonds are in the saddle. I modeled my life after Uncle Kenneth and that saddle would have been handed down to me if she hadn't gotten sick. Gems and diamonds that once draped her neckline, now are in the hands of a crook."

"Just like when you adopted Ringo, you'll hand your things down to him, I bet."

Painting a grim face, Doc said, "Breaks my heart to see diamonds fall in the hands of Showman Wagoner."

"Let's find a way to win it back or I can kill Showman Wagoner like in the Old West, fastest gun wins or just take the saddle, as a modern day pirate."

"Let's get it back, Chuck."

"I'm in, Gilbert. I'm going to love this shootout."

Oil from a person's hand was said to devalue the leather, if handled improperly. On a farm in West Virginia, in the hands of a collector was another Roosevelt saddle, crafted for a coal tycoon and delivered by Uncle Kenneth, sporting the same number of diamonds as the saddle in Barringer. At age 81, Uncle Kenneth used Doc's Army Rough Rider design, taking just under ten years to collect the diamonds and craft a second World-Class saddle, making history in the art of saddlery for American collectors, too.

Other than diamonds and leather, popular colors at McCarthy's Barn were tasteful red, white, and blue colors, the kind men favored. Various flavors of chocolates were shipped to the gift shop, updating McCarthy's as a world-class attraction by the fall of '97, even though Doc hated to admit anything good Showman Wagner had done for the community, he said it that way.

Popping up like daisies on a spring day, Barringer grew because of McCarthy's Dance Hall and other businesses followed, adding horse trails that weaved between log cabins and hotels made the town more authentic and attractive. Steak houses and diners were built alongside BBQ restaurants on Eastway Drive, to accommodate the flood of tourism that lined up in Barringer; good news for the town. Barringer was nominated as an All-American City, the summer prior to Doc and Ringo's arrival to the horse town.

Local newspapers printed how Showman Wagoner planned to make Barringer "The Cheyenne of the East," and within five years "Teddy Roosevelt Days" would be established in North Carolina, where Barringer would become a town known for "Pretty Horses and Beautiful Women."

Just as towns like Branson, Missouri and Park City, Utah and Santa Fe, New Mexico were well established in their own niches, Barringer stood in lush green grass, where white picket fences were linked, farm-to-farm, and pristine stone walls and stables were painted stunning white and black colors. The town was a picture of considerable wealth and beauty that fascinated travelers enough to visit and buy property.

***

Walking through the double smoked doors of McCarthy's Dance Hall, Tipp found the wanted man, the one Brandi was excited to embrace.

"Hey, Ringo Bare," said Tipp, who strolled to a corner booth. "This is the place to ponder life, huh?"

"Tipp, my brother, I heard you were my next of kin." Ringo adjusted his black cowboy hat and offered him a manly hug and shoulder slap. Do I have any more brothers and sisters running around the Great South?"

Tipp sat across from Ringo.

"No way or I would have known about it by now. Mickey talks too much." Tipp propped up his legs in the long booth and listened.

"We share the same father, I heard," said Ringo, who saw their features and mannerisms to be alike. "That would make us half-brothers, I believe?"

Brushing his blonde hair back, Tipp nodded.

"My grandfather and I knew we needed to meet you in person to talk things out."

"Well, I'm glad you did, Tipp. Mystery solved. Doc isn't too happy about it, though."

"And Mickey knew you wouldn't meet us at The Tobacco Barn in Savannah, so we've been on the hunt to find you. Mickey even flew over Clem Cline's ranch when you and Doc were on the tailgate of a truck."

"I had watermelon wine in my hand when Mickey Starr flew overhead in the red helicopter, huh?" With a fired up face, Ringo asked, "So, did you buy the saddles out of freakin' pity for me or what?"

"No, sir, Ringo!" The music got loud. "That is a legitimate order. We must have those saddles for the Thanksgiving Parade, for sure."

Not seeing the similarities before, but in the light of McCarthy's, their facial features were uncanny and brotherly looking, mistaken for twins, perhaps. Both had well defined jaw bones, sandy blonde hair, and strong frames, and they were about the same height. However, Tipp was a little older than Ringo, not by much, though.

"What brought this on, I mean, hunting me down?" He rotated a beer bottle in his hand, leaning forward for an answer.

"You were on television a few years ago in Waco and Mickey felt it was time to track you down. Pomona kept in touch with him over holidays, and Mickey felt compelled to contact you, face-to-face, and not by phone."

Ringo hadn't heard from his mother but three times in nearly ten years, and even the sound of her name stung him, but he hoped she was doing well.

"My mother has the right connections, I see."

After admiring the novelty shops and western wear of such a grand establishment, Brandi pushed Ringo's legs on the floor and hugged him.

"Ringo, do you mind if my brick house sits beside you?"

"I'm sorry about that. I was being an ass."

"You have a sweet side, too, I bet?" said Brandi. "We can start where we left off, unzipping my dress later." Brandi whispered something in Ringo's ear that made him smile, squeezing his legs under the table. "And that's a promise, cowboy."

"So, you know about me being part of the Starr family, huh?"

"Yeah, I have known for a few years now and I think it's great. You can move to Savannah, start a whole new life with me, Ringo. And your father Danny Starr, he's a great guy. Will you give him a chance to be your friend and father?"

Adjusting his hat, "How could he be a great man!" sounded Ringo. "He left us broke. No offence, Tipp, Danny

Starr could have made this "family thing" better twenty years ago, before I became famous."

"You and Dad will have time to work through the contempt," said Tipp, rubbing his hands. "Kick his ass if you have to," fist bumping him. "Hell, I'll help ya do it, for being a Deadbeat Dad and a big jerk."

Brandi kissed him. "Mister Ringo, could you spin me around the dance floor tonight and hold me tight?"

"I would doll, but a mad bull messed up my foot a few years ago, and well, I don't Texas Two-Step much."

"I'm sure you do a few other things well," dragging her fingernails down the back of his neck. "You can tell me later. I'm tired of guessing about you."

Then she waltzed to the dance floor alone. But not for long, accepting the hand of a noble cowboy with good vision, who held her close.

"Dad will be in Savannah in a few days and," said Tipp looking Ringo in the eye, "he'd like you to be there, if you will?"

"That's not good for me, Tipp. I appreciate the invitation. I need more time and good beer to wash this news away."

Tipp's face turned sour.

"We are having a big party, it'd be cool if you would consider being there, that's all. Think it over and take your time, buddy."

"Where's he been?"

"He lives in South Africa."

"What does he do there?"

"At first, my father worked in the seafood industry for Mickey, off the waters of Cape Town, and two years later, he sold his boats and felt a call to the mission field. He hasn't been to Savannah since my grandmother passed away."

"Our father, he's a godly servant, helps other people with food and medicine in the mission field, right?" Ringo brushed his thin beard.

"Yeah, doing the Lord's work."

After a few minutes, Ringo gave him the benefit of the doubt and couldn't restrain his tongue any longer.

"He was helping other people when his own son was nearly homeless." Ringo scoffed and sighed in disgust. "If it wasn't for Doctor Greenway taking me in, feeding me when my mother ran off, I would've been an orphan in Texas, long before I was a teenager. He's a hell of a man for doing that for me."

"Our father is a different man now."

"It's not a good idea to see him right now, Tipp. Let's go shoot some pool, talk horses, and pretty women. Looks like I'll order a pitcher of beer for my new brother, Tipp Starr. They toasted. Welcome to Barringer."

***

After a half hour of pool, Tipp won the first one and Ringo aimed at the eight ball for the win. Up walked a tall, clean cut man, broad and cocky, thin hair and sparse beard, and dark eyebrows. Beside him, two guys stood in dark glasses, like bodyguards at the airport who followed him around and handled his business when he snapped his fingers to do so.

"Get your hand off the eight ball, Showman." Ringo gripped the pool stick and stood tall, proud, and ready to fight.

"Showman Wagoner," said Tipp. "How've you been?"

Slamming the ball in the corner pocket with his hand, "You boys got another game ready?" Showman pointed his pool stick at the bull rider. "How about you, Ringo Bare? You feelin' froggy and ready to lose some money?"

"I don't lose, especially to you."

Wiping his lower lip, "I saw you get crushed like an aluminium can by War Wagon," tapping his chest, "of which, to my favor, I bought the bull at a good price from a man in Bruceville-Eddy, Texas, who raised the price on the bull once it kicked your ass."

The round bodyguard elbowed the skinny one, and both snickered like football players cheering on the starters.

"Takes a real rough rider to climb on a bull," said Ringo, who eyed his first shot at Showman Wagoner, the man who was on the magazine cover he found in Texas.

Showman chuckled. "I bet it was lots of work, snapping Ringo Bare back together again after he fell off the War Wagon train."

Rounded cheeks on Showman's slick face formed, bobbing his head like a dashboard dummy on a bumpy Route 97 highway, and laughing behind him were his amused guards.

"It takes a man to ride a bull, not just own one," said Tipp, watching Showman's every move while Ringo racked the table. "There's no better rider in the world than Ringo Bare, I guarantee that." Tipp rubbed a $1000 in front of his lips.

"Are you Mickey's puppet, Tipp Starr?" asked Showman. "Flashing that seafood money around like it's a napkin. Hope you got more than lunch money to bet."

"You better watch your damn mouth!" said Ringo, stepping up toward Showman's face. "Don't worry Tipp Starr, Showman's an instigator, talks a lot of smack, but he's afraid to back it up. Clem Cline saw him piss his pants when he was a kid trying to ride bulls, thirty years ago."

Showman walked up close to the bull rider and stared him in his face. With a sudden reflex quicker than a horse kick, Ringo's fist curled, and his arm crossed his body.

"Smack!" Showman's head whipped and he fell down.

"I believe you broke his damn nose," said Tipp, spalling at Showman's injury.

Ringo was taught that move by Doc, long before he strapped himself on his first bull. Blood splattered when Ringo's hand connected, knocking out one of Showman's teeth and loosening a few others.

"Pop! Pop!" Tipp hit the other two men, staggering the bodyguards.

Showman, grabbing his lip, spouted, "My grandmother hits harder than Ringo." Blood rolled down his face, smirking through the pain and pulling up his bodyguards. "Got ourselves a couple of hard ass fighters, don't we?"

"I let you live, didn't I?" Ringo formed a second fist.

One of Showman's bodyguards swung for Tipp's head and missed. Then in a split second, Tipp clubbed him in the throat with a pool stick, left him choking and gasping for air.

Rushing into the game room were five men, spreading their arms to stop the fight, and blocking any connection between the men.

"Hey, what the hell is going on?" A big man joined Ringo, and yelled, "Break it up, I said!" spinning around in a circle and shouting with his arms stretched out to divide Showman and Ringo.

"Hey! That's enough!" A host of other men raced up beside the famous bull rider and Tipp, who now stood with a pool stick in each hand, breathing heavily in the large game room.

The guard from McCarthy's Dance Hall shielded Showman from Ringo's reach, stepping between the fighters. Wagoner's blood dripped from inside of his mouth, targeting Ringo in his sight and thumbing blood from the corner of his mouth, he scoffed and laughed.

"This bull rider has some fire in his gut. Ha-ha-ha," said Showman. "Wow! We got a sailor and bull rider who think their Barringer bad asses." Showman shook his fist at the half-brothers.

"We have witnesses and blood to prove it, Showman," said Ringo, rolling his hand down the brim of his cowboy hat and smirking at his opponents.

"I came here looking for Doc Greenway, but I'm glad I met you, Ringo Bare. I own the meanest bull in the world and he's in my barn, that's why I'm here," said Showman, walking around the pool table. "I got $100,000 says you can't ride him for ten seconds."

Ringo knew the rule was eight seconds and ten seconds on a bull was a nightmare from hell and felt like an eternity, too, taking it back to the old school days of bull riding in Barringer.

"What bull do you own?" asked Ringo.

"No Man's Land."

"The Brand of Honor." Ringo raised his head.

Turning to the crowd, Showman placed his hand behind his ear, then widened his arms. "My friends, did that challenge just silence the Golden Bare?" Then he turned his back to Ringo and Tipp, "Boys, Ringo doesn't have the mojo for No Man's Land, does he?" The man rolled a cigar in his hand, spinning back, "Do ya, Ringo?"

"If you put up the money," pointing across the room, "and that Teddy Roosevelt diamond saddle, I'm in, Harley "Showman" Wag-O-Ner."

"Hell no!" sounded Showman.

Tipp walked away. Ringo threw the broken stick on the table and followed Tipp.

"He doesn't have the money, folks." Tipp laughed and raised his hands. "He's not Mickey Starr, Ringo. Let's get out of here."

"I'll call your bluff, Ringo. Your busted foot won't make it three seconds." Chewing on his cigar, Showman paced toward the men in confidence. "I got your money and the diamond saddle, Ringo. You are freakin' bluffing and a no show, anyway. You can't ride or you'd be in Las Vegas, taking home the championship, right now?"

Taking off his cowboy hat and spinning around to a good sized crowd, "You folks just witnessed this bet!" said Ringo. "I can ride No Man's Land, boys. Thank you, Showman." Ringo flipped his hat on his head. "Get your bull ready, Showman."

Tipp grabbed his half-brother's shoulder.

Raising his hands, "Ringo said, he can do it. Showman, let's line it up, get the camera crews ready, and call Big Ray Brown and Max Sheridan, too. This will be a hell of a ride."

Flashing his hand toward the crowd, Showman stood beside the diamond saddle. "Do you need to talk this over with Doc Greenway before you say *yes*, Baby Bare?" He asked, blowing smoke into the air.

"You bring the money and the bull; I will ride him." Ringo waved at Showman. "Name the time and place."

"Listen, it's at Barringer Stockyards. You just make sure you tell Doc I'll be glad to take his money again and keep Kenneth Greenway's diamond saddle safe in my hands." Showman cupped his hands, "The event is the Saturday after Thanksgiving. Bring cash. No Monopoly money, boys."

Tipp pulled Brandi off the dance floor.

In a haze of memory, glossy dark eyes, and the ugly black face of No Man's Land haunted Ringo's mind. It was the only mad bull he didn't draw on the circuit and he knew little about the animal. Uncertain of his own ability, having not ridden a bull since War Wagon wrecked him, he regretted taking the deal, and thought about it. However, he'd be the laughing stock of Barringer if he didn't show up and turned down the challenge. Mouthing and cursing Ringo and Tipp at the door, Showman threatened them several times before they left the building.

"One more thing, Showman, and then we'll leave," said Ringo. "You need to see the large animal vet."

"Why?"

Holding his cowboy hat high, Ringo continued, "He specializes in jackasses and he'll love you."

"What's going on here?" whispered Brandi to Tipp.

Opening the truck door for Brandi, Ringo said, "Get in! I'll tell you on the way back to Doc's house."

Tipp drove back to Doc's house alone and Brandi rode with Ringo, where he stopped in Troutman at the nearest gas station because Brandi had a sweet tooth again.

"Hey, boo!" a lady spoke.

"Sarah Ann?" Ringo tugged on his collar. "What are you doing all dressed up?"

"On a date with Karl Robinson, he's in the truck."

Ringo and Sarah Ann stood in an isle where no one could see them, placing his hat on her head.

"What was the kiss for?"

"I've been thinking about you."

Looking at Ringo, "Honey?" said Brandi. "Let's go back to our place. Hi, Sarah Ann, are you buying cleaning supplies for your maid service tonight?"

"Why'd you kiss me when you're on a date with Brandi?"

"We're not dating." Brandi smacked her lips. "We're just midnight lovers and afternoon delights, aren't we, Ringo?"

"We are not either one. Don't believe her, she's just teasing you."

"It's nice having Ringo down the hall, when I need my dress unzipped or a late night massage. He's got my back and big hands, too." Brandi winked. "You can't deny that can you, Bull Rider?"

"You are just a guest at Doc's house and we're not lovers."

"You promised you'd take me out for bread pudding, Ringo?" said Brandi, moving her nails down the curve of his biceps. "Or are we going to that steak house again tonight?"

"We're not going out at all," said Ringo, walking near Sarah Ann. "Stop making up things, Brandi."

Taking a deep breath, Brandi kissed Ringo and winked at Sarah Ann, massaging his shoulders. "After Ringo wins the money, he'll move to Savannah, we'll start a family, right cowboy?"

He sounded with a stern voice, "Wrong." A hopeful smile melted from Sarah Ann's face.

Without hesitating, Sarah Ann touched Brandi's clothes. "Girl, you'd be a perfect stripper, you stay half undressed most of the day, anyway."

"Don't you have some cows to milk in the barn?"

"Brandi, what magazine said you'd put on a few pounds after your Louisiana trip, tell me again, please?"

Stepping between the ladies before the claws came out, Ringo showed each lady to their respective vehicle. After the errands, he drove Brandi back to Doc's house, practiced his saxophone to keep from talking to anyone about bull riding or relationships or the Starr family, especially he didn't want to discuss No Man's Land with anyone but Clem Cline.

23

The Bull Stops Here

A week had passed since Tipp, Brandi, and Mickey returned to Savannah, leaving friends behind in the golden brown autumnal colors of North Carolina, they had to return to their business. The first Saturday of November '97, Mickey felt the need to call Ringo before he headed to the Thanksgiving Day Parade in New York City, and Mickey's Tobacco Barn champion horses were slated to be the first animals in the parade, ahead of celebrities, yellow inflatable cats, and slow pacing cartoon characters. Brandi and her modeling agency, a long list of fashionable women from the Big Apple and other places, had promised to ride the horses, rain, sleet, or snow, and Mickey and Tipp agreed.

"No." said Doc, answering directly. "Ringo's not here, Mick. "Yeah, two more saddles, and your order will be ready for horses." Doc told the man, in a less business-like manner.

"I don't think you boys are going to make it, Creole."

Raising his voice, "We'll make the order deadline, Mickey Starr."

"Tipp will be in Barringer next week. Hey, I hope you don't embarrass me, Doc. That would be bad for business." Mickey slammed the phone.

***

Dressed in black boots and dark gloves, Chuck walked through Doc's home, smiling, and sat between Ringo and Doc, who were glued to the television. Suddenly, in a bold move, Chuck turned the football game off at halftime and held the remote control.

"What the hell, brother?"

"Well, I did it," said Chuck, unzipping his coat, laughing, and coughing, even shaking when he told the truth.

Doc slowly sat up in his recliner and listened when his brother shook and trembled in mid-sentence.

"You did what?"

"I made my way behind security last night at Wagoner's Barn & Stables," shaking his head and zig zagging his hand in a maze design on the table top.

Ringo gulped his beer. "This guy is my superhero."

"I touched the legendary bull No Man's Land, and I can still smell the bull. Here are a few photos to prove his whereabouts, Ringo. Now we're a team, buddy, ain't we?"

Passing the pictures around the room, Ringo said, "Look at that massive bull, Doc," forming a lump in his throat. "Chuck could break into Fort Knox."

"Don't tempt me, if they got Kentucky Bourbon locked up beside gold bars, I'll do it."

Planting his feet on the floor, Doc leaned forward with his eyes glued to his brother. "So, Ringo, you must've taken Showman's bet on riding the bull?" The doctor threw his hat across the room. "Some guy at Troutman Hardware was telling customers that a Texas cowboy had accepted the bet. Were you going to ever tell me?"

"Yeah. I was going to tell you."

"That's a damn mountain of a bull, and the most muscular animal I have ever seen." Doc knew Clem Cline owned hundreds of bulls; none were this bulky and massive. "He's an Australian Charbray," said Doc, studying the photo, "weighing 1900 pounds, at least, a blatant bull." Rubbing his face, Doc took a deep breath, "Showman Wagoner was on television last week saying how no one could ride his monster bull. He was setting you up at McCarthy's Dance Hall. Damn it, boy, didn't you see it coming?"

"Ringo can ride him, brother!"

"I can ride 'em, Doc."

Stomping the floor, a half dozen times, Doc paced the floor and rubbed his head. "When will you start training?" Doc rolled up the newspaper and whacked his hand.

"Tomorrow," said Ringo, chugging a beer.

Slapping his hand, "Put the beer away and start today."

Chuck followed the two men to the kitchen, "I'll need a beer while you two men talk this bull crap out." His younger brother headed upstairs.

"Is this bucking bull a competition or a bet?"

"Bet." Ringo leaned back. "Huge wager."

"Charity work, huh?" asked Doc, getting loud. "Just for *funzy* on television. Is that what your generation calls it now? I'm sure it will be on the radio and television."

"Big Ray Brown and Sheridan are headed to Barringer," said Chuck, burping. "And some movie star bull rider named Max Sheridan, that's him, they will be promoting the event.

Gripping a tall salt shaker, Chuck tapped it like microphone and sounded,

"It's The Great Eight Second Ride Show, starring Ringo Bare as himself, hanging on for dear life. Let's not forget his faithful sidekick, the banker and Creole legend, Doctor Gilbert Greenway. Let's welcome these two suckers to the Barringer Stockyards. How 'bout it, Doc, can Ringo Bare ride No Man's Land?"

In a room of silence, "This is no time to play games, brother."

Chuck stood in the doorway between the living room and the kitchen. "Ummm, the Town of Barringer sends their best wishes and most of them are coming out to watch Ringo die." Still blocking the doorway he continued. "Everyone is looking forward to seeing you ride No Man's Land for $100,000, Ringo. Makes for good tourism in a small town, plus Uncle Kenneth's diamond saddle is part of the bet, Gilbert."

Doc turned to Ringo, "Got a $100,000 to your name, Ringo?"

The bull rider turned and looked out the window.

"Now we have no chance in hell of getting the diamond saddle back since our *hero* has only days to train himself," insinuated Doc, turning his head from Ringo.

Snapping his finger, Chuck announced, "Ummm, the funeral director said to call his office, he has options for Ringo."

"Joe Hatman?" asked Doc.

"Yeah. Joe wants Ringo to pick a pine box and pillow."

"Could you go back to New Orleans?" blurted Ringo, turning red.

"Who would've told Doc about your wager?" asked Chuck, who found a seat, kicking up his leg. "And who would have finished the last four saddle bags while you were running around with the Starr family, and making out with Brandi?"

"So, Mr. Ringo, you got the money to spare, if you don't ride this damn bull?" Doc inquired, gazing out the window.

"I'm not going to lose, though."

Doc looked at Chuck, bent over in a big laugh.

"I got the money, boys." Chuck drank his beer.

"You got bread, brother? Don't tell me how you got it."

"I got your back, Ringo. He'll win, he's the best."

"Your odds of winning are next to zero, unless Clem Cline can fly in from Texas and train your ass," said Doc, pacing around the room. "But he questions the fact that his crazy wife burnt down his house, so he's a bit schizo, anyway."

"You burnt down Uncle Clem's home?" asked Chuck.

"No." said Ringo. "His crazy wife burnt down our farmhouse. It's a long story."

"The humble cowboy will insist on a limousine ride at the airport," said Doc, sighing on the back deck, "and his normal room atop the Barringer Bed & Breakfast, just like he did when Uncle Kenneth died."

In a low voice, "I can win the money and I can ride this bull. I know his style and know what I did wrong with War Wagon, too. It won't happen again, Doc."

"Yeah," dropping his head, "I do too!" said Doc. "You got wrecked and nearly died, and I thanked the clowns for saving your life."

"You cannot win without Doc Greenway and Clem Cline," said Chuck, pulling on the beads of his pirate goatee. "I'll tell you that much! Ain't no damn coin flip goin' to help you on this one, hot dog. Much less a wish you well handshake from your rich poppy, Mickey Starr. And fist bumping Volt Hendricks after he sings the National Anthem, well, that won't help you much either, big boy. Though, he's a cool guy." Chuck raised his beer. "I met him once in New Orleans."

"Three weeks." Doc eyed the calendar. "That's not much time to get that old timer, Clem Cline to Barringer and get you in shape to ride that cowboy killer bull, No Man's Land."

"I'm going to handle this tank and win Uncle Kenneth's diamond saddle for you, Doc," said Ringo, turning up a serious face, hugging him.

Doc turned to Ringo, smiling and grabbed his shoulder.

"Do you have the same fire in your belly?"

"I thought about that day for three years."

"But from here on out, you are cut off from making saddles. No beer. No more late nights or chasing women."

Raising his hand, Chuck added, "I'll volunteer to do those things for you, Ringo," covering his heart. "Especially that last one, I can start today, pick up your slack."

"This is big money; you don't have it in the bank." Doc reminded Ringo. "I'm not letting my brother fund your mistakes. Sorry Chuck, he's on his own."

"He can just get a check from his filthy rich Poppy Mickey Starr, or he could ask his half-brother with that million dollar home in downtown Savannah, to untuck some pocket change."

Chuck laughed when he said it, but they stopped when he spoke of Brandi's brickhouse. Doc and Ringo weren't amused.

"Why the hell are you taking me off making saddles?"

"Why?" asked Doc, stretching his arms out toward Ringo. "You have to get yourself out of this damn mess, so you don't have to pay for it. Plus, you will be blasted all over the television if you get wrecked again. This time, things won't be favorable with your foot. So, it's best if you listen to Clem Cline."

"My crippled foot will be just fine!" Ringo stormed out and slammed the front door behind him.

"If you need me, I'll be helping my brother with saddles, I guess!" said Chuck, laughing. "Don't worry about me." He watched Ringo jet down the driveway.

Doc looked at Chuck in a confused state.

"So, you dig the saddlery business now?"

"Yeah, man," said Chuck, flipping the yellow porch light on the wall. "Got to do it," opening another beer, "if you're going to keep that boy from getting his ass killed on that monster bull. You know, that's one he can't ride, right?"

Doc didn't answer.

"Brother, that bull will wreck him. That's a deadly creator, fire shoots out of his nostrils when he sees a man."

"It's going to be a long couple of weeks."

Touching the calendar, Doc wrote Clem Cline's name on a napkin and called him immediately. The two men said no more than a sentence or two as they walked to the saddlery shop.

With new leather in each hand, Chuck said, "He's riding for Kenneth's Teddy Roosevelt saddle. The leather ain't worth a nickel, but the diamonds are something to see, big brother."

Doc turned and opened the door.

"Kenneth sold that saddle to cover Aunt Sandy's hospital bills. It was the only way, but it's time to win it back." Doc watched the horses he'd just had delivered thundering across the rolling hillside and thought of his Uncle Kenneth, a fine man who loved saddles as much as he loved horses. "He would have left that saddle to me in his will. Ringo needs to win and win big for us all."

***

Pouring lemonade, Doc remembered a conversation with his uncle in the late 60s when he helped build the barn for Kenneth and learned the craft of saddlery. He had hundreds of conversations with his Uncle Kenneth at the barn, but one changed his life. Not knowing it at the time, Barringer became an important part of Doc's life, in many ways, the best part.

Doc remembered his words, "Gilbert?" said Uncle Kenneth, holding a sheet of paper. "You're an excellent artist. I can teach you something that might make you some money, one of these days, follow me to the barn."

In those days, Uncle Kenneth was short and stocky, had broad shoulders and worked daylight 'til dark. Most of his uncle's time was spent making saddles and studying stones and gems he'd found around the globe. Uncle Kenneth tried to master the craft, adding diamonds and sapphires, so wealthy folks would purchase saddles for horse shows or maybe a gem museum would see his saddles as valuable, he said.

As a teenager, Gilbert was cocky, but skilled and agreed. "I can design a few things for you."

Hammering the legs solid to a saddle stand, Uncle Kenneth requested Gilbert take part in what he'd planned for a long time, a diagram partly penned in a notebook, but needed something else to finish it. His uncle looked at him in a curious manner, "Would you design a Teddy Roosevelt saddle for me, from horn to stirrup and do not leave out a single detail, Gilbert."

"You mean, President Teddy Roosevelt's saddle?" taking the pen in his right hand.

"I have the President's saddle design. And don't ask me how I got it, but it's the original Rough Rider design from his Army days."

"I can design the saddle, inch by inch, patterned just as his butt was mounted on his horse, Little Texas. It's an honor to handle the artwork and saddlery for you, Uncle Kenneth."

"Get as close as you can to the original saddle design."

His uncle was the man who encouraged Gilbert to become a doctor. "It doesn't have to be perfect, but Sandy would love to see the saddle decorated in diamonds. It's her surprise anniversary gift from me."

"You really want diamonds on her saddle?"

"I'd like to take Sandy through the woods on our anniversary, riding the new mare I bought her in Love Valley. We've been in love a long time, son." Kenneth had a big contagious smile and told him something else. "I hope you might consider spending the summer working on the barn and designing saddles for us, how 'bout it, Gilbert?"

"I'll make it for her and design it, diamond by diamond. Yeah, I'd love to stay the summer and move in, if you'll have me?"

"Good man." Uncle Kenneth hugged and squeezed Gilbert so hard, it popped his back. "Barringer is a good town. I hope you will live here, too. Some people forget it's even here. Your saddle will put Barringer on the map and we'd love to have you stay, son."

Doc remembered how he called him "Son" and respected his talents and opinions, even encouraging him to attend Tulane. Genuine love and being made special, was something Gilbert cherished and understood from that day forward. That's why he had an unsettling desire for the saddle, it was for the man that "loved him and called him son" and meant it.

Sitting at a homemade drafting table, Gilbert worked at a faster pace than his uncle did. They both made plans to build an additional section onto the back of his farmhouse, but the new barn seemed to be more logical and traditional, far away from his wife's Scripture studies and piano playing, Sandy needed her space just like the men did. Day and night, it took Gilbert three days to design the Rough Rider saddle for him.

Years had passed and the design was almost forgotten before Kenneth felt Gilbert was an expert, the Dark Side Saddlery Edition had enough leather for two saddles. When Uncle Kenneth was finished; one saddle ended up in West Virginia while Gilbert served in the Army, Kenneth sold the second one to the wealthy Wagoner family, the same year he penned letters to his son:

***

Dear Gilbert,

I hope the Army is treating you well. Sandy and I pray for you half the day and cry the other half. We see what is happening in Vietnam on the television and read the reports in the newspaper. Come home soon.

I finished the Teddy Roosevelt saddle this week, it turned out exactly the same as your design, from horn to stirrups. When I added the diamonds to the leather, there was a coal mining tycoon from West Virginia paid enough for the saddle to cover your tuition at Tulane University, if the Army doesn't cover the room and board. That's good news, Gilbert. We love you and come home soon, son.

Love,
Momma Sandy and Uncle Kenneth

***

In 1994, the Roosevelt saddle was appraised at $100, 000. Kenneth meant the world to Doc Greenway, so he needed to settle the score with Showman and have Clem Cline train Ringo. While Doc was living in Texas on Clem Cline's ranch, Kenneth finished the second diamond saddle, a vivid dream from the late 60s had come true, designed on more than a napkin.

***

Chuck snapped his fingers in Doc's ear.

"Hey, brother, wake up."

"I was in prayer."

"Well, good." Chuck smirked, rubbing his face. "Hope that thirty minute nap of prayer brought you into some favor with the Lord."

Doc walked over to Chuck's desk, scanning layers of stacked Bordeaux cowhides, and paced the shop.

"I've seen the Darkside Teddy Roosevelt saddle at McCarthy's Dance Hall. Women gather around it like honey bees," said Chuck, smiling. "Do you have a plan "B" if Ringo fails to ride the bull?"

"Took him years to make it after I shipped him leather from Temple, but the old man did it. I've never seen the Teddy Roosevelt saddle, but I drafted it thirty years ago."

"Let's go see the saddle, brother." Chuck put his arm around him. "The saddle Kenneth made is worth as much as my home in New Orleans."

The two men sat at the kitchen table, where Doc decided to ask Clem Cline to reconsider and fly to Barringer. To have him by his side would be pivotal in reducing a few notches of uncertainty and bumps on Ringo's head, too. Finishing what Doc could do on the saddles, and without delay Chuck guaranteed he'd personally meet Uncle Clem Cline at Charlotte Douglas Airport. Clem's favorite room overlooking the duck ponds and the tall cedars was available at the Barringer B & B, offering him the inspiration needed to coach Ringo back to professional status.

"Uncle Clem agreed to train Ringo; he's on his way," said Doc, pouring tea in a glass. "We must get Ringo professionally trained since he has been inactive for a while. If he wants to have a snowball's chance in hell of winning the money and staying alive, we need Clem Cline, right here. The important question is," said Doc, scratching his head, "where can we get a bucking bull?"

"Yesterday, I saw a rodeo in Troutman, and I'll bet a glass of Cliff's Classic Old-Fashioned, they'll have one."

"I'll talk to the owner before Clem Cline lands and plan something for Ringo in the morning; good eye." Doc agreed. "With Ringo's reputation, they may let him borrow a mechanical bull, if they have one that works."

24

Breakfast in Troutman

Across from the depot where the train once made frequent stops in the Town of Troutman, a hub outside Barringer, where Perth Road joined Highway 21 and the road forked under the red light, was a small business sector. People from three counties drove into town for pulled pork barbeque, New York style pizza, and the best ice cream money could buy. To the right of the depot, was where Doc had his morning coffee and pancakes. The place was where a dozen arrowheads were unearthed, left behind by the Catawba Indians. On the corner, still lively, was Vega's Dance Hall, built in 1977 and alongside it were a few good diners.

Half past nine, was when a friend of Doc's recognized him sitting alone at the bar, cowboy hat snug to his head, sipping on hot coffee. He listened as the waitress spoke of the hundred longhorn steers that were slowly becoming an attraction in the Town of Barringer, too. The owners of the Troutman Diner found longhorns to be more profitable than selling dill infused goat cheese and milking Guernsey dairy cows twice a day, just to turn a profit.

"Well, well, well, aren't you just everywhere?" said Sarah Ann, giggling at her neighbor.

"Where's Ringo and little Miss Brandi, getting groomed or did he put her out to pasture with the rest of the heifers, he dated?"

Doc held a cup of coffee with both hands. "Sarah Ann," turning his face toward her, "they're getting married. Didn't your parents tell you?"

"Married?" losing the grip of her notepad and pen.

"Brandi said to make sure you got the first invitation, though. I have it on my living room table for you."

"How blind is he? She's not the woman for him, I am..."

"I'm just kidding you, Sarah Ann. He's parking the truck; he'll be right in. You might want to tell Ringo about you being the woman for him, before he goes and marries Brandi, though."

"You're in big trouble with me, Doc Greenway."

Grinning, he covered his laugh and apologized to stay on her Christmas list. The bull rider walked in, sitting beside Doc.

"Hey, Sarah Ann," said Ringo, smiling, "I guess Doc told you the good news." He faced her in his usual chair. "Don't you think it's great news?"

"If Brandi moved to Ireland, that'd be wonderful news."

"I'm headed to the post office and the bank," said Doc, tipping his hat to the waitress. "Wrap my food to take home, Ringo."

Waving his hand, "You got it."

"You mean, bull riding?" said Sarah Ann, standing beside him. "I called Doc's house, he said you were training to ride a massive bull with a guy named Clem Cline from Texas."

"My muscles ache."

"Rumor has it, they sold five thousand tickets to the Barringer Stockyards for some big event with your name on the billboard. Some say it's your last ride, though."

"What do others say?" accepting his water.

"They have money bet against you."

Chuckling, Ringo whispered in her ear, "I'll have to show 'em different, won't I? Meet me at McCarthy's, by the mechanical bull, say eight o' clock tonight."

"Let's see what you got." Sarah Ann winked. "I've heard you brag, but can you ride?" She felt close to him again. "I'll meet you, watch you fall on your butt. You got me curious and let's make it seven."

"Alright," pulling her inside his arms. "It's a date."

"Kiss me, cowboy."

Without hesitation, he pulled her behind a panel for privacy, the world slowed up in his imagination as they touched. Triggering his nose was her delicate perfume of mandarin that commanded his attention, caught in her aesthetic beauty, he did just as she requested of him. They kissed. Pressing her cherry lips and making revolutions together, romantic, and yet intimate. Convinced by her tight embrace, opening her eyes, sneaking one last kiss, they were officially a couple. He was in love. Neither of them wanted the trance to end, which brought upon a sensation from both, a subtle moment, one that hadn't happened before between them. Far more sobering and gentler, the simpleness of a kiss, elated him and closed her eyes.

Later, at McCarthy's Dance Hall, dressed in black and white cowboy hats and boots, matched in style and fashion as if they were signed up for a dance competition, Ringo, and Sarah Ann locked arms at the door. Moments later, he escorted her to the one thing he felt confident about, even before leaving Texas, being a bull rider.

In weeks past, the agitation of the mechanical bull, turning and twisting under his seat, made him restless in a western corral, and lured him to where he was most comfortable and felt at home. Aside from the diamond saddle at McCarthy's Dance Hall, the mechanical bull drew the largest spectators to Barringer.

From the moment the bull started to function without a rider reminded him of the last time he landed his boots on the dusty soil at Conrad Cavender's ranch, in Louisiana. Ringo stopped. Then like a comet in the sky, War Wagon, bull 134, flashed in his mind from his last ride in Waco, Texas, remembering the nasty smell of the bull, the black glossy eyes of the fierce animal staring him down in the bucket chute, he angled in a blank stare. Ringo was locked in a nightmare, stuck in the dark side of a demon that wouldn't leave him alone until he conquered it.

The man operating the lever teased Ringo. "I know who you are, boy, that big-time bull rider from Texas. Do you have your courage back, Cowardly Lion?"

Without being intimidated, Ringo knew what he wanted to do with his life. "We'll see, won't we."

"You are that wanna be guy, Ringo Bare."

"Huh?" Ringo scoffed, walking toward the man.

"I'd like to see you ride him," encouraged Sarah Ann. "Wait! Three years ago, I was in a western store in Mooresville, a small crowd of kids cheered for you on television. Some of them even wore your t-shirt, the one with your picture on the front."

"T-shirts? I hope not." He blinked his eyes. "Were they good pictures?"

"I didn't buy one." She giggled, propping her boot on the rail, and winked at him. "I might buy one now."

"You must be my only fan." The more he watched the mechanical bull, memorizing the operator's hand movements, whipping, and spinning the machine in the same five changes, the more he wanted to ride it.

"Maybe some other time," said Ringo, tipping his hat.

The large man working the level shouted, "Showman Wagoner was right about Ringo Bare, 'Ringo ain't rough enough to ride in Carolina' right, cowboy?" The man tossed a stuffed animal at Ringo that hit him in the shoulder. "For the pretty lady, not the bull rider."

Sarah Ann stopped, tugging Ringo's solid arm. Her long lashes encapsulated his heart when she touched him.

"Dial it up, operator." Ringo adjusted his hat and belt. She kissed him twice. "Be back in a minute, that bull needs a rider."

Mounting the mechanical bull, all he could see was War Wagon, and what the *Temple Daily Telegram* printed 'RINGO BARE FELL OFF THE WAGON.'"

Gripping the bull, his dreadful attempt at Black Rio caused him to contemplate his action. Then Ringo positioned his legs and upper body in the bull, *I'll prove them wrong*, he told himself. A small crowd gathered around the black mechanical bull to watch him ride for the first time in three years.

"Let's see what you got, Tex!" A tall man shouted from the crowd. "Let's pretend this machine is No Man's Land, Ringo," howling and laughing at the bull rider.

Sarah Ann winked at Ringo, watching the bull rider lock his hand into the spine of the mechanical animal and nodded.

A guard walked up beside the operator. "Russell, don't take it easy on this ol' Texas boy, he's a professional bull rider, kick his ass and kick it good." The two men tapped bottles.

Blocking the negative words out of his mind as best he could because he'd grown used to that type of chatter at events for motivation, Ringo slapped his hand in the rope, nodding his head to the big round operator with a flush face, who held a stubby cigar and a sarcastic smirk on his round face.

"Cowboy Up."

"That bull will wreck you, but you are my hero!" A beautiful lady turned up her collar and blew him a kiss.

Becoming jealous, Sarah Ann blew him two kisses.

"Ringo's a wallet maker, not a bull rider!" called a round man in the corner.

"Let's go Ringo!" shouted Sarah Ann, waving and holding a heart necklace he'd bought her. "Listen to me, not them."

"You better follow your sweetheart," said a drunk lady, who shook a cowbell. "She's cute with that golden hair."

The bull started out slow, cut left under him, back up and dropped, turning right and then a swift left again. Ringo steadied his position and found his groove as a professional bull rider again, gripping his hat, twisting, turning, and controlling his breathing as his heart thumped his chest. He signaled as he controlled his rhythm and balance, when the operator upgraded the machine with a slight push, shaking Ringo like a rag doll, the machine vibrated again. The bull rider pulled his body to the center with all his strength, leaning when he needed to correct his balance, trying as if he was on a real bull in Waco, years earlier.

Five seconds into the ride, the bull turned to his weak side, the crowd sighed, and Ringo recovered his balance above his bad leg. The operator slowed the machine down to fake the rough rider out and again the bull rider was able to adjust his hat back between turns and dives. With a crooked smirk on his face as if he'd robbed a bank, the machine operator thrusted the lever to throw him off as the bull slowed down and the crowd cheered for Ringo. Victorious! Ringo landed on the soft cushioning, held up both his hands, waved and smiled. The large crowd whistled and cheered after he'd completed his eight second ride, in an effortless ride, shouting, "Ringo! Ringo! Ringo! He's back."

Looking at the operator smirk, Sarah Ann yelled, "Ringo! Watch out!"

Whipping the joystick in his hand, the round operator knocked Ringo against the railing, laughing, and throwing his arms up as if his actions were innocent. Zooming in as the operator handled his cigar, he waved in Ringo's face.

"Hey, you're a dirty crook, I should knock you out."

Ringo jumped out of the way of the second intentional swing as the backend of the bull dipped toward his bad leg.

Dodging the bull, Sarah Ann held up his hand and he carried her to the smooth hardwood floor for his first dance in years. Before her boots landed gently, she kissed him, humming in excitement after what he'd done to impress her meant something to them both.

"Told you," pointing, "I'd ride that bull."

"You're the best I've seen." A male line dancer patted his shoulder, "I watched you ride in Lynchburg, you won it all."

Another man said, "My money is on Ringo Bare ridin' No Man's Land. I'll change my bet with my bookie."

Wrapping her arms around Ringo during a slow song, Sarah Ann whispered, "That was an unbelievable ride."

After two songs they walked outside in the moonlight, Ringo tucked something from his blue jean pocket, hugging under thousands of beaming stars that seemed to favor him from heaven. Sarah Ann watched his hand working deep in his pocket, grinning as if he was searching for a coin.

She glanced at his palm. "What's this?"

"It's too early for wedding bells, and I can't sing like Volt Hendricks, but ...." opening his hand. "My grandfather handed me the keys to a little log cabin in Elkin."

"Is this Mickey Starr's log cabin?"

"Do you want to go?" twirling the key around his finger.

Sarah Ann gripped his hand and her eyes sparkled.

"Wow!" massaging his arms. "The two of us in a romantic log cabin together, Hmmm? I'm not sure."

Walking over to his truck, "I thought we might take a drive, see what Elkin looks like on a Friday night."

"Maybe?" Her head dropped. "I can't go, though. I have to feed the horses early in the morning."

"I'll call Doc, he'll feed your horses."

"You are an eager gentleman, aren't you?"

"I love being with you. Plus, there's a house full of leg lamps, Tipp told me when I got the keys."

"You better not play with the leg lamps. Let's hurry before I change my mind. My legs need a warm fireplace."

"I'll park my truck at my uncle's house in Troutman and you can drive the '56 Apache on our first road trip together."

Mountains were sky high, tall, and round, streams were full of trout, honey bubbled from beehives, and cabins were booked a year in advance.

At the wheel, Ringo said, "Tipp said, it seems as though you are touching the stars in Elkin, where you can walk from the porch and ride the clouds to the moon."

"When I was a little girl my father told me about Elkin, North Carolina," said Sarah Ann, leaning on him as he drove, "it's a place where you can pull a long string that connects to flashing and flickering stars in an endless sky that seems to be the glittering floor of heaven itself."

"We could make it our new home?"

25

Sweet November

Down a narrow patch of land where a graveled road was the only sound they heard, rolling his truck to a stop, and making a sharp turn between two dozen cedars, stood a fearless twelve point buck. Shifting the truck into park beside a broad evergreen thicket as long as a football field, the lovely couple had made it into a secluded wilderness.

Atop a wide spread hill, they walked the length of a fresh, new cobbled stone pathway, heavy fog drifted through the valley, and Sarah Ann pulled him to the rustic log home. At first glance, two dark stained doors were centerpieces of aged-old quality, restored to their former glory, as if it were the gate entrance to heaven. Just as Mickey said, it was a true sense of comfort and rustic-style, tucked away as if it was meant to be hidden. It was surrounded by the beauty of nature, for folks who cherished secluded cabins and adored the many wonders of flora and fauna, far from urban places, threaded naturally with tranquility.

"It's almost heaven, here, in Elkin," whispered Sarah Ann, moving slowly as two whitetail deer darted from the yard into the darkness of a pine thicket until midnight. "I love this place."

Under the lonesome streetlamp, Ringo surveyed the steady flowing rock waterfall which made its way out of the

Appalachian Mountains, mentioning how it would be a cool place to hook a rainbow trout or take a summer swim.

"There's a note nailed to the door." She unhooked the paper and aimed her flashlight on the page, moving inside the great room to read the paper. Walking up beside her, Ringo heard Mickey's voice through the words he'd written a week earlier:

Grandson,

I knew you'd like to see my log cabin. I like it too. Hope you two would stay a while, I lined up seven bottles of Andy Oliver wine in the refrigerator for a nightcap, fresh hen eggs are in the door for breakfast, just in case you stay until sunup. Something tells me you will wake up in Elkin. This is the first note from your old grandpa, and I hope you will be a true gentleman and join us in Savannah.

Stay cool,
Mickey

Turning the page over Mickey's deep voice rang in his head, "My grandfather thinks of everything, doesn't he?"

Flipping over the note, she said, "There's something written on the back of the page."

Ringo read it aloud:

Don't party too much because I need you to finish my damn saddles and don't forget the matching saddle bags, son. I had the neighbor buy two dozen red roses for the table because I knew Ringo would forget. Tipp always forgets and I figured you two were just alike, brothers, for sure. Thank me later, Sarah Ann.

"Why Ringo Bare, he knows you already, doesn't he?"

"He does. That's why Mickey Starr is a legend."

He examined the dark fireplace, from the hardwood floor to the hearth, all it needed was a glowing fire. Holding a box of matches, he watched her dance and familiarized herself with the cabin like she planned to stay a while, but it was her nosey nature. She changed radio channels until she found her favorite station in North Wilkesboro. There was hardly a moment when Sarah Ann wasn't convivial, spinning and singing, who knew songs, years from before she was born. Taking after her grandmother, she adopted her traditional nature, *more of a friend each day*, he thought, *sweet as bread pudding, too.*

"This is going to be special." She whispered in his ear.

"Here's the world famous leg lamp," he laughed, and made it glow. "Her leg is so smooth."

"It's a plastic play thing, Ringo, not touchy-feely, cowboy."

With a sweet voice, "Here's another note taped on the lamp," unfolding the paper.

"***Be a gentleman, Ringo.*** **Always be a gentleman, young man**" Sarah Ann pitched him the note as she danced.

"You missed the back of the note, he said,

"Rub the lamp leg for good luck, Bull Rider."

The note reminded him to do something. Reaching in his pocket, he flipped the coin while she looked around the log cabin at the pictures, and books were lined, shelf after shelf, and the place resonated romantically. She thumbed the hardback covers until her eyes found Hemingway, Fitzgerald, and

Lippincott, and a handful of other hardback novels stood in the bookcase.

Seeing the coin hit his hands, she watched him work his hands, and asked, "Was it heads or tails, Ringo?"

"Heads." He fell back on the sofa laughing as her eyes watched his abs flex when he laughed, tight as an ironing board since he'd been preparing his body for Clem Cline's training.

"It better be." She bit a piece of cheese. "We need some luck, you especially."

"How'd you know?"

"Doc mentioned your silly superstition and corny coin flips a long time ago." She leaned on the brown sofa beside him, kicking up her sock feet with a book in her hands. Her glasses made her look studious as she twirled her golden hair as it covered the pages, humming to the music as she read.

"You were checking up on me months ago, weren't you?"

He kissed her forehead and massaged her shoulders. "If you haven't noticed, I'm nosey." She changed the subject, turning the novel to the end. "Have you read this book?"

The bull rider moved to the fireplace, finally striking a match he'd found on the oak hearth after the first attempt failed.

Scanning the title of the book cover, "Nope." He grinned. "I don't read much." He fanned the flames and blew under the grate. "What's it about, anyway?"

"Hemingway takes a trip to Spain." She said excitedly. "He joins his friends at a festival and watches "Running with the Bulls," making a few friends in the process.

"Sounds cool."

"You'd like it." Her eyes brightened. "I bet you would."

Ringo collected pillows and placed them behind her head and under her feet, fluffing the third pillow for her arm and draping a thin blanket across her legs.

"I'll have to read it, of course, if it's about bulls and a Spanish festival, I might like it." The fire was warm enough for him to take a break, climbing under the covers as she leaned on him.

"What's happening in the story?"

"In the end, Jake puts his arm around Brett, and tells her how they would have had a *wonderful time* together in Madrid."

"Isn't it pretty to think so," said Ringo.

"You lied to me!" She gently slapped his shoulder. "You've read this book, haven't you? That's the last page."

"I'm an educated man when it comes to bulls."

"When it comes to bull crap, you mean."

Rolling away from her laughing, she slapped his hips and rear. "I can't lie to you. It was Doc, he made me read the darn novel after I hurt my foot and couldn't ride any longer. I spent a week in bed with classic literature and a saxophone by my bed."

"But you can ride, right? I mean, ride a real live bull, not just a plastic swiveling bull machine?"

"Yeah, sort of."

"A hundred people saw you ride tonight, like a professional again. You beat the eight second buzzer."

Pulling her close, he kissed her. "Let's not talk about bulls tonight. I want to know more about you."

"Good idea."

She removed her long sleeve shirt when the house heated up, two large purple and blue marks were on her arms.

"Where did you get those bruises?"

"I must have hit my arm feeding the horses."

"Now you are lying to me, aren't you?"

She pulled her shirt back over her body as she forgot about the marks on her arms and walked into the kitchen. He knew she was hiding something, the small part of her arm had hand marks as if someone had grabbed her with all their strength and meant to leave a mark.

They talked and kissed until two in the morning, where they fell asleep on a bear rug from Canada, surrounded by large, fluffy pillows Sarah Ann had stacked up as if she was in an oversized bed.

The smell of strong coffee opened her eyes as she picked up the pillows and collected wine glasses from their romantic night together. After eggs and biscuits, Ringo saddled up two horses for a ride along the mountain range, trailing for two hours down Sundance Run, turning behind Mickey's property. Then she surprised him on the summit with a long kiss atop horses, taking him by surprise, it was the most romantic thing she'd done or seen for that matter. They didn't realize how cold it was until they removed the saddles and watched the heat rise from the backs of the horses inside the barn. The brisk mountain air had picked up, he fed the horses while she planned lunch.

When Sarah Ann's pale hands became cold to the touch, he rushed her inside and washed them in warm water. Then he fixed a spread of ham and tomato sandwiches, plated sea salt chips and served her for a change. To warm her body, she moved about the log cabin, washing their dirty clothes from the horse ride while doing yoga. Dark fell on Elkin Mountain as they returned from walking around the pond, they held hands and were congenial.

When they started the truck a nine point buck picked green grass and stood fearless forty yards away. They agreed it was a wonderful place and how beautiful the porch rails and even the fireplace would look decorated in the glow of Christmas lights.

When Ringo returned to Troutman, he dropped her off at her uncle's home, then had one stop before he headed back to Doc's place. He knocked on the door of a home he'd never been to on Shinnville Road. Opening the door slowly was a thin young man who stepped out on the porch, Ringo's eyes were bloodshot with anger, the same as when War Wagon bucked him off, years earlier.

Ringo examined him in a casual way, sizing him up.

"Are you, Robinson?"

"Yeah, why?"

"Pop!"

The young man was belted with a blast to the face that sent him flying into the front yard and on his back, grabbing his busted lip, he yelled, "Hey, man! What the hell was that for?"

"You touch Sarah Ann again and I'll break your neck. You got that?"

"I didn't date her. That was my twin brother's girlfriend, Karl."

A second young man walked outside and looked at his brother on the ground, Ringo rushed to where he stood.

"Karl Robinson?"

He nodded when his name was spoken.

"Smack! Pop! Thump!"

The thin young man landed on the lawn beside his brother. Ringo landed punches before he caught his breath. Karl looked at his twin brother, the smaller of the two, who tried to understand what just happened.

Pointing at Kyle, "You can tell him why I hit you both."

As he slammed his truck door at the Robinson's, Ringo was elated about the romantic getaway with Sarah Ann, causing new energy and confidence to flood his training as he listened to her favorite radio station, preparing his mind for Clem Cline's training. Chuck was in the shop, finishing the last saddle for Mickey, then Doc stuck his head inside the screen door and smacked his hands together.

His gloves popped at Ringo.

"Are you ready to start bull riding again?" asked Doc, his teeth shone, then the whites of his eyes became enlarged. "What the hell is the ice pack doing on your right hand?"

"I hit a guy in the jaw." His knuckles had two cuts and were swollen. "Hit two guys, if you're counting."

"Did you get in a bar fight again?"

Ringo extended his hand and flexed his fingers.

"No. It's a long story."

Handing Ringo a fresh ice pack, Doc commented,

"That was the same hand you cut in Louisiana, right?" as he checked his knuckles, and sat across from his son. "O' Lordy, here we go again. It's money down the drain."

"Yeah, I know." Ringo leaned in his chair against the wall. "That was at Conrad Cavender's ranch, you shouldn't have bet on me."

"Now, we have a week before you lose your grip and embarrass your damn self on television. You might get hooked in the process. I'm concerned, that's all."

Kicking the chair across the room, "I'll be fine! He won't wreck me this time! Bet all the money you got on me, please do!"

Doc took Ringo's hand and pressed it flat, remembering what he'd learned in medical school at Tulane. It helped.

"Keep it under ice. Thank God, it's not broken," popping him in the shoulder.

"Feels busted up and hurts like hell."

"Let Sarah Ann kiss it for you, hot lips. Her red lips will heal things." Letting the screen door slam behind him, shouting out into the back field, "Chuck, we might have a snowball's chance in hell, if the boy can ride!"

A red headed woodpecker pounded holes in a cedar tree, like he was cheering them on or building a pine box for Ringo, the doctor couldn't decide what the bird was doing.

"What are you getting so loud about, brother?"

"Ringo busted up his hand again."

"There was a bar fight?" He stood and stared at his brother. "I'm disappointed, no one called me to the rescue?" pulling on his goatee and drawing back his hand. "Thump!" grunting in pain.

"Now why did you go and hit the wall, Chuck?"

"Wish I could have been there to help him in the bar fight." He lifted the fake patch from his eye and offered wild and crazy eyes. Doc shook his head in amazement.

"I'm sure we'll have to fight our way out of Barringer Stockyards, win, lose, or die." Doc handed Chuck a cold beer from the shop ice chest. "Here, it's going to be a *sweet* November."

26

Meet Bogart

Training included a five mile run in the morning, building up Ringo's wind and lightening the load for confidence and to respect the sport of bull riding again. His breakfast was a mystical blend before six in the morning, laced with eggs, steel cut oats, potatoes, toast, red peppers, and a large bite of ginseng. The bull rider pulled up a chair and examined a different type of food on the table.

"What the heck is this crap?" said Ringo, emptying his lungs with a sigh. "Smells good, though."

"Something I call, "Build the Bull Rider" and don't you laugh, just eat it and ride the damn bull. You're a champion, and a champion you are to me, son."

Separating his food in sections, "Why are there red peppers and Chinese ginseng on my plate, may I ask?"

"Since you owe me $5,000 and a motorhome mirror from Louisiana and you agreed to follow my training to a tee, it's best to not question the cook." Doc cocked his head and squinted his eyes at Ringo. "And remember, you haven't paid it back yet. So, I wouldn't be in contempt of my meals."

"Why the heck do we need a Liberty Bell in the kitchen? Heck, there's a rooster and four hens in the backyard."

"Don't question my madness or discount my experience, okay? Clem Cline taught me, and if he says we need a bell and chickens, we buy it for him. Clean your plate and love his coaching methods."

"You and Clem have gone Kevorkian on me, Doc."

A dinner bell was made out of a coffee can, turned upside down, tied with leather on a wooden post, and inside it was a metal spoon found on the Chisholm Trail. Doc had been up half the night planning his training, like a football coach, dreaming about winning the game with the inverted veer. The old man hadn't shaved in a week. But he plated food and poured his infamous power water over ice and slid it across the table, just like Chuck taught him to be a good bartender.

"What in the world is in this pitcher?" The bull rider lifted the beverage to his line of sight, examining the liquid at sunrise.

"Salt, sweet water, orange slices, and a Creamsicle." Doc replied, raising his hand. "Plus, chunks of fresh coconut, I like coconut, okay."

"Did Rocky Balboa drink this crap?"

"Rocky wasn't a bull rider. You'll be bigger, faster, and stronger listening to me." Doc tipped his cowboy hat.

"I'm not sure if there's poison in the green eggs and ham, either."

"Food coloring, maybe?"

The phone rang. Doc smiled.

"You're coughing, Clem."

"Doc, I'm sick as a dog, and I couldn't train a hamster on a spinning wheel today, bud."

"Call me when you feel better. Relax and rest."

"I'm with you, in spirit and prayer, my friend."

Doc hung up the phone with a long face. Ringo stopped chewing and dropped his head.

"Well, well," said Doc, "Clem Cline has fallen ill. I have another idea to get you trained before you meet that monster bull." Ringo was a professional, but he lacked motivation, and Doc knew it would be best if he had someone other than him to push Ringo.

Early that morning, Doc and Ringo took a country road past a harvested corn field and two soybean patches, trailing off the hill through thick laurel and high grass, and under sky high pines and rushing streams, to meet the slender "Corrientes Cattleman," Juan "Bogart" Perez, the man only bull rider in Barringer from El Paso, Texas. Therefore, without delay, and having no formal reservations needed to introduce him to his friend, they agreed to meet Bogart.

Ringo and Doc stepped out of the truck, turning around as ten motorcycles thundered like hell on wheels, rolling up behind them were big men, who wore red bandanas. Three classic cars jumped on air ride systems and two vans full of Spanish Angels made the journey to meet the champion bull rider. Within a few minutes, Ringo was surrounded, signing autographs for ladies.

"Where's Bogart?" questioned Doc.

Someone jumped behind Doc, slamming him and Ringo against the Apache truck, waving a long knife.

"Hey, leave them along, me amigos," shouted a stout Mexican man in black sunglasses, covered in ink and wore a black denim vest.

"Bogart?" said Doc, smiling. "¡Hombre salvaje!"

One of the men picked up Doc from the ground and the other man held a knife to Ringo's throat, returning the blade to a leather case made by Kenneth Greenway, pocketing their weapons when Bogart shook his head.

"Let's ride!" announced Juan Bogart. "It's the great Ringo Bare from Texas!" stomping out a short cigar in the clay soil, clapping his hands, signaled a man ready to coach.

The men raised their hands, pacing behind Bogart, shouting, "Tequila! Tequila! Tequila!"

Women cheered, wooed, and surrounded Ringo again. When shots were fired by a big Mexican, the ladies left the bull riders' side. Spectators walked through a tall barn to the other side, stepping into a ring surrounded by bleachers and waited on Bogart to command the platform. He spoke in Spanish to raise the wild crowd and invited his friends to watch a real Texan ride, making history in Barringer.

Hoy vemos a un jinete profesional con el nombre de Ringo Bare. Necesitará un trago antes de comenzar. Saca el Jersey de leche de vaca.

Men leaned back on the bleachers and laughed at the bull rider. Doc, fluent in Spanish, grabbed his belly and knew what to expect, too.

"What are they saying?" Ringo stood beside Bogart.

"Amigo, you will have to wear a blindfold." Doc held the cloth and announced the rules to the crowd. "Tendrás que estar con los ojos vendados." When they released a black bull the size of War Wagon in the corral, Ringo loosened his collar and sleeves.

"What the heck?" said Ringo, with a shocked look on his face. He started to walk away when two big Mexican men stepped up, blocking his retreat, and turned him around.

"Hey," said Bogart, reaching for his black bandana. "Put this on your face, Ringo," speaking with a thick accent, "and tie a good knot."

Bogart tied an extra knot, jerked his hand, and walked Ringo down to the chute. The bull rider climbed over the railing on a heavy animal, the ladies chanted, "Ringo! Ringo! Ringo!"

Doc grabbed his shoulder. "You ready, Ringo?"

Nervous as heck for a professional, feet pointed straight, Ringo hadn't been on a bull in years. Other than a mechanical bull, he had no experience being blindfolded, but knew what to do. The bull rider mounted the animal, pulled his hide, tightened the rope, and whiffed the smell of the animal.

"Cowboy Up!" Holding the rail, nodding, and slapping Ringo's helmet, the man counted down in Spanish. Then the wide bucket chute gate swung open. The crowd screamed and rolled in the bleachers. The animal was motionless. Snatching his bandana, "This is a damn cow!" Ringo yelled, smiling, and a bit relieved, he rested.

About that time, a man ran to pull the Jersey milk cow behind the gate to safety, Ringo jumped off the animal in the center of the ring. Raising his hands, Bogart gave the signal, two men opened a large chute and released the second meanest bull on the planet.

"These people have paid good money to watch you die!" shouted Bogart. "Don't disappoint them, Ringo."

Running like a wild man, Ringo climbed out of the dusty arena, and respected Bogart, making his heart hungry for bull riding again.

"I won't. *What the hell did I just say?*" watching the large animal run and jump around the ring. The glossy black eyes of the bull reminded Ringo of War Wagon, but it was a tidal wave of realization, too.

Bogart grabbed his arm and pulled him up on the platform. "I brought you to see the meanest one in Barringer." "You have a wild confidence about you, I like it. I heard you broke Black Rio and a dozen other horses in your wilder days."

Men opened the gate for a bull running wildly, and within a few minutes, the animal was brought to the bucket chute where Ringo was hanging on the rails.

"Cowboy up!" said Ringo.

Rocking back and forth until the bull settled down in the chute, Ringo nodded, and with a solid grip, Bogart coached his men to count in their native tongue. The gate was sealed tight. This time it wasn't the Jersey milk cow under his hide, but a bull ready to kill him that rattled the gate and chute, if he had the chance to hook him, the animal would have done so.

One amigo counted, "Uno, dos, tres," spinning and bucking, "cuatro, cinco, seis!"

The crowd cheered and shared whiskey, smoking, and taking shots of a fiery Mexican tequila. Clowns picked up Ringo off the ground, his crippled foot was almost unknown to the spectators who seemed to be impressed with his riding.

"He has courage. I can train him until Clem Cline gets better, Doc." Bogart called the doctor over to his side. "Have Ringo here every day for a week and bring Clem Cline with you next time. He's a true bull rider. I can get him ready for No Man's Land," shaking hands with Doc.

"No one knows that bull better than I do," said Bogart.

"Yeah. Is that right?" Doc removed his gloves.

"I raised No Man's Land," said Bogart, laughing. "Right here, in Barringer, he's a killer bull. I'm the only one who knows how to win that creator over and get a good ride out of him."

"You sold him to Showman Wagoner?"

"I bought a condo on Lake Norman with his money." Bogart grinned.

"Good deal." Doc howled, shaking hands. Then Bogart yelled and so did his amigos. "I got the right Texan, didn't I?"

"Clem Cline is a better man, but he's a sick man."

Doc whistled at Ringo to meet him at the barn. Ringo trotted to the center of the barn to where Doc stood alone.

"What the hell was all of this for?"

"It was a big test. You passed. He's willing to work with us and train your second class ass until Clem Cline gets his butt out of the Barringer B & B."

"The good news, right? I didn't die."

The crowd loaded up, promising to return for the next training session. Bogart's friends met Ringo, some sober and others were drunk, but they were excited to know the Texas bull rider.

As Doc and Ringo walked back to the truck, Doc said, "Clem needs to get better soon. He would have laughed his ass off about the Jersey cow."

"It was Clem Cline's hair raising idea, too. Don't worry, though, they captured today on film for him." Ringo watched the lines of motorcycles disappear in the distance, waving and thundering down the dirt road on their black Hogs.

"We have the best bull riding coach from El Paso, right here, in Barringer until Clem Cline regains his health," said Doc, cranking the Apache truck. "And a good bull that will kill you, that is, if he gets the chance to hook you."

"He's a wild coach. Brave, too."

"Respect him, he was a Grand Champion in Mexico City, in his day. Doc stared at Ringo. "His hermanos will stand with you when things get out of hand in Barringer, too. This isn't McCarthy's mechanical bull or some Wild West Show, it's real, life or death, for these guys."

The bull rider rolled down the window and let his face feel the cool November air, soaking up the rolling countryside of Barringer, alive again.

"Do you think I can ride No Man's Land?"

"Take it seriously. I don't want these guys on my back when you get arrogant and say, 'Bless your little heart, Bogart', nodding and smiling. So, don't do it, cowboy, unless you want to be tied behind a flying motorcycle."

Throwing his arm up on the seat, them pushing Doc's shoulder, "You didn't answer my question, did ya?"

"I did inside my big head."

"I'm cool. You don't have to say what you feel. Life gets tough from here on out."

Driving back to the saddlery shop, "But I made you tough enough to ride that bull, though."

Slamming the door and laughing, "What the heck, you made me tough?" throwing his hat at Doc. "I made myself tough."

"Good. Now show everyone you can ride the bull."

"I'll do my best, old man."

"Stop calling me, old!"

27

Didn't Like You Much

The stretch of ground from Sarah Ann's house to her pole barn was muddy from a hard rain that lasted for hours. Standing in the doorway with mocha coffee in her hand; the time on the clock changed, but she'd kept her schedule the same, falling back an hour, which made no difference to Sarah Ann's effort on the family farm.

Dark as the center of a deep tunnel on the Blue Ridge Parkway before sunrise, Sarah Ann was the type of lady who worked regardless of time, weather, or feelings. Amid her foamy coffee, she heard a turkey gobbling at the edge of a nearby hayfield. Destined to be a golden morning, the sun eased its way through the tall evergreens until the glow of light made visible the silvery fog that hovered in the valleys of Barringer that time of day.

In mid-November, Doc and Ringo dropped Clem Cline off at the Barringer B & B, he felt under the weather again after a mid-morning training session. Later, after returning from a late training session at Bogart's farm, Ringo marked his arm in black ink, which meant he stayed on the bull until the buzzer sounded, six out of seven times.

Good ole dependable Chuck tacked the last piece of leather to the tenth saddle, which meant the completion of

Mickey Starr's Bordeaux leather saddles and saddle bags. The finest wine color finish ever seen in Barringer or any place, for that matter.

More of a brother than Doc pinned him out to be, Chuck had grown up since his younger and wilder days in New Orleans and his brother appreciated his dedication to the Bordeaux saddles as well. Chuck took a deep breath and smelled the strong pleasing fragrance that had taken over in the leather shop and inside his nostrils, he was proud. Pure leather. Western. Chuck cleaned the shop, sweeping and organizing the saddles with the Saddles of Barringer brand name on a rectangular leather tag, draping from horn to fender on a string of tied leather. It was the first time he felt close to Doc in thirty years.

For the next few days Doc and Chuck focused their time, not on polished Bordeaux saddles and saddle bags, but on training and conditioning Ringo for the ride of his life, setting goals for him, from the business side of selling leather and making money between rides.

Four days before Thanksgiving, Mickey called Doc, he was due to send Tipp to Barringer the next day, settling the agreement they'd made at the Carousel Bar months earlier. The custom-made vintage Bordeaux saddles and matching saddle bags still stood as the agreement; the highest-quality craftsmanship Doc had ever handled. Uncle Kenneth and Sandy would have hugged Gilbert and wept, wrapping him up for what he'd done on their farm.

Ringo walked into the leather shop and the bull rider finished the final task, tugging the billet straps and polishing the fenders until they were glossy on each side. Chuck laughed and knuckled his head for being courageous and not the jerk he once said he would become. With a handshake and a manly hug, they agreed to be life-long friends.

While Doc grilled three steaks and spicy baked beans, mixed with a slice of cornbread for each man in a small celebration of their accomplishments, Ringo read the newspaper and became preoccupied with a section that caught his attention.

"If you have extra coffee," said Ringo, "I'd like to take Sarah Ann a cup and the newspaper."

He was losing that boy to the spell of love, Doc thought. "You are a true gentleman. Did I teach you that?" Doc made another pot of Colombian coffee, handpicked by Juan Valdez, of course, Sarah Ann's favorite blend. "Give me five minutes, lover boy. Try not to get wrecked by that lady, either."

A chilly wind blew into Barringer from the Great Smoky Mountains, dropping temperatures cold enough for gloves and a thin cap, Ringo had an idea. The bull rider knocked on the barn door with his boot and smiled.

"I brought you something." She wrapped her hands around him and thanked him with a long kiss. Her golden hair had grown longer by fall, pulling her ponytail forward for another intimate moment, she held his hand.

"I love hot coffee with vanilla creamer on a chilly morning." Sarah Ann sat on the bench near the horse stall, leaning back, gazing at Ringo. "To be honest, you are a true lifesaver. I'm not used to someone catering to me."

Leaves were tumbling across the field and into the barn.

"Reminds me of Central Texas, the wind from the Rockies has the same brisk effect in Temple," handing her a folded newspaper, he turned it to the page he wanted her to see.

"What's this?"

"There's a dance at Vega's Dance Hall tonight?" he said, folding the newspaper in her lap. She leaned on his shoulder. "We don't have time to practice, it's tonight."

She rubbed his hands. "I'm not sure I can make it."

"Why not?" Ringo was shocked.

"What about your foot?"

"I'm fine." He stood with a handful of grain in his hands for her horses. "There's a prize for the winning couple, what do you say?" Ringo poured the bucket of grain into the red trough for Applesauce. "The mare had her colt, I see."

Her head dropped. "I can't go." Tears fell.

"I wasn't asking you," he said, grinning. "I was just showing you the local paper."

"When you first moved here, I didn't like you much, especially your friendship with Brandi, but now I really hate you for not asking me to the dance." She snapped her eyebrows together and sipped her coffee.

"I'm just joking with you, but now since you hate me, I will walk around Vega's Dance Hall alone."

"I don't hate you," she said, wiping her tears. "But you can make it better for me, if you like?"

"Sarah Ann, would you be my date?"

"No. I'm busy reading the newspaper and shoveling manure," looking at him with a cute smile. "But if I read while you shovel, then we could be dancing by eight."

"No deal."

"What?"

Standing tall, "You get dressed up, give yourself plenty of time and I'll handle the barn. You can read later."

For a moment, they danced and kissed. Her eyes closed and a warm sensation ran over her neck, turning her face a soft pink color.

***

Doc knew about the dance and how pivotal a woman she could be in Ringo's life, especially being influential and pretty, holding her own with him, it was a plus. While Ringo was in the shower singing a Marty Robbins song about El Paso, Doc and Chuck, on the other hand, did something special for him. The Greenway Brothers polished the bull rider's best pair of black boots, Chuck reflected light from his ropers that made Doc jealous, handing him his boots as well. Chuck grabbed his belly and they spoke about how good it was to hang out again, while Doc's boots were being polished.

"Why Doctor Greenway, what's this?" Ringo shouted from across the room.

"He ain't the only one who gives a damn about you, Ringo," said Chuck, who stood in the doorway. "Look at the glossy shine on those boots, Bull Rider?"

"The boots look like mirrors." Ringo checked his reflection. "I didn't know old boots could look like the ace of spades."

The brothers headed down stairs. They spoke about how much better he'd look in a picture with Sarah Ann on his side. Ringo shaved, checked his pressed pants, snapped his silver buttons in the mirror, and slipped on his black ropers. Checked his bad foot that was sprained from being thrown and bucked for the past three weeks. Ringo tapped his watch and flipped a coin, smiling at the fortunate flip.

Chuck handed Ringo a small box, big as his hand.

"Just a little something from your Uncle Chuck."

Ringo uncapped the box.

"Is this a black on black native American bolo tie?"

"Best Cherokee rope and stone I've ever stolen," he chuckled. "Well, I wanted to steal it, but it's actually the only one I have ever... Okay. Hell, I traded for the damn thing. Now are you happy?"

"Are you serious?"

Walking in the kitchen, Chuck said, "Troutman Pawn & Loan sure liked it when I traded your El Paso cowboy boots for that American bolo tie."

"Is that pirate joking, Doc?"

"Well, I'm not sure."

Gulping his beer, "No. I had to pay extra to get them to take your smelly boots. So there, hush, and go dance with that lady."

"My brother is just messing with you." Doc coughed from laughing and hoped Ringo still had his cowboy boots in the closet. "Here's part of my appreciation for your dedication to Clem Cline and Juan Bogart, take the keys to my Ford truck since your Chevy Apache is in the shop."

"I'd rather take the motorhome, but...*tonight* I'll make an exception and suffer through driving a Ford."

"Are you wearing the fancy blaze orange underwear I bought you?" Clem asked, walking in the back door. "Might bring you some luck."

"Clem Cline? Did you come over to see me off on this date?"

"Heck, no. I heard there was good food here. Maybe some of that leftover Texas Cowboy Stew, you burnt my damn house down with in the summer."

They laughed for a half hour as Clem Cline stole the evening with his stories about Ringo and Uncle Kenneth and growing up on a ranch in Texas.

"He doesn't need luck," said Doc. "Ringo's our lucky charm!" adjusting his belt and looking him in the eyes. Doc walked with Ringo outside and the only light they could see across the field was Sarah Ann's room.

Ringo pulled on the ropes of his bolo tie. "Clem Cline has made me laugh for ten years," he said.

Handing him a cold box, "She'll need a corsage, Ringo."

"Wow! You saved my life. I appreciate you taking me in. You are the man; you didn't have to be."

Crossing his arms, Doc lowered his head, "For fifteen years I've been your father, plus you were born on a Tuesday. I know better than anyone, Bull Rider. Now, go dance with that lady."

As Ringo walked down the driveway, Doc thought about all the great years with Ringo, sniffing and he knew they were days that would last in his heart forever.

Turning around Ringo asked, "Why did you care all these years, Doc?"

"You were standing in the rain when your mother left us together. Just you and me in a cold, rough world and no one else, so I promised myself I'd become the father I didn't have to be, even better than Clem and Kenneth were, for that matter." Doc had a lump in his throat. "Now it's your turn, Son. I didn't bring you into this world but brought you this far. Be more than her date, be the gentleman other men admire."

"If this night goes well, you'll be a grandfather."

"I better not go that good. Keep your horse inside the barn."

Doc walked Ringo out to his truck, "Here, flip this coin. See if it brings you any luck?"

"Keep it. I have a wonderful lady and the finest father in the country, I don't need a silly superstition. Got what I need."

Doc nodded in agreement.

"You're a great man, Ringo."

"I'll trade this Ford truck tonight when it breaks down, get you a real Chevy truck by morning, Dad."

"Get the heck outta here."

***

In style and attractive, Sarah Ann stood tall in a red velvet dress, cut to the thigh, buttoned, was a jet black vest, and black shiny boots polished like mirrors in a fashion magazine. Thirty minutes into the competition Ringo and Sarah Ann danced as if no one else was watching them, spinning "in a world of romance," a fine moment to witness, for those that did.

Sweat dripped from Ringo's forehead, and in her own way, Sarah Ann just glistened, two stepping and scooting on the dance hall floor at Vega's Dance Hall, in rhyme and style. She was happy. In a moment of astonishment, they found each other, more than anything, more than music and moment; the beginning of a love story was good for them both.

Her heels hit the hardwood floor like a team of roofers, pounding in the midst of the excitement, natural and sure footed, yet with grace and certainty of talent. Positioning his black cowboy hat low, spinning her with force, made her long golden hair whip, a sense of touch and beauty combined. In a state of submission, when she batted her dark lashes over her soft hazel eyes, he lost his breath. Three judges were glued to Ringo and Sarah Ann as they kept in step, missing only a few points. The bull rider blocked the crowd with his cowboy hat, private and like a true gentleman, he kissed her at the end of the movement.

She was radiant. The way she carried herself, from the inside out, the kindest soul in the community, making her even more attractive to him and he knew it, too. Ringo wrapped her up tight, kissing her after the dip as the crowd roared in the last thrilling moment of the dance. They took second place. After midnight Ringo and Sarah Ann walked outside to cool off, laughing and spinning, still in motion. Ringo recognized someone standing in front of Doc's Ford truck.

"We thought we'd find you here, Ringo the Dingo."

"Is it Karl and Kyle or Kyle and Karl?" said Ringo, pointing at the twins. "I can't remember which one of you that I knocked out first." Both brothers had black eyes and one had a gash on his top lip.

"Kyle, what are you doing with that ball bat?" asked Sarah Ann.

"He's not going to do a damn thing, are ya?" said Ringo.

"Crunch." Kyle busted Doc's headlight with the bulk of the bat.

"Take a swing at me!" yelled Ringo. "You didn't play baseball, did you, hero?"

The baseball bat went over Ringo's head. Belting Kyle with a right cross, Ringo caught him off balance, kicking him, like Doc taught him to defend himself from bullies.

"I believe he broke my arm!" yelled Kyle, rolling in the grass.

Karl jumped at Ringo and grabbed him off guard. Picking up the baseball bat, Sarah Ann swung like she did in softball, ten years earlier.

"Crack!" The bat hit Karl and then she struck Kyle.

"Oh, my God!" said Sarah Ann. "I heard his leg snap."

Rolling beside his brother, Karl moaned and groaned.

She flipped the bat on her shoulder as if she'd hit a homerun in the World Series, hopping in the truck and holding Ringo's hand. They won. The bull rider navigated through the Carolina countryside like they won the war together. Scooting closer to the bull rider, she yelled, "Let's go. Let's go."

"They won't be running after us."

"Is the fire still burning at the log cabin?" asked Sarah Ann. He turned on her favorite radio station and jingled the cabin keys. With one headlight, he drove to their favorite hideaway.

"There's a warm fire and a bear rug."

"We better ice a bottle of Andy Oliver wine, too, for the hot tub," said Sarah Ann. "I didn't bring a bathing suit."

"My bolo tie will be warm enough to cover you."

"You wish!" Leaning on his shoulder, she fell asleep.

***

On the night of the dance, Doc walked up to Showman Wagoner's mansion, and rang the doorbell. Showman's cocky smile widened as he slicked his hair back and with a condescending look, said, "Why Doctor "Tulane" Greenway?" toying with his gold diver's watch and flashing his sapphire ring. "What the hell are you doing here with a pirate?"

"I'd like to double my bet on Ringo riding No Man's Land. That's why we're here!"

Walking up behind Doc, Chuck flashed his own black diver's watch, a bit bigger, and made visible his dark tiger eye rings to match Showman's as well. "You got an extra $100,000 cash in an ol' dirty sock, don't ya, Showman?" taking off his dark sunglasses and flipping a coin.

Thumbing his chin, Showman answered, "I got the bread, see if your cracker jacks are bluffing me. I've got $100,000 that says my champion bull wrecks Ringo and he dies at Barringer Stockyards."

"He might really have the money, brother, huh?" stepping in Showman's face. "Well, I'm lovin' this bet," said Doc. "That's a hell of a deal. Much better than we'd planned for, Chuck."

"What time do you have, Showman?" said Chuck, admiring his gold piece. "Would you care to put up that fake watch as part of the bet, too? I'm a collector in New Orleans."

"Though, I suspect you've never seen a real collector's watch, right, not one like this diver's watch?" Showman handed it to him. "Admire the gold, partner."

Doc stepped closer.

"So, you feelin' your bull will kick Ringo's ass?"

"I'll put up the gold watch, the Roosevelt diamond saddle, and the money we spoke about on my bull." Showman ran his hand over a handful of bills in front of the brothers. "That's how confident I am, Gilbert."

"Even better." Doc thumped the stack of cash; it was twice as much. "I'm glad we had this meeting, and my brother needs a gold watch for his Pirate Bar, more than you do."

"It pays to know wealthy people," said Chuck, handing his watch back to him.

Doc offered his hand. Showman refused. They stared at each other like gunfighters, locking eyes for a few seconds. Chuck grabbed his hand.

"By God," said Chuck, pressing with all his strength, "you'll take my hand and my brother's hand, when we make a deal. Right here! Right now! Then we will leave, you get my drift, Harley?"

The Greenway Brothers stood firm.

"You're breaking my damn hand!" moaned Showman.

Doc's teeth gritted. Then Doc gripped his other hand.

"Make sure you bring the bank with you on Saturday night," said Doc, grunting and releasing his hand. "Don't forget

Kenneth Greenway's saddle, the fancy watch, and the money, you got that Showman?"

"Don't try to leave town," said Chuck, releasing his hand and stepping off the front porch, gandering at the veranda. He laughed at Showman, adjusting his shoulders and black vest.

"You stinkin' Cajuns, get the hell off my damn land!"

28

Romance Mountain

The grand log cabin was glowing with a tall fire in a short amount of time, making the house a warm and welcoming home for the night. The nearest neighbor was a mile away and the phone was inoperable. Private. Romantic. Dry wood popped and crackled in the fireplace, he used the same method of lighting paper rolls and kindling that had worked once before when they visited the log cabin.

Opening the storage closet, Sarah Ann found a stack of decorations packed away in boxes. Within an hour, the cabin was decorated for the holidays. She called it "Romance Mountain," a home away from home.

Still, there were beverages in the fridge and a few snacks they'd agreed on at a convenience store, mainly popcorn, soda, and lots of chocolate. Once settled in from the drizzling rain, Sarah Ann poured her favorite wine, a brand from the vines of Virginia, called Andy Oliver. It was Pinot Noir, a "good red" she favored from the Shenandoah Valley.

Other than the fireplace flickering and a lit candle that moved when she walked by, they felt fond of the place. The couple could see their reflection in the kitchen window and in the mirror as the candle flickered in the background. Walking up behind her and placing his hands around her hips, Ringo was a head taller than Sarah Ann, causing her to turn around inside his arms. She removed his cowboy hat and he lifted her up on the countertop, letting her lead in passion.

"Little lady, like Burt Reynolds said in the Smokey and the Bandit movie, 'My cowboy hat only comes off for one thing and one thing only,' touching her chin.

"Mine is on the hat rack, Ringo Bare. I've seen that movie, too."

They laughed. He took a deep breath and didn't know if she was kidding or not, but he felt comfortable. "Lady, where'd you learn to swing a baseball bat like that?"

"You're not the only one with talent, you know."

"I'm not the only dancer, either," he smiled. "You have a few moves yourself. Much quicker than I dreamed."

"Are you too tired to make another dream come true?"

Carrying her over to the giant sofa, he felt her legs were cold. He kissed her and covered her in a blanket, one handmade, and large enough for one more.

"What dream?"

"Just a little dream, I had." She was nervous for the first time with him, even her feet were cold. He found a heavy pair of blue socks, pulling them snug up to her smooth calves.

"I remember the first time I saw you," massaging her legs and feet.

"Walking the dog?"

"Nope." He sat up and faced her. "That was the second time."

"I was standing on the porch, Doc nudged my arm and showed me where you were in the field."

"You looked my way, huh?"

"Let me finish. The sun was setting low behind the tall pines, you were looking down in the valley on horseback. Do you remember that?"

"That was a pretty orange sunset, I remember the day." She laughed. "I was wondering who the jerk guy was with the giant Texas flag on the motorhome in the driveway."

"But you were waving and flirting with me."

"I wasn't trying to get your attention." She moved around on the sofa. "Give me some credit. My horse stepped in a nest of yellow jackets and I was swatting bees buzzing my head."

"What?" nearly spitting out his drink. "I thought you were flirting with me, for sure. Doc told me that much."

"I was trying to get out of there. So, you thought I was flirting, huh? Boy, that's cocky on your first day in Barringer."

His face turned red, nodding, and drinking his beer.

"You were trying to see if I was watching you or not, Ringo?"

Leaning over laughing, "What about the day at the shop when you walked up behind me?"

"Spotted you working," gripping his arm and laughing, "I thought you might need some lemonade and a shirt on your back."

"The sun was melting me, so I took off my shirt. In a strange coincidence, a lady hands me lemonade"

"You were half naked and looked thirsty."

He poured her a glass of Andy Oliver wine.

"You saved my life with the lemonade."

"I was concerned about your hydration."

"Hmm?" removing his vest. "Did I look like this?"

"Where's the suspenders, Tex?" She kissed him and softly ran her hand down his face.

"I was hanging the new door for the saddle shop."

"You were showing off your body, cause you knew I was nearby."

Sarah Ann brushed wine from her lips. "I had a lucky horseshoe over my head, you know. I wanted to make a memory."

"If you ride No Man's Land, you will be a hero, and that's not luck, it's talent."

"If not?"

"I believe in you, more than you know." She gripped his hand. "You're the best in the world at bull riding and kissing." She kissed his shoulders. "This is the biggest thing you have done in years; your body is ready, and your muscles are tight from training, too."

"You are a gracious woman for looking after me."

"I've never done this before," she confessed. "What I said about having a dream? This is all new."

They didn't speak about making love much after midnight. Later, sometime around three in the morning she shivered, Ringo found a moose print quilt, from the larger of the two bedrooms, he kissed her and covered her up. Remembering her request, he cupped his hand behind the flickering candle flame and extinguished the fire. He took the thinner of the two blankets for himself. Kneeling on the floor, he built a cozy fire, with enough wood that would last until morning.

When she rolled over, he pushed the pillow back under her head, combing her hair to the side, Ringo finished the wine and watched her sleep in peace. The only glimmer of light by morning was what was left of the glowing embers that had burned down, gray ashes had fallen under the grate. He made another fire and watched her sleep.

Seeing his kindness with the blanket and pillow, she kissed him, pressing her finger against his lips. "I hope we have many more good mornings together."

"Isn't it awesome to think about." He held her close. "Did I make the dream come true?"

"It was close, but we may have to try it again."

Later, as the sun made its way between the evergreen forest and oaks, glowing in the openness of the cabin, he gazed out the wide window as a skiff of snow lightened the lawn. She sat in the wide window and they watched the wind make the snow dance across the front lawn. In communion, deer returned and so did rabbits and birds. Yet warm and cozy, inside his arms, she enveloped him under a blanket, and they made love and fell deeper in love.

As she napped, Ringo surprised her with strawberry covered pancakes and chocolate milk, something he knew she favored. Playing her favorite jazz song on the saxophone somehow lured her out of the foggy shower. Something he'd practiced and planned, days earlier. When Ringo moved away from the fireplace, two red stockings hung from the mantel, her name was penned inside a heart on the larger red stocking.

29

Sidebar Between Brothers

Late November was enough for a long sleeve shirt and jacket, and by that time of year, there were more leaves on the ground than in the bare treetops. All that was hanging on the limbs were the evergreens and a few oak leaves that refused to submit to the chill of autumn.

After Mickey commissioned Tipp to settle the debt for the vintage Bordeaux saddlebags and matching saddles, Doc, Chuck, Ringo, and Tipp, loaded the saddles in a long van with "The Tobacco Barn" name on the side of the vehicle. Chuck and Doc shook hands with Tipp. Then the Greenway Brothers headed back inside the leather shop.

"Ringo," said Tipp.

Walking to the end of a gravel driveway, Ringo stood under the wide oaks to see what was on Tipp's mind.

"What's up?" Ringo tucked his gloves into his pockets.

"After the Thanksgiving parade, Mickey is flying from New York City to Charlotte, then a limo will deliver him to the Barringer Stockyards to watch you ride. He said to tell you, he wouldn't miss it for the world."

Unfolding his hand from his pocket, Tipp dropped something in his hand.

"Keys. More keys?" The bull rider was confused.

"Mickey has a condo at Tybee Island. It's prime real estate at sunup. You can see the ocean and drink all the Moon River Beer you want." Tipp tapped his gold watch and filled his lungs full of the cool air. "I love this time of year; it's meant for family."

Spinning the Tybee Island keys around his finger, Ringo asked, "It's a big condo on the ocean, and why me?"

"He'd like you to live there free of charge. No questions asked. It's a gift of gratitude to his grandson, and for as long as you would like to stay there. The place is yours now."

"What about Sarah Ann?" he asked, adjusting his hat. "We have plans to be together."

"The condo is yours to keep." Tipp assured him. "Brandi has a beach body; lives two doors down, though. Of course, you know that already. I gotta go, cowboy. Take the "Brickhouse" and leave the farmgirl." Rubbing his hands together, Tipp shrugged his shoulders and nodded in confidence.

"Hey, Tipp," pitching the condo keys back at him, "keep the damn condo."

Scanning the property, he and Doc had together, fields were cleared, a new leather shop attached to the barn, and new gravel from the hardtop to the road, with plans for new pavement. He felt welcomed in Barringer as much as he did at Clem Cline's ranch. In deep thought, Ringo walked toward his truck and Tipp pulled up beside him.

"One more thing, Ringo, before you turn us down."

"Hmm. Yeah?"

"He'd like you to manage The Tobacco Barn, it's a six-figure salary. You'd teach the youth in Savannah how to ride bulls and horses. The kicker, you'll make three times what Doc pays you to run Saddles of Barringer."

"I don't make much here. There's no stock options."

Tipp snickered, snapping his fingers.

"Mickey Starr matches his stock dollar for dollar."

"Good for you, fisherman."

Tipp handed him a business card.

"Here, take my cell phone number, call when you want to talk business. Barringer isn't Wall Street and Hoover." Tipp grinned and looked away. "Mickey is planning big bull riding events on Saturdays. Plus, after you ride No Man's Land, you'll just sign autographs, kiss babies, and travel with Brandi, from town to town. You might reconsider the condo key, and... think it over, Ringo."

"Barringer is a good town, though. I'll keep the cabin."

"Well," stretching his arms, "I'm sure Barringer has its perks. But Mickey is serious about you moving to Tybee Island, taking over as CEO. I ran the numbers, you'll make more money than anyone in the company has ever made, rough rider."

"What do you do for our grandfather?"

"I manage Starr Fishing Company, America's oldest fishing business. We fish with forty boats now, doubling our fleet after the storm hit. Volt Hendricks works for us now."

Ringo nodded. "Sounds tempting, brother."

"It's gold bars for Christmas, buddy. Come join me. Barringer doesn't have an ocean of money yet."

"Let me think about it." Ringo tucked Tipp's number inside his wallet. "Hey, Tipp, it's good to have a brother."

"Yeah, Mickey is planning on sending you and Brandi to Andy Oliver Vineyards for Valentine's Day. He plans to buy the vineyard next year, anyway, and you'll get another log cabin." Tipp checked the time. "Well, I let that one slip out, didn't I, brother?"

"Andy Oliver is high class, Tipp."

"No more Cajun beans and rusty buckets like that '56 Chevy Apache truck. It's seafood and Cadillacs, Cowboy Ringo."

"It's a cool classic truck, though."

"That's a good one to restore in Mickey's garage." Tipp laughed and rolled his vehicle. "Well, let's show off your Bordeaux saddles in New York City, how about that?"

"Tell Mickey, he has my attention."

Tipp leaned out the window, and waved, "Join us and roll like a celebrity."

"Tell Mickey, I'll see him on Saturday."

"Ride the damn bull, Ringo!" Tipp pulled out of Barringer en route to New York City.

***

Working the morning shift at the soup kitchen, Sarah Ann handed out baked hens, green beans, and slices of turkey in Troutman, serving veterans and the homeless for Thanksgiving. Something she had done since she was in high school.

Back at home, Doc and Chuck prepared their own feast, while Ringo made prime rib for his girlfriend, attempting to surprise her with one of her favorites, Sarah Ann came home after lunch exhausted. Chuck and Doc played back the recording of Mickey and his team of models riding in the parade, to see their saddles on television again. Brandi and her friends marched Friesian Horses ahead of a group from Wyoming County, West Virginia, a beautiful team of horses and ladies were well admired.

Seeing the custom Bordeaux saddles and saddle bags on television made the Greenway Brothers excited. On the other hand, Ringo walked the trails near Lake Norman State Park, found a bench to rest and watched a handful of boats sail the main channel. Thursday had been a pleasant Thanksgiving Day with Sarah Ann's family, he thought, among other things.

Friday morning, Doc wanted to take Ringo to see the bull he was set to ride at the Barringer Stockyards, now open to the public. They walked around the corrals, amazed at the only spotted bull with a massive dark brindle coat. The animal had dark eyes the color of West Virginia coal and ugly horns, too, No Man's Land, was a deadly bull that had wrecked a long list of tough cowboys. Doc examined the breed of the bucking bull, that snorted three yards away and turned his eyes and horns toward Ringo's hawk eyes. More than ever, Doc couldn't wipe away his uneasy concern for Ringo, and didn't know deep down if Ringo could ride the bull or not. Penned was one of the finest breeds he'd ever seen at any rodeo or ranch, and Juan Bogart raised the animal and sold the monster bull for an undisclosed amount to Showman Wagoner. Studying the behavior of the animal, Ringo let the bull smell him and they met for the first time before feeding time. Neither of them were pleased.

"When you look at the bull, stare him down," said Doc. "Like you are doing now, you will be bigger than the bull."

Ringo rested his foot on the rail.

"He's a top bred, for sure."

"Ringo, hey, you rode that bull's father in 1990. Heck, you were in high school, back then. That's a piece of cake for you."

"Yeah. That's right. Devil's Slingshot is the sire of No Man's Land." He tipped his hat to Doc and winked.

"Let's get the heck out of here. You got this bull."

"I'm hungry."

No Man's Land was the meanest and nastiest bull Doc had ever seen in his life. He built confidence in Ringo's mind by telling him he'd ridden the bull's father, when he wasn't sure himself, but he said the words anyway, for the sake of his courage.

"You're a champion," said Doc, hitting his fist in his hand. "Don't be intimidated by the damn thing when you drop down in the bucket chute." He pushed Ringo against the wall of the tunnel underneath the arena to encourage him. "Ride it like a hobo on a hayride."

"I'll land on my feet."

"Chuck is headed back to New Orleans. He found love."

"He's a damn good man. Let's invite Sarah Ann over for dessert and coffee then. How about it?"

Doc uncovered bread pudding from the oven.

"Chuck made this for you and Sarah Ann, a little parting gift for your courage and dedication."

"I bet this one has a splash of Chuck's Bourbon in it?"

"Three tea spoons. Then Chuck finished the rest, 'Like a good Pirate should,' he said."

Seeing him laugh and enjoy himself with Sarah Ann caused Doc to roll a hundred thoughts through his mind about how Ringo had grown up around him, far from a young boy on the back of a pony, to being one of the top ranked bull riders in the world. He was proud of him showing an altruistic soul for others.

30

Meanest Bull in the World

With great anticipation, hotels were booked weeks in advance and restaurants were packed with fans excited to witness the "Meanest Bull in the World," penned in Barringer, North Carolina. Twenty-two thousand seats were sold at the Barringer Stockyards, the media praised the bull more than the bull rider, which was expected since Ringo had been absent from the sport for more than three years.

Because of Mickey's parade recommendations, Saddles of Barringer had taken orders for western saddles from thirty-three states and the United Kingdom. An Englishman, the owner of the Famous Seven Oak Paddocks expressed an interest in English saddles for fox hunting, in which Doc had considered a design, but not confirmed it with Ringo yet. After consulting with his partner about the numerous orders, Doc called the man in the U.K.

"Old Chap, Doc," said the Englishmen. "We're interested in stamping Saddles of Barringer on English saddles for show jumping and hunt seat events."

"Ringo is mainly into western saddles, but being an avid horseman, he'll make horse racing saddles and Polo saddles for your daughter's event." He proudly told the man from Seven Oaks.

The Englishman was grateful and wired the money. As a result, Doc and Ringo reserved two tickets for his new friends.

"Aye," returned the Englishman. "See you at the show, good chap."

Ringo spent the last few nights in prayer and meditation alongside Sarah Ann, making her coffee when she woke up. She voiced her thoughts about him becoming a flying ragdoll by the power vested in No Man's Land, hooked, or trampled to death. For Ringo, it was too late to turn back now, and he would not retreat, anyway. Clem and Bogart would kill him if he resigned.

"The show must go on." He eagerly told her.

****

"I'm Big Ray Brown from Eddy, Texas."

"And I'm Max Sheridan from Luckenbach, Texas," adjusting their microphones for the big event. "I've seen a few large crowds from Las Vegas to the Big Sky Country in my twenty nine years of commentating, but this crowd is eager to witness history being made, right here, in Barringer, North Carolina."

Twirling his pen in his hand, Big Ray announced, "I think this showdown will land Barringer on the map for future bull riding events. What can we expect to see from this bull, Max?"

"Barringer, well, it's a bull riding town right now," adjusting his microphone close to his lips as he spoke. "In the grand slam event of bull riding, the underdog Ringo Bare attempts to ride No Man's Land, the meanest bull since Wild Bodacious."

"And don't forget Bushwhacker from Denver."

"This steer is 1900 pounds, and he hates the smell of a bull rider's cologne, despising the feel of leather, ironically. No bull rider has even ridden this Australian Charbray for eight seconds, a giant steer, throwing seventy-one professional bull riders off before the buzzer. He's a deadly creature."

"The big question is, can Ringo Bare ride him, right here and right now, in Barringer?"

"Bull riders have limped away with broken ribs and two dozen have been carried out of arenas on stretchers, all over the country." Max scanned the large crowd. "All I can do is count the odds against the rough rider #21 Ringo Bare on this pitch black night in Barringer. The venue doesn't seem to matter to No Man's Land, the bull hates bull riders and cowboys alike."

Max poured coffee in his large cup and offered Big Ray some brew, who waved it off. Max tipped his hat to people he knew from Texas and Oklahoma, who'd made the long trip to North Carolina.

"We've seen this bull before in Del Rio, Waco, and at Wild Bill's arena, out in Cody, Wyoming. He nearly killed Tito Samuels in Archdale last summer. Some good cowboys have attempted him and lived to tell about it. First timers, well, they try to make a name for themselves with No Man's Land and with seventy-one outs, not one bull rider has stayed on this animal's back for the count."

Max gripped his cigar.

"The unanswered question, can Ringo Bare be the first, Big Ray?"

Ray tried to get comfortable in his chair.

"I don't know. Riders have paid the price each time, from broken arms to busted ribs and one man was drug like shag carpet across the Texas soil in Waco, but for Ringo, I truly hope so."

He removed his hat as Volt Hendricks nailed the National Anthem. Then they watched ladies riding horses around the arena holding the American flag and the North Carolina flag whipping in the breeze.

"But this showdown has brought fans to North Carolina from as far west as Montana and Arizona and as far south as Central America, a few have joined us from Brazil."

Curling his lip, Max elbowed Big Ray Brown.

"In the front row, I see the legendary Mickey Starr from Savannah, who made the trip from the Big Apple."

Big Ray adjusted his specs, shaped his brown signature cowboy hat, and observed the massive crowd of political figures and popular journalists, who aimed to print one for the books at Barringer Stockyards.

"The fact is," said Ray, grunting, "this bull hasn't been ridden for eight seconds, he has thrown cowboys before the count. Postponed the career of Jeff Woods, just two weeks ago in Huntington, and the week before that took down Larry Ford in Abilene. I remember "Risky" Rambo Sneed, out in Tulsa, he had a heck of a time with this bull. No one has ever made the eight second mark with this bull or gotten past five seconds, for that matter."

Rolling a signature Tobacco Barn Cigar sent by Mickey Starr to the commentators, Big Ray said, "But tonight, we are going old school with ten seconds on the clock!" The crowd roared. Big Ray wiped the sweat from his forehead and kept spectators amused.

"How's Ringo Bare going to hang on for ten seconds; half that time is the longest any cowboy can brag about riding this bull?" Max flipped his clipboard. "Jose Gonzales from Brazil, he made it five seconds at the stockyards in Fort Worth, two months ago. Other riders were dropped in three seconds, bouncing like a stick man on a trampoline."

"I can't answer that one, but this ride will change his life," said Big Ray, handling his cigar.

Max shuffled in his seat. "I can tell you this much, it's going to be a once in a lifetime showdown. Fans have poured in spirit and support for Ringo Bare, who's a tough cowboy from Texas."

"Today, Ringo can cash in big. I've heard the prize money has doubled if he can hang on for the count. Also, let's not forget Kenneth Greenway's diamond studded Teddy Roosevelt saddle, which is being guarded in the back of that chuckwagon by the North Carolina State Police." Max changed hands with the microphone. "If he can hang on without touching the bull, that is."

Big Ray leaned forward.

"The famous saddle," said Big Ray, "designed by the late Kenneth Greenway will go home with Ringo Bare or stay in the hands of Showman Wagoner, who is seated with his girlfriend, Samantha, in the VIP section."

"But if he can't handle No Man's Land, the saddle and prize money might leave Barringer. *The Statesville Record and*

Landmark newspaper reported, the saddle will be shipped to Wyoming with the honorable Showman Wagoner, where visitors will pay to see Teddy Roosevelt's Rough Rider saddle in his new Great West Museum."

Big Ray, a heavy, round man spun his chair around, and sighed, "Showman Wagoner keeps the prize money, but the fans came here to cheer for Ringo Bare." Big Ray told him. "I'd like to see it happen. Redemption."

"After that tough ride on War Wagon a few years ago, Ringo hasn't been back on the circuit. This is a bright light in a dark world for this cowboy and I hope he walks away a winner."

"It's the unknown that keeps the loyal fans coming out to arenas for all the marbles and it's exciting, too."

"We have ten minutes until the showdown." Max stood. "Let's take a short break."

***

Doc walked underneath the tunnel where Ringo was seated in a small room designed to house bull riders and the Cowboy Church on weekends. Doc leaned back on a bail of straw and waited for Sarah Ann to kiss Ringo, and after she left, Doc knocked on the thin door.

"How are you doing, Ringo?"

"Fine."

Ringo placed his cowboy boots in the dirt.

"Mickey stopped by to check on me." Ringo shaped his cowboy hat and couldn't look at Doc, who knew something was up. "He wished me... good luck, too."

Doc straddled a folded chair.

"What else did he say?" His eyes were locked on Ringo, like he'd gotten a bad report from his physician.

"Said he flew in from New York to watch his grandson." The bull rider sat up tall. "Told me, he'd like to see me on Monday morning in Savannah. He offered me a big deal to work for him, too, Doc."

Doc's face turned flush red, rubbing his head, and sighing.

"Surprise, huh? He wants you to join the famous Starr family business." Doc threw his gloves against the wall. "What'd you tell him?"

"I said I'd know more after the ride." Ringo brushed his hands together, taped and gloved up, like he did before each ride. "Lots of pressure before a big ride."

"Life's full of pressure and how you handle the situation makes you a man or a mouse."

Doc unbuttoned his long sleeve shirt, rolled up and exposed the inside of his left forearm where the bull rider could see it.

"Where'd you get that tattoo? That's your first one."

"Barringer." He nodded. "The day you announced to the world, you were going to ride No Man's Land."

"What does it say?" Ringo moved in close and stretched his arm out, yanking his long sleeve, tight to the elbow - Ringo Bare - my Son."

"Doc, that's pretty cool. That rocks."

They gripped and embraced each other. Uncertainty and emotions were locked inside each man. Regardless of the next step, Ringo saw it with his own eyes, and he was proud.

"I would've accepted a dang postcard, instead. I believe that's the most anyone has ever thought of me and I don't know what to say."

"Just do what Clem Cline taught you. Either way, you walk away my hero." Doc buttoned his shirt sleeve back up. "This tattoo is just ink and I love ya, Son. There's more on my heart."

"Love ya, too, Doc."

Adjusting his collar, Doc buttoned his coat, too. It was the first time either of them had spoken from their heart about how they felt in a long time. Wondering where Ringo would spend Christmas, Doc hoped it was in Barringer.

"No matter what Mickey tells you," Doc eyed Ringo, gripping his shoulder, "his son may be your biological father, but who's been here for you? When you climb on that animal in a few minutes...." He turned, opening the door. "We've been on this ride together, and I'm still on your side."

"I'll ride for you."

"Ride for yourself today."

"You didn't have to get a damn tattoo, though."

"Saddles and ink and you, that's all I know." Doc shook Ringo's hand. "We've forged our way through a hundred hardships, and I'm still here." Then he nodded and kept walking into the bright light of the tunnel, stopping at the end.

"Savannah or Barringer?"

His silhouette disappeared after he rolled his hand off the brim of his hat. Ringo had five minutes. Flipping a coin over in his palm, he left it in the room for the next Rough Rider. The knock of the horseshoe against the hollow wooden door brought back memories of his years as a teenager when Ringo first met Doc. They spent days nailing horseshoes to the barn and said the Lord's Prayer together, so it was worth repeating again, in that moment. He did it.

***

Doc sat between Sarah Ann and Clem Cline, who was beside Juan Bogart, and they listened to Clem tell funny stories about Ringo growing up on his Central Texas ranch.

In the summer of '84, Doc bought Ringo his first chestnut Quarter Horse, had three white socks and a long white face, a stallion he'd bought in the Town of Christmas, Texas. Ringo broke it to ride in three days. At that point, Doc knew he had more courage than most men, recalling the first day Ringo was trained to ride a bull by Clem Cline.

"Hold on tight," said Clem. "He likes to run left first and leap. Learn his pattern, Ringo, ride like you want to be remembered."

In a bit of fear for the kid, Doc rang his hands in his favorite pair of gloves and pulled 'em with his teeth when he got nervous.

"Turn him loose," said Doc.

Ringo kicked the bucking bull in the ribs with considerable hope to command him, causing the heel of his boot to widen the eyes on the animal.

"I got him." Ringo mumbled over the mouthpiece, adjusting his helmet, nodding underneath his outfit weighing on his head and chest. He looked ready, at least. Doc and Mike eyed each other, not sure if it was a good idea or not, but they studied the boy. Mike was Clem's son, who held the gate for riders and counted down, too.

"Watch that boy ride, Clem!" Doc yelled.

"He's got potential!" Clem yelled back.

"He's holdin' his own, Dad." Mike watched the young bull rider. Clem stood on the gate watching the bull spin and leap.

"He could be great with a little training."

The bull spun on a hard left, Ringo hit the dirt after seven and a half seconds. Out of the mouth of a sharp washed up bull rider named Showman Wagoner, who watched him ride from the driver's side of his pickup truck and became jealous, and shouted, "He'll never make it, Clem," closing the truck door and walking toward where the men were positioned. "Might be another Clem Cline wanna be," Showman laughed.

"Showman Wagoner," said Clem Cline, "you get your damn stuff and leave my property. Don't ever come back!"

"Ringo Bare is one of the best paseo de toros I've ever seen." Clem told Showman and Doc. "What do you think?"

Doc spoke with his deep voice, "Did good today, didn't he?"

Clem looked at his son and then Doc with a big smile.

"Mike, can we make him better, though?"

The young man walked up to Ringo and held him up on his shoulders as Ringo raised his hands above his head, the happiest smile Doc had ever seen on a kid appeared on Ringo's face.

"We can make Ringo Bare great."

"If he's as bull headed and stubborn...." said Clem. "He'll just get hurt and cause us a bunch of emergency room visits, turning Doc's wallet upside down." He swung a rope over his shoulder.

The wind blew slightly out of Morgan's Point, Doc pushed Ringo's hat down on his head. Clem walked up close to Doc, and Clem said, "He's a fine boy. I wanted him on my team, and he made the cut."

Doc untied their horses and planned to go home.

"Thank you for letting him ride, Clem, but we'll just stick to ropin' calves and cleaning stalls, back at my place and maybe raise a few longhorns this year."

Pivoting and walking back toward the corral, Ringo said,

"Hey, Doc!" His voice changed from alto to bass, turning the faces of the men in his direction. "I wanna to be a bull rider and a damn Rough Rider, like you guys."

Standing in dusty jeans that would have to be washed twice, young Ringo tightened his pants to his hips and carried Clem's rope on his shoulder. Between the barn and corral, Ringo shouted, "I'm not some milk cow blues boy or some barn jockey." The kid adjusted his hat. "I'm a dang bull rider, gentlemen."

"Are you sure, son?" Clem Cline walked fast toward the kid. "Are you positive about what you're saying to us? One day, you'll walk into an arena, it will be you and a wild bull, roped up."

"Can I ride him again?"

"I think he's got courage!" Mike yelled. "Hot damn, he's a champion. I knew it the first time I saw him."

"I don't work with cry-babies or sissies, Doc." Clem Cline threw a rope from one hand to the other. "Prove it, Ringo."

"Ain't no cry baby, neither." Ringo bit his mouth guard and fastened his helmet even tighter.

"Either he's stupid as hell or he's awfully brave." Mike dropped him in the bucket chute atop the bull.

"Let's get him a bigger bull." Clem Cline grinned. "Who is this rough rider boy, anyway, Doc?"

"He's my son, I just adopted him."

***

That was the day that flashed in Ringo's mind at the same time Clem Cline told the story to everyone seated in their section, only minutes before he climbed aboard a bigger bull, No Man's Land. The bull rider heard the crowd getting louder and louder as the arena reached maximum capacity. Easing forward Ringo paced from the inside depth of the dark tunnel, waiting on Big Ray Brown to call his name and number.

The tunnel was not much bigger than a one car garage, filled with straw and smelled of hay, one just like he'd witnessed ten years earlier at White Hall Ranch, Texas, owned by world famous Clem Cline. Ringo embraced what time he had left in the tunnel before showtime and recited more than one prayer. Big Ray Brown nudged Max Sheridan's arm inside the booth.

Big Ray stood.

"Look who just walked out the tunnel."

Max placed both hands on the table and stood beside Big Ray Brown, who had a great anticipation for what was about to take place in Barringer.

"The long-lost bull rider, we haven't seen in over three years." Max's voice amplified with each word across the arena. "He's here, in Barringer, North Carolina, the star of the show!"

Big Ray pressed his heels against the floor and shouted, "This man needs no introduction, he's the toughest bull rider on the planet." Big Ray lifted his microphone from the table, "Ringo, Ringo, Ringo Bare #21!"

Over twenty-two thousand fans rose to their feet, and chanted, "Ringo! Ringo! Ringo! Ringo! Ringo!"

A second overpowering comment from Max Sheridan lifted the crowd, a roar sounded across the long valley of Barringer, and the packed arena tipped the Richter scale.

"We haven't seen him since Waco, Texas, where he busted up his foot and now he walks with confidence."

Ringo walked onto the large platform, raising his hands to the crowd, waving at friends and fans, scanning the arena as the lights hit him. Trained by Clem Cline to locate the bull, right out of the tunnel, and not worry about the crowd, he did just that, and then he found his friends.

"He looks stronger than ever." Big Ray told Max.

"Ringo has stayed in shape." Max added, taking his seat. "Where's he been keeping himself?"

Big Ray ran his finger across the program.

"This paper says he moved from Temple, Texas, a few months ago and now lives in Barringer, North Carolina." Nodding, Big Ray rubbed his chin. "I had no idea."

A tall thin minister walked up to Ringo with his hand out, touching the cross and then he slapped the bull rider's shoulder. "Lots of folks praying for you, young man."

Ringo shook the hand of the gray haired man accepting the sincerity in his wrinkled face and the calmness in his voice relaxed him.

"I'll take prayer." Ringo spoke into his gloves as he waved at Sarah Ann, raising his other hand. "Pastor, I may need you again soon." The minister was nowhere to be found. Disappeared. He scanned nearby seats, but he was gone.

Fans wore t-shirts with Ringo's picture on the front and back. Little old ladies, kids, veterans, and young kids held up their cowboy hats and signs with his name in bold print. Rodeo queens from days gone by and ladies with crowns had their own special section. Ringo lifted his hands, tipping his hat and waving back at Sarah Ann, as he neared his way to find the large bucking bull everyone had come to see him ride.

Another ten paces separated Ringo from the bucket chute where "No Man's Land" would soon be positioned, a bull known to shake the graves of the dead, they said. Bulls smelled bull riders from a short distance. Twenty feet away and close enough to smell Showman Wagoner's cologne, was seated the nemesis to all bull riders. With a great amount of money on the line, Showman cupped his hands to his face. "There's no way in hell you can ride my bull," he heckled, looking at his friends. "He'll eat you for lunch, Ringo."

Stepping close to the bull, the young man he fought with outside Vega's Dance Hall, Kyle said, "No Man's Land will break your legs, Teddy Bare."

Ignoring misfits and critics, Ringo used rejection as a form of fuel, to set greater goals for himself and a new purpose of determination raged within his gut, by that point.

Recognizing a familiar face, one friendly and kind, Ringo said, "Why Clem Cline, I didn't think you attended bull riding events?"

At his age, less and less events were attended by Clem Cline; Other than mentoring Ringo, the last one he cared about was with Lane Frost in 1989. Out of respect for the former champ, who balanced himself with a cane, crippled from years of handling steers and horses, but he proudly stood for Ringo when he walked by him.

"I came to see that Teddy Roosevelt saddle my brother made." He laughed. "I didn't know you'd be here, Ringo Bare."

"Thanks, World Champion of '46 and '56."

The old man snapped his fingers and winked.

Ringo stood tall and greeted his long-time friend and coach. Clem Cline's frame was bent over by that time in his life, where a long career of action and war horses had made him a well-known figure. He moved at a fraction of his once rapid speed and hyperactive pace, it showed in his fragile state and in the way his arm wobbled when he positioned himself at his seat. Ringo's circle of friends were few, but they were some of the toughest he'd ever seen, and as sincere to him as a team of ministers.

"I hoped you would be here."

Clem Cline cleaned his glasses and wiped his tears.

"Wouldn't miss it for the world, Champ."

***

Standing tall above the chute, Ringo dropped down over the massive hide of the animal and for the first time in his life, Ringo felt bigger than the bull. The bull rider mumbled a quick prayer. He climbed aboard, rattling the gate at his feet which made it nearly impossible to grip the leather or to find a good position. No Man's Land hated the sight of any cowboy with silver spurs or breathed for that matter. Much less the tightness of a smooth rope wrapped around his belly and back. For the first time in a long time, cameras flashed Ringo's face on the big screen and on television for his fans at home.

"This is a long-awaited matchup between man and beast." Max leaned over his desk. "Overdue in the world of bull riding, and we need more men of courage and honor, to step up.

Big Ray eyed the second hand on his watch, and sounded, "We are only seconds away from this showtime. I see Ringo is trying to find his position in the bucket chute."

"He's down on the animal, making his presence known on the hide of No Man's Land."

"Folks, we're witnessing a historic moment in bull riding." Big Ray twisted and bit his nails to find comfort in the last unsettling moments of adjustment for Ringo, a strange habit he'd formed over three decades commentating rodeos.

"He's warming up the rosin on the rope." Max rolled the program. "This keeps the rider's hand from popping out of the bull rope's handle, causing a disqualification."

Thousands of people watched Ringo straddle the bull and make adjustments to the rope, pulling tight into the back of the bull, just like riders had done for decades, locking his muscles in a secure grip of the rope.

"Ladies and Gentlemen!" Max shouted, "No Man's Land hates hotdog cowboys as much as he hates other bulls."

"Go get him Ringo!" shouted a man from the third row.

"He's my hero!" a little boy sounded, holding up his hat and waving a Texas flag.

Slapping his left hand tight as he'd ever held a rope on the back of a bucking bull, Ringo Bare wrapped a rope around his side and bit deep into his mouthpiece until his teeth cut into the black plastic crevices. His mind was clear. One man stood on the top of the gate to help tighten the rope around the bull. Uncomfortable in the riding vest, Ringo said the Lord's Prayer as fast as he could. He nodded slowly, a normal signal with his head, rounding his eyes, and now in position.

A young man in a straw cowboy hat stood on the ground and pulled a heavy rope with enough force to open the gate as twenty-two thousand screaming fans came to witness history. Not a scuffle of boots of any kind existed in the stands, male or female, it was like church during the invitation time. The latch clicked, metal to metal, the pastor prayed, and the bucking bull raged out of the chute, twisting, and turning, like the animal was stepping on flaming coals from the depths of hell.

In amazement, Max Sheridan looked at Big Ray Brown with wide eyes, then he yelled, "We got ourselves a war!"

Big Ray chewed his gum, "Come on, Ringo."

The two announcers stood in awe.

Ringo hung on for dear life. Clowns in orange and white spotted suits took their positions behind wooden barrels, people stopped eating to watch the champion, who had been absent from television for far too long.

No Man's Land left the earth, twisting in a full circle twice and whipping his head left then right, cutting his hooves into the earth to throw Ringo off his back.

"Five seconds have passed," said Max. "Halfway."

"Nine seconds!" Ray counted aloud.

The bull cut left and then leaped and stretched out his body, off the ground again. Airborne. His long and thin tail whipped his rear. Fans could see the bull standing at a vertical leap, two tons of the meanest bull in the world had Ringo whipping like a rag doll, hooves planted deep in the Carolina clay, where the bull rider looked like a chicken on a chain.

Tears rolled down both sides of Sarah Ann's face, her hand covered her mouth and stood motionless. Then she screamed, "Ohhhhh Ringo!" A thundering awe sounded, and the crowd stood, flat footed and motionless.

The bull threw Ringo forward where one of the horns hooked him in the chest. His face hit in the dirt and dust clouded around him. Horns from the bull raked over his back. Then the body of the bull slammed down into the ground. No one could tell if he was stabbed by a hoof or not.

Big Ray Brown removed his cowboy hat and wiped beads of sweat, gripping Max's shoulder in astonishment. The two of them stood, shoulder to shoulder, Max staggered as another bull rider was down for the count.

"He took another big hit, didn't he?" said Big Ray.

Clowns whistled and shuffled around wooden barrels to prevent the bull from crippling Ringo, the place was silent as Ringo remained motionless, but he was alive.

"He did it!" Big Ray announced. "He rode No Man's Land for the count. "He's the first bull rider to do it! But it doesn't look good for Ringo Bare, so far."

"Ringo!" shouted Sarah Ann. "Ringo!" She cried and screamed, moving down to the first row of the arena for a better look.

Two painted up clowns watched the massive bull disappear behind the swinging gate into the depths of the corral. Without hesitation, they were the first to reach Ringo, his body atop the dirt and immediately they flagged for help.

31

The Recommendation

Leaves covered country roads and city streets in that part of North Carolina in late November, and a familiar winding road, one that led Sarah Ann to Mickey's Elkin log cabin was less occupied and private that time of year. The neighbors dog barked as they stepped outside the truck. Ringo greeted the animal with a biscuit he'd saved when he realized where she'd taken him after the hospital visit. She kissed him again, turning a big smile on his face.

Three days had passed since the showdown in Barringer, and the large crowd had packed up and left, but Sarah Ann wasn't about to leave his side. This time, it was to rest, not for horseback riding, exploring the Blue Ridge Mountains, or to rename the mountain, for the sake of romance.

Ringo had hardly spoken to anyone, only a few words to Sarah Ann were said. Nothing had been mentioned about the prize money or about Doc or where Clem Cline was until that point. Under the recommendation of the doctor, the bull rider was to rest, far from the media and cameras, hidden away. Doc recommended she take Ringo to Elkin, a place he wouldn't mind visiting, anyway. His eyes lifted and his face curled a bright smile about how she whistled when she made turkey sandwiches and poured sweet tea for Ringo.

Taking a seat at the table and holding his head, Ringo asked, "What the heck happened to me?"

"It was the best ride the world has ever seen. Big Ray Brown and Max Sheridan are still talking about it on the radio. Pictures of the ride are plastered on the front page and online."

"Here, wanna read it?"

'Ringo Bare conquered No Man's Land.' "We won?" asked Ringo.

"Yes. You won it all."

Ringo shook his legs slowly, still in some pain.

"Well, how was the ride, cowboy?"

"Showman protested. Judges spent ten minutes reviewing the tape, counting, and recounting the split seconds leading up to when your body went forward. The bull reared up and your head collided with the bull's head. I thought I'd lost you."

"What was my time?"

"Ten seconds."

"I can't believe I rode that bull."

She handed him sweet tea. "You won! You earned it."

"Where's Doc and Clem Cline?"

"Texas. Doc's trying to buy back Clem Cline's ranch before it hits the real estate market. Clem is getting too old to handle cattle and horses. His son, Mike, well, he wants him out of the ranching business."

Hugging her, Ringo exhaled, "Best news I have heard in a long, long time. I won."

Tears rolled down her face like a leaky faucet.

"The bad part, Clem Cline had a heart attack after the ride, he'd bet $100,000 with a Las Vegas bookie, and became so excited, he clutched his chest and fell beside Doc."

Ringo held Sarah Ann's hands.

"This has turned into a big mess, hasn't it?"

"It has been tough on Doc. Then Clem Cline demanded he die in Texas, and nowhere else, but Texas. That's when Doc took him to Temple, Texas." Sarah Ann hugged him. "I told Doc we'd be here, if he needed to get a message to us."

"What about Showman Wagner?"

"He escaped to Wyoming with the Teddy Roosevelt diamond saddle and the prize money." Ringo closed his eyes in disgust. "He told the media he was going to close Barringer Stockyards and move his office to Wyoming."

Clutching his forehead, Ringo told her.

"I thought the bull was going to hit the ground, cut left and he came back up, I was off balance over top of the bull, too far. He knocked my lights out when he bucked, felt like a train wreck. The next thing I remember, I woke up in the hospital, in and out ever since, and felt better when I saw you through the glass."

"You were unconscious for several days."

"Is that when Doc flew to Texas?"

"Yeah. He'll call when he gets Clem Cline settled."

"Now what?"

"Mickey, Tipp, and your sweet little Brandi called from Savannah." Sarah Ann rolled her eyes.

Ringo pushed his plate away.

"What did Mickey say?"

"He wants you to move to Tybee Island." She dropped her fork. "Take over The Famous Tobacco Barn, he built a few years ago, that seems to be doing well, he said."

"Tipp mentioned that last week."

"Savannah? Temple? Barringer?" Sarah Ann stared at him. "I'm staying here, but where are you going next, Ringo?"

"My head hurts. I don't know, yet."

"When will you know? I need to know."

She left the table with her wine glass, walking over to the window, and crossed her arms. Then stood at the fireplace.

"Maybe by Christmas, I'll have a plan. I'm not sure."

She couldn't hold in her thoughts any longer and with a sarcastic voice uttered, "The newspaper said you are moving to Savannah. Do you have plans with Brandi and Mickey?"

Sarah Ann emptied her glass.

"Wow!" Ringo waved his hands. "I'm with you, babe."

Pacing to the living room, Ringo steadied himself beside her and let her cool down.

"Brandi called twice. She thinks you and her had a *love connection* at Doc's when you unzipped her dress," adding a sassy tone, 'I had a special moment with my bull rider,' at least that's what Brandi said to me on the phone."

"No moment. Nothing was special."

"Well, good."

Wrapping his arms around her, he kissed her. "I love you."

She cried happy tears. "I love you too, Ringo. I thought I'd lost my first love."

He swept her long hair from her face and kissed her again. "I'm your last love, too."

Pressing against him, "Seriously, are you moving to Georgia or Texas?" sighing and rubbing his back.

"I love you, Sarah Ann. I'm staying in Barringer and making love to you. If I have any energy left, I'll make a few saddles, in no particular order, though." He promised.

"Do you plan on marrying me or is this another eight second ride and then you are off on another journey?" Her voice was stern. "Do you want to talk about marriage?" Sarah Ann raised her brow.

"Plus, I didn't know Doc was moving back to Texas." Ringo sat on the big sofa and fell back. "O' God, this is all big news to me. Remember I was knocked out."

She touched his nose. "Oh, my gosh!" she said, with eagerness, "You don't know about your orders, do you?"

He adjusted his cowboy hat and leaned forward. "What are you talking about?"

"You have a big business to run in Barringer. Orders came in from all over the country while you were in the hospital. There are lots of orders. You can thank Big Ray Brown and Max Sheridan, for promoting Saddles of Barringer on their new radio show." She handed him a clipboard full of papers.

"There must be forty requests here. That's about $80,000 in saddles."

"If he plans to move to Texas, maybe you could buy Doc's farm in Barringer? Pay for it yourself, right?"

"Hmm?"

He looked out the window and they walked outside, flipping through the orders. Sarah Ann counted the orders and walked across the porch with her clipboard.

"This is wonderful news. You can make a lot of money, Ringo. You could teach me to make handbags."

"It's not Handbags of Barringer, it's saddles."

They had a big laugh and more wine.

"I need to meet with Doc, see if he wants to sell it."

"If you want us to stay together, then we have to stay in North Carolina. That's my final answer."

"Looks like I'll be running the saddlery company alone."

They sat beside each other on the front steps for an hour talking about future plans and what they'd like to do.

"There's a check from Mickey Starr inside the envelope. You should be able to make a considerable deposit."

"Doc will not sell his Uncle Kenneth's farm, will he?"

"Why not?" holding his hand. "Aren't you his son and business partner?"

The tattoo on Doc's forearm flashed in Ringo's mind and he grinned and kissed her. The afternoon sun was warm as they talked about their ideas and how they could increase the business with riding lessons and breeding horses, too. She had a hundred ideas, and he had no idea how much smarter she was until the day at the log cabin. He told her, without hesitation, too. "Yeah. I need to talk to Doc, in person." He closed his eyes. "See what he says."

"Mickey would lend you the money, I bet?" Sarah Ann remarked, squeezing his hand. "I understand Doc is terribly jealous of Mickey Starr, and your father. Now that Doc is moving, he knows you will partner with Mickey and Tipp's style of living. He might think you have your sights on Tybee Island, too."

"He'll roundhouse kick me if I borrow a penny from Mickey Starr."

Racking his hands through his blonde hair and lifting his head, Ringo pounded his fist against the banister.

"We need to go to Texas, Sarah Ann."

"You want me with you?"

"Yeah. Talk to Doc, get his advice and see what he wants to do about Showman Wagoner, who skipped town with the prize money."

"You can call him, just the same. He's looking after Clem Cline, anyway."

"We could check on Clem while we are out there."

"I'm going with you to Texas?"

"Yeah. I can't be anywhere without you."

"That's what I wanted to hear."

They watched three deer run from the yard into the woods, two were doe, twisting their ears and one was a buck. Ringo explained what rutting season was all about in November. They watched wildlife meander on the trails that lead to a stream flowing into the small lake, as he thought about what he needed to do, making a list of questions on the clipboard.

Hugging him, she said, "We need to plan to do more things together since we are admittingly in love."

"Let's share a bottle of Andy Oliver, the white bottle this time."

"Good idea. I'll pour." He used a tool for the cork. "Doc has been more of a father to you than Mickey or your biological father has been around, that's for sure. Doc's a good man."

Ringo finished a glass of wine in two drinks. "We'll pack in the morning."

She wrapped her arms around him, squeezing and feeling relieved, "Seriously, are you in love?"

He kissed her. "Ever since you were waving at me on your horse with the bees buzzing, well, I've been in love."

"There were no bees." She covered her laugh. "I was flirting with you, but I didn't see Doc with you. I'm embarrassed that you'll tell him."

"I knew it! Doc said you were flirting."

She twisted her hips, walking to the kitchen and poured them another glass of Andy Oliver, the white was her second favorite, paired with cheese and crackers of any kind.

"You mean, it's a family thing?"

Nodding, "I hope to, don't you, babe?"

Turning down the lights low, she struck a match, lit a candle, and checked her figure in a rustic mirror. Ringo took the wine glass out of her hand and sat it down. They kissed and made love. Dark clouds moved into Elkin, moving puffy clouds, a change to cooler times they'd grown to enjoy in the Blue Ridge Mountains, especially being wrapped in the warmth of a big bear rug, settled beside a cozy fire.

"Is that snow on the neighbor's dog?"

Later, Sarah Ann petted snowflakes from the dog in the doorway. The lady saw the flakes dropping like shredded cotton balls, and snow blanketed the hillside of Elkin for the second time.

"It's romantic." She covered her body and stood in the window. "I love snow. We can walk from the porch to the snow clouds and glide across the sky to the moon in Elkin."

"Cover yourself, you are mooning the rabbits."

Ringo snapped a picture. The flickering light of the fireplace was the only light in the room as the dog sat between them on the floor. Sarah Ann opened the curtains as wide as the window would allow. Other than the skiff of snow, the first heavy snow of the season lasted until morning. The dog fell asleep on a rug in front of the fireplace on a night he wished would never end, falling asleep in his arms on the sofa was Sarah Ann, and he was content.

Later, Ringo let the dog out and he didn't return. They talked and didn't sleep much. More ideas crossed his mind about what would happen in Temple once they landed. The next morning Ringo met with his travel agent and bought two tickets to Texas.

32

With Great Expectations

Texas was the place Sarah Ann dreamed about on the plane ride. Nervous as a back row Baptist talking to a minister, Ringo dreaded his meeting with Doc. However, he had a new desire to rest and recline, back in Texas, and to hear Doc's thoughts and plans. He hoped Selena didn't show up.

Yet, it was saddlery and bull riding that made him proud of himself again, and no doubt, he was in love. Ringo meditated more after the concussion, like hard charging football players did after a major collision, or how a coal miner coped with being covered up in an explosion. With great expectations, Ringo realized how life altering events played a role in change, sending him down an unexpected road.

Ringo and Sarah Ann finally made it to Clem Cline's White Hall Ranch, where a hundred horses and cattle lined the fence when they arrived, just like the animals were welcoming him home.

"Well, bull rider, come in. Look who lived to walk and talk again." Doc hugged him. "Sarah Ann, welcome to Temple, Texas."

"Temple is a beautiful place." Doc took her coat. "I wanted to see Waco and shop, but another time."

Doc wrapped Ringo in a big bear hug and made sure he was still in good health, examining the bull rider, head to toe.

"I'm goin' to live." Ringo hugged Sarah Ann. "The doctor recommended I find another line of work, though, like golf or making saddles."

Clem Cline walked to the barn with a cane that kept him propped up. "I thought you were practicing to be one of those store mannequins and registering yourself as a professional tackling dummy." Clem Cline rested his hand on Ringo's shoulder as the bull rider guided him up the steps.

"There's no tougher cowboy than Ringo Bare," said Doc. They all agreed.

"I bet you two are hungry. They don't give enough food on an airplane to keep a chipmunk alive," Clem said. With a sharp voice, he addressed Ringo. "Boy, I warned you about keeping your balance on that dang bull, didn't I?"

"Being in mid-air on a mad bull, I didn't have time to react or pose for a photograph."

"We are starving," said Sarah Ann, lifting her nose. "A Carolina girl knows good cooking, just like Texans."

"I make a mean Texas Cowboy Stew and cornbread," said Clem, laughing, who told the entire story to Sarah Ann about how the house burned down, joking, and blaming Ringo for the flames. Singing, Clem Cline belted out, "He didn't start the fire, but his stew's been burnin' since the world's been turning."

Good times were had by all.

Walking up to Ringo and Sarah Ann, Doc jammed his hands inside gloves and rolled up his collar with a curious look on his face, shivering. "How are you two love birds doing?"

"Doing fine," answered Sarah Ann, elbowing Ringo.

"O' that reminds me," said Ringo, "Doc, you got a minute?"

"Step into my outdoor barn office."

Sarah Ann helped Clem Cline with the kitchen while the two men talked, and she hoped Ringo wasn't discussing Brandi's good looks or Selena's Spanish dancing. Firing up his truck, Ringo said, "Let's check on the windmill."

"What's on your mind?"

"I need a place to live."

"I know you hit your head on that bull, but you live on my farm in Barringer."

Ringo sighed and kept driving.

"That's your farm, not mine." The bull rider adjusted his hat. "Plus, we have a partnership, don't we, back in Barringer, not in Texas? I heard you were buying Clem Cline's ranch."

Rolling down the window, Doc said, "I think I'm moving back to Texas. Clem Cline made me a deal on his ranch, so I'll be here. You build some revenue in the saddlery company and we'll talk. You can have the stuff in Uncle Kenneth's shed, the saddlery shop, two old trucks, and how 'bout that for being a good father?"

"I'd like to buy the place from you."

Gazing at the baby blue sky, Doc stepped out of the truck and rolled a quarter over his fingers at the fence and thought about the importance of a man's independence. He stared at the coin and thought about how far Ringo had come, and he felt Clem Cline, not only was a huge part of his success, but he'd been there for Ringo, too. "My place in Barringer is not for sale, Ringo. I will not sell Uncle Kenneth's property to you or anyone else. You got that? Maybe later, but not right now."

"You don't need it." Ringo hit his shoulder. "I need a place to settle down, Dad, Sarah Ann and I are serious." Ringo viewed Clem Cline's White Hall Ranch. "I need a place just like this one." The men sat on the tailgate. "You got this place now and what do I have?"

Looking out across the land, they spoke of what potential was left in the Barringer farm and how more fences and horses were needed, and how to add more value to the real estate in the spring, just the way Clem Cline built his ranch, barn by barn, horse by horse.

"Think it over, Ringo, you may not want to live beside your in-laws." Doc grinned and chuckled. "They will dig into your personal affairs, tell you what blue jeans to wear to the Troutman Diner. I've seen it happen. That's just my thoughts on the matter. Congratulations on the way you handled No Man's Land, made you a world champion again, didn't it?"

"I credit Clem Cline and Juan Bogart and Doc Greenway." Ringo propped his leg on the fence just like Doc had his foot on the rail. "They reminded me about courage, risk and reward. Something you taught me when I came to live with you."

"There was no prouder moment in my life than when Big Ray Brown shouted, 'Ringo Bare has just been named Bull Rider of the Year' and you earned it. You made people believe in you again. They played your video on all the sports channels for several days. People are still asking about you, and talking about you, even here, in Temple."

"Felt good to win one for you." Taking off his hat, Ringo felt the evening sun warm his face, handling his thin beard. "I read the newspaper at DFW, and in January Showman Wagoner is donating the Teddy Roosevelt saddle to a museum in Cheyenne."

"He can't do that!" Doc kicked the fence. "You won the diamond saddle, fair and square. You spent your ten seconds on the meanest bull in the world and everyone saw you ride the bull. When you were on the stretcher, a man saw Showman on television grabbing the payoff and leaving Barringer. That's when that rip-off millionaire grabbed the saddle, the money, and flew his private jet to Wyoming."

"We need to stop him."

"He'd love to get back at us and make a donation before we can find him. Then we'd never see it again." Ringo bit a piece of straw from a bale and leaned back in the truck bed.
"That's my uncle's saddle and it belongs in Barringer."

Ringo stood.

"Let's go to Wyoming, how about it?"

"Yeah, let's go collect our earnings, take what's ours!"

The wind spun the blades on the windmill, clouds slid in front of the sun and tumble weeds rolled north into the fence, and that moment changed everything, in motion again. Doc and

Saddles of Barringer

Ringo formulated a plan on a napkin, right on his tailgate, father to son.

"We can put him in his place," said Ringo, rubbing his chin with a pen and talking about Wyoming.

"You and I could leave for Cheyenne in the morning and surprise him."

Ringo spat out the straw.

"You mean, talk it over with Showman like a used car salesman, man-to-man." laughed Doc. "He'll have guard dogs and guns pointed at us. You want Sarah Ann to go to Cheyenne or fly back to North Carolina?"

"I know there's no wedding bells or rings right now, but there could be soon. She's come this far with your ugly bull riding butt." Doc laughed. "And she's a great lady. You need her a great deal more than she needs you, I'll tell you that much."

Ringo chuckled and let Doc know it was good to have her in Texas with him. "You call it?"

"No." He pushed his shoulder. "You call it."

"Heads! We're going to Wyoming, old man, and handling our business with Showman Wagoner."

"Tails. We send Chuck Greenway to Cheyenne with a bottle of Bourbon and a machine gun and see what happens."

Doc drove back to Clem Cline's big house. Ringo held the door, Doc yelled, "We are going to Wyoming, folks!"

Reading the newspaper after his Texas Cowboy Stew, Ringo said, "The newspaper says Showman will sell the saddle to a Wyoming collector by the end of the year, a deal has been done."

"That's my brother's design," said Clem Cline.

***

There wasn't a man more knowledgeable about bulls, or liquor, or horses than Clem Cline. The unknown did not exist to him, a collector of relics and a few other things. Unable to harness horses and train bull riders meant something to Clem Cline, and for him, traveling was better than Sunday supper at the White House.

Chewing his tobacco, Clem Cline said, "Every man has his own price and his own vice. I have a hit list of dislikes for Showman Wagoner, harboring it for a long damn time."

Inside his towering barn, he had hay and straw for bedding, and from time to time, he'd reach in a dusty milk bucket when someone needed a snort of firewater, a liquid remedy, for stress and other such illnesses.

Later, Clem Cline took a break from feeding cattle and horses, saw Doc walk through the west end of the barn, surprised to see his sour face, standing with his hands jammed in his pockets. After a heart attack, Clem Cline wasn't about to slow down to hear his confession or even throw sand in the air to test the wind. When friends needed Clem Cline, he was beside them with advice and a few dollars.

"What the hell has gotten into you, Doc?" Clem reached deep into the third shelf, moved a few oil cans and a metal funnel, knocking off enough dust to cover a grave, and pulling a dozen mason jars forward to find what he'd tucked away, years ago.

"Nothing. I'm fine, Uncle Clem."

"You've lost some color in your face, but I got the remedy for any problems, though." Clem called Doc to take a seat. In a spirited voice he asked, "What's killing you, anyway? Speak up, young man when I talk to you."

"I need Uncle Kenneth's saddle from Showman Wagoner. Me and the bull rider are leaving early in the morning for Wyoming."

"Well, let's go get the damn thing." Clem pulled the barn door tight, the wind picked up out of the west, which reminded them of what the Cowboy State would be like. "Why is the leather and horn so important to you, anyway?"

"There's something underneath the fenders of the saddle." Doc tapped his glasses. "Not sure what it is, your brother stitched it inside the leather."

"Like what, Doc?" he asked, canting his head, and stopping long enough to adjust his hearing aid.

"It's a letter from Uncle Kenneth." Clem Cline stopped walking to examine Doc's wrinkled face for the truth.

"Letter, huh?"

"Inside the leather fenders, I designed it that way." Doc walked beside him. "I am the only one who knows about it."

"Keep it that way," Clem insisted. "Let's get packed, ride our horses to Wyoming; we have some trouble to discover."

Clem Cline paced slowly from the barn to his grand collection of cowboy boots, some were sixty years, kept in a large showroom room in his elaborate home.

"I get to take the Chisholm Trail on horseback." He told his friends. Clem Cline yanked a long string that made the room glow, displaying a rare collection of saddles and boots. The old timer sat and slipped on a pair he'd bought in Waco in 1956, two days after he won the Bull Riding World Championship, equal to a coveted western store. His collection was impressive, to say the least.

"Nah, not on horseback, like in the film *Lonesome Dove*." Doc snickered. "We'll take your new Suburban." Doc paced around the room examining leather boots and saddles still with tags on the horns. Like Kenneth, he thought leather came from heaven. "No one can out do you on leather boots, Clem."

"This collection needs to be in a museum," said Clem, handle his old pair of boots. "And when I die, it stays with the house, nephew."

"Your brother's diamond saddle needs to be right beside your collection, too." Doc told him in private.

"Horseback, now that would be a more traditional way to ride into Cheyenne, waving pistols and shooting up the damn place." Clem turned off the light to the room and locked the door. "Next time, I will bring my guns and holster."

His mind had faded pretty bad since Doc and Ringo moved to Barringer. "I'll ask Ringo and Sarah Ann," said Clem, strapping a holster to his hips, "if they'd rather ride horses or take my Suburban to Wyoming, see what the consensus is in this house?"

Everyone laughed.

"My friends," said Clem, standing straight as an arrow, "just as the sun shines after the dark, the light of good is brighter than any darkness. You remember my words, friends."

***

Two days later, snow fell like fluffy cotton balls when they reached the city limits of Cheyenne. Still talking about the mouth-watering steak dinner they'd wolfed down in Amarillo, the four of them were ready to do whatever it took to recover Uncle Kenneth's diamond saddle. Pride. Justice. Revenge. Satisfaction. Waiting a long time to settle the score, Doc imagined Showman Wagoner laughing in his face at the Waco Poker Championship, in 1991.

Bright as a Jerusalem star, city streets and glowing lights made Cheyenne a Christmas town, just like shaking a snow globe amid a mountainous western town, it was sweet, a picture of serenity. While Clem Cline handed out his favorite Texas Bourbon to Ringo and Sarah Ann, Doc planned his special ops mission as if he was in the Army again. To his right, Clem Cline told more stories than one man should even know, and his head was full of ideas on how to retrieve the saddle and the money.

Admiring the Laramie Mountains from the window seat, Sarah Ann fell in love with the place and how the wide valleys stretched from the hills to the plains, was her Christmas card for the season.

"Cheyenne will either bend us in embarrassment or it will be our most glorious day," said Doc.

Either way, he wasn't riding the famous Carousel Bar, nor was it kicking back with a bottle of Andy Oliver in Elkin, but it was the most pivotal moment Doc had anticipated in a long while, a true battle with his adversary.

Eagerly knocking on Showman Wagner's mansion, Doc faced a tall butler, who had a scare on his face, dressed in black and white, running his eyes about Doc's frame with curiosity.

"Good evening, sir," said the butler. "May I help you?"

"Is Showman Wagoner at home?"

"Yeah. I'm right here." Stepping in front of his hired hand, Showman Wagoner appeared. "Well, you found me, Doc. You have come to get even. I thought my fake ads in the newspaper would lure you to Wyoming. That's what happens when you own the newspaper."

Clutching his fist, Doc asked, "You got time for a hand of cards?"

"Yeah. Where's my manners? Sure, come in. I happen to have guests who'd love to take your money, Doc."

"My pleasure."

"I have something of yours, I think you'd love to see, anyway."

Waving his hand at Ringo, Sarah Ann, and Clem Cline to enter the doorway, Doc advised them not to eat or drink what was offered.

"I thought you'd join me much sooner, though." Showman saw Doc's crew pacing with him as no introductions or exchanges were made in the long corridor. "Hope you brought some money with you." Showman closed the door behind his guests.

"Best of five, and it's $10,000 per hand?" Showman buttoned his suit and waited in suspense. "Will you be joining the game, Doc?"

"You knew me from Temple and double crossed me in New Orleans with Big Easy Boys," said Doc, watching his every move. "I'm back for more in Wyoming."

Though Clem Cline wanted to blow the place sky high, Doc decided to walk right in the front, taking him at his own game. Next, they walked in a line through three rooms, down a dark hallway until they reached the room where Showman locked the door behind them. The group followed Doc's eyes and hand signals.

"Welcome Ringo Bare and the ancient bull rider, Clem Cline." Showman scoffed and turned to Sarah Ann. "Who's this golden honeycomb with the nice, curvy figure, huh?"

Doc grabbed Ringo's arm before he took a swing.

"Wait! Hold on, Ringo! You could kill him with your left hand if I'd let you."

"This ain't Barringer or some Wild West show, boys." Showman locked the door. "Now, you're on my turf and I make up the rules in Cheyenne and change them if I want to."

"You haven't changed, Showman?" said Clem Cline, unrolling his cash for the game. "Still pissing down your leg and running from bulls, like you did when your rich daddy sent you to my ranch in 1965. You pissed on yourself when I draped you over the bull, made your daddy mad as hell, too."

They all laughed. Doc Greenway slid on his dark glasses at the card table and scanned the doors and windows.

Still standing and sounding out a loud whistle, Showman removed his hand from his lips, three large men stepped up behind him. One man tapped his gun and stared at Doc and his friends. Tapping his cane, Clem Cline pointed at the men, acting as if he was shooting a long rifle. Sarah Ann and Ringo encouraged the rifleman with their applause.

"Need me to handle this guy, Boss?" asked a big guard.

They stared at Doc, like he was waiting for a gunfight to take place, and he knew they were outnumbered as more men entered the room, back and forth, signaling Ringo with four fingers to settle down.

"No. This group is from Barringer, North Carolina, they've traveled a long way to make a donation into my pockets." Showman Wagoner lit a cigar, taking a puff and blowing smoke into the tall room, laughing. "They're pissed off because we didn't give Ringo Bare his *glory day* after he rode a bull for the first time in three years."

"We are here to collect our winnings and have fun, gentlemen." Doc took off his glasses. "Relax and deal."

"Years ago, I beat Doc at poker, he's been chasing me from town to town, trying to regain his losses, mapping out his pot of gold as an average poker player, that's all."

"The bank will back him." Clem Cline slapped his jacket pockets. "And I'm the damn bank, Harley Wagoner."

Nodding at his friend, Doc recognized that Clem Cline's pockets were stuffed, a dangerous blessing on another man's turf.

Doc waved for his friends to move closer so he could talk to Ringo and Clem Cline, if he needed them. There was a large chair, one bigger than the rest, Showman adjusted his seat at the head of a card table, smoking and sipping whiskey.

"Why Ringo Bare?" said Showman, chuckling and looking and his armed guards. "Did you like the way my bull wrecked you, flipping you like a cat on a trampoline in the end, at Barringer Stockyards?"

"I rode your bull, didn't I? Where's my damn money?"

"You sure acted dead in the dirt at the end."

Showman smoked his cigar and laughed.

"Let's play Blackjack, boys." Doc tilted his dark glasses.

"That takes three more players." Clem Cline told them.

"Now we're gettin' down to business, he's a wise man." Showman blurted out to the crowd and flagged his guards to retrieve the others.

Three men barged through the swinging doors and took their seats. One man who wore a red bowtie whipped out cards and chips, handing each man two cards. His cards turned an ace of spades and the other one was face down.

"I knew you had more players. Their seats were still warm when I touched them," said Doc, who placed his $10,000 on the table.

Folding her lips, Sarah Ann nudged Ringo. "Your father is good."

"That's why he's called Doctor Tulane."

All the players stacked money on the table.

"Get these men a drink," Showman ordered his butler. The servant paced to the kitchen and returned with bottles of beer from the Rockies.

"No brew for me." Doc concentrated on his game. Not being a man of strong drink or any drink, Doc declined the butler's bottle.

"Pour the others something strong!" yelled Showman. "Bourbon from High West, Utah, please. Bring out the good stuff for our guests, especially Goldilocks and Ringo Bare."

"I'll have High West from Utah," said Clem Cline, who flagged down the butler. His friends knew he'd violated the major rule.

Everyone had a drink, but Doc wasn't there for the party. His eyes never cut from the table and he didn't even subject himself to a glass of water in fear of being poisoned by the devil that lived inside Showman. Doc Greenway capitalized, taking the first round, which caused Showman to pace around the room for five minutes.

"Piss your leg again, Showman." Clem Cline lifted his High West Bourbon to the host and laughed.

The tallest bodyguard returned behind Showman Wagoner, placing a black briefcase on a nearby table, the man pressed two buttons, the latch clicked, and the case popped open.

"Here's a quarter of a million," said Showman Wagoner, rolling his cigar in his hand. "As promised, I'm all in, boys."

The guard kept the briefcase in his hand as they played.

"You boys are serious." Clem Cline encouraged them.

"High rollers club," said Sarah Ann.

"Took a long time to get here." Doc turned over his cash. "I'm having fun in Cheyenne, aren't you, Wagoner." He eyed his enemy. "What about it, Show?"

"Bring out my Teddy Roosevelt diamond saddle," said Doc. "You know, the one you stole in Barringer."

"Honey?" yelled Showman. "Could you bring in Kenneth Greenway's diamond studded saddle, please. Our old friends would like to see it up close." A stunning bleached blonde walked through the door and stood.

"Pomona Bare?" Doc took off his glasses. "I thought you were dead, Mrs. Bare?"

"My sister died."

"I am sorry, Pomona." Doc stared at her.

"This is your mother?" asked Sarah Ann. "She's the most beautiful woman I've ever seen."

"I don't have a mother," said Ringo, staring at her.

"Thought I taught you better than that Ringo?" said Pomona. "Be respectful to a lady, right?"

"Hard to teach me when you're sleeping around," said her son. "I see that hasn't changed much for you, sleeping beauty."

"Well, well, friends," said Showman, taking his next two cards. "Isn't this a hell of a family reunion? The lady, ex-boyfriend, dumbass bull rider, and the old man named C.C. have graced us with their friendship."

Ringo flung a beer bottle at Showman's head. Clem Cline tapped the real gun on his hip and looked at the guard.

"That son of a bitch will pay!" Showman wiped blood from his cut.

"I can throw better than I can ride."

Ringo flipped his wrist. Showman pitched his cards in the air. Clem turned his arm over and aimed his gun.

"Ringo!" said Clem Cline. "We came to play cards, not wreck the mares and little boys who piss on themselves. Did Showman piss on himself again?"

"Deal!" Doc told the man. "Pass 'em out, dealer."

"Pomona?" Doc flipped her a coin. "Here, you left this coin for your son a few years ago, remember?"

She nodded and looked at Ringo.

"Let's get back to the card game." Clem Cline sounded.

***

After an hour Doc had lost two games and won two games and a short break was taken. The poker room was as quiet as a Monday morning church in an abandoned ghost town. Showman stood.

"Let's take another smoke break, boys," said Showman.

The card dealer raised both hands, and spoke his first words, "No one leaves this room until this is settled." The large man wore a red bowtie and had dark eyes. "I haven't seen a game this good since Waco."

His name was unknown, but he didn't trust anyone, especially Showman or the wild eyes of Clem Cline. Pomona re-entered the room in a sparkling white dress. "Who's winning?"

"Tied." Clem Cline told her. "One more game, gal, and we are out of your bleached blonde hair. Showman has won the last two hands and Doc won two rounds."

Not speaking a word in two games, holding his emotions to himself, Doc focused on his cards, hands folded, he seemed relaxed in his chair. Both Showman and Doc wore dark sunglasses and leaned forward looking at each other, scanning the cards they were dealt. The other players ran out of luck.

"Hit me!" said Doc, tapping the green felt table.

His head raised and his throat was dry, bobbing his head as if he needed a better hand, Doc hesitated. The exit door behind Ringo was shut and across from him, and an unknown door from which everyone kept moving in and out, seemed to be the last option for an exit.

Without cameras, no recording happened as far as Doc could tell because Ringo spotted his father scanning the room between rounds, just like he had taught his son to do in the motorhome before they parked the vehicle in the French Quarter. Doc taught Ringo to find a jumping off point on the bull, and Clem Cline turned and knew the game was about to end. Everyone but Sarah Ann was looking for the best exit plan when the last two cards were revealed. Sarah Ann was amazed at how beautiful Pomona was standing in the sequin dress.

As uninvited guests, Doc knew it would be dangerous getting everyone down the long hall, through the three large rooms to the Suburban before they were clubbed and dropped off in the snow atop of the Laramie Mountains. Risk. Reward. Knowing it would be difficult to waltz out the door as if they were in Las Vegas, it wasn't about to happen in Cheyenne either, for Doc; the rules had changed on a snowy turf. The slowest of the group was Clem Cline, who carried a cane, some High West Bourbon, who was a fighter in his younger years. But the man could never be underestimated in a pinch.

"Everything all right, Gilbert Greenway?" Showman eyed the dealer and then observed Doc, grinning, and laughing as if he were bluffing, or he had a hot hand again.

"Fine." Doc took a deep breath. "Cowboy Up!" which was the signal for his crew to ready themselves to ride out of the room.

"Haven't seen this much money since I beat Chuck at his Pirate Bar in New Orleans, years ago or maybe it was another pirate on duty?" Showman leaned forward toward Doc. Chuck said, 'But this is Gilbert's part of the inheritance, and it helped make him a better businessman.'

Laughing and moving his body, Showman's tanned face which seemed out of place in the whiteout of Wyoming, turned up a smile as he flipped his cigar in his lips.

"My part, huh?" Doc folded his glasses, placing them in his shirt, and zipped his coat to his neckline.

"Ha-Ha-Ha-Ha." Laughed Showman alongside his guards. "Some of this money should have been in your pocket, years ago then. It's all brotherly love, of course."

"Bastard!" yelled Doc. "I've always hated you!"

"But you seem to always follow me and so do your women." Showman crushed his cigar, taunting his opponent.

"Deal the damn cards!" said Ringo. "Let's go!"

"Call," said Doc.

Showman pushed the shiny diamond saddle to the side of the room, a briefcase was on the table, and all Doc thought about was Sandy crying and having to part with her diamonds and Kenneth's favorite saddle.

The dealer flipped the cards. "Let's see the cards," said Clem.

"Ace!" Ringo shouted. "Nine of hearts for Showman."

"Nineteen." Pomona whispered.

The room was thick with tension, men mumbled, and Doc tapped his cards. Others folded, but not Doc Greenway.

"Let's see 'em, Doc." The dealer moved his hands.

Pointing his hand, Showman stood and leaned over the table, palms sweaty as if he'd worked out.

"Ace of hearts and ace of spades." Sarah Ann said.

"20!" yelled Clem Cline. "You beat his ass again."

"Yes! Yes! Yes." Ringo jumped and punched the air. "Damn it, he's good!"

Ducking a powerful right cross from Showman, was Ringo who watched his father's hand, as if he was about to shake Doc's hand. Hitting Showman Wagoner between the eyes, was no other than Doc Greenway, knocking his opponent backwards, a long overdue message he'd been waiting to deliver.

"We win!" said Sarah Ann, jumping.

"Put down the gun, guard!" said Clem Cline.

Using their coats to collect the money, Clem and Sarah Ann stuffed their jackets with what was promised to Doc and Ringo. Doc collected the gold watch from the table for Chuck. They eased backwards out the door and down the hall, like Doc and Clem had practiced in the barn. Flipping the diamond saddle over his back, Doc held out his hand for Pomona, who latched onto Gilbert Greenway's arm like she did under the yellow umbrella, years ago, in 1982.

"Damn you, Pomona!" sounded Showman.

"I got the Rough Rider saddle and my lady. She's a bonus, Showman. See ya!"

"Doc!" said Pomona, who was shocked. "After all these years, you are still a kind gentlemen. I dreamed you'd come for me." Kissing him on the cheek, Pomona held his arm tight.

"Not so fast, Doc!" Showman whipped a knife toward Doc's head, blocking the weapon with the saddle fender.

"That's Ringo's diamond saddle now."

Stabbing at Doc's side and missing with a second knife, Showman saw Ringo lunging at him with his bad foot, making contact with his arm and slamming Showman against the wall.

Helping Clem Cline make some speed down the hall, Sarah Ann and Pomona tugged with all she had to get the big guy moving to the vehicle.

Moaning and staggering, "That son of a bitch just broke my arm," shouted Showman at Ringo. "Kill him!"

Showman's men picked up their guns and fired three shots down the hall. Being the last two to escape, Doc and Ringo made it to the Suburban, where Sarah Ann had the vehicle running and took off.

"Clem?" said Doc, holding his uncle. "You're bleeding!" who was seated in the backseat beside the old man.

Slumping over, "I'm hit under the arm. Burns like brandy on a barbed wire cut, nephew."

Guards fired more shots that were embedded into the doors of the vehicle. No one else was hit as they raced away. Driving and weaving into the passing lane, Sarah Ann eluded the gunmen and rushed Clem Cline to the nearest hospital in Cheyenne, where his blood pressure dropped.

"How's Clem?" Ringo held a long face.

"Clem Cline is dead." Doc fell in a chair.

Sarah Ann and Pomona screamed and wept. After reporting what happened to the authorities, Sarah Ann, Ringo, and Pomona were released. Later, on a flight from Cheyenne to Charlotte, Ringo and his mother found reconciliation and forgiveness to be a humbling experience, while Sarah Ann sat between them, as mediator.

Making the long drive from Cheyenne to Clem Cline's ranch, Doc felt alone in Temple, Texas. Later, Clem Cline was honored with a twenty-one-gun salute and buried beside Aunt Rita, his wife of fifty years.

Over 5,000 people wept at the funeral of Clemson Regal Cline. Doc jumped when the twenty-one-gun salute was fired, and for days the sounds of gunfire shook him at night in a panic. More than an uncle was lost, Clem Cline, was a great friend, too. Clem wouldn't sell Doc his land, he gifted it to him, and Mike agreed, pending total access to cattle and land, if needed. Doc paid Mike a good price for the ranch, anyway, and covered the taxes on the property before he left Texas.

Talking to Clem's son over breakfast in Austin, Mike said, "Heaven must've needed another cowboy, to take Clem Cline away from us."

"He's with Uncle Kenneth now."

On the drive from Texas to Barringer, broken-hearted, Doc remembered how Clem Cline had taught him how to cook Texas Cowboy Stew and Doc taught him how to fix Shrimp Gumbo, an even trade and they became close. Two simple lessons that meant the world to them both, far more than cattle and horses, they became best friends, too.

The G.I. Bill paid Gilbert's way through medical school, but it was his uncles, Kenneth, and Clem, two half-brothers, who sent him money each month at Tulane University. Doc never forgot part of his life, a simple gift of kindness.

***

Back in Barringer, days before Christmas, Doc carefully removed the diamonds and the fenders from the Teddy Roosevelt Rough Rider saddle and had them appraised in Troutman, the diamonds were well over a hundred grand, the lady told him. His Uncle Kenneth was the only saddlery master from North Carolina to ever be considered for the Smithsonian Museum.

***

On Christmas Eve, snow fell for the first time in years, blanketing Barringer, Doc imagined his Uncle Kenneth kissing the diamonds and crying as he shined the leather and dusted the gemstones for the last time before he sold the Teddy Roosevelt saddle to the Wagoner family. Knocking on the door of the saddle shop with eggnog in each hand, Ringo asked, "What did Uncle Kenneth's letter say?"

Sitting on a stool with his glasses on his nose, Doc spun around and faced his son with an envelope in his hands, and in a low voice replied, "I didn't open it yet."

"Use my cutter."

Pressing the envelope against the wooden countertop, he eased the blade until a clean cut snipped the end and the letter with his uncle's handwriting gently slid into his hand.

Doc read it aloud.

"A good man said, 'A soft, easy life is not worth living, if it impairs the brain, heart, and muscle. We must dare to be great; and we must realize that greatness is the fruit of toil and sacrifice and high courage. For us is the life of action, of strenuous performance of duty; let us lie in the harness, striving mightily;

let us rather run the risk of wearing out than rusting out.' No better words have been spoken," said Doc.

"Did Uncle Kenneth write those words?"

"No." Doc shook his head. "Ringo, these are the words of the ultimate Army Rough Rider, the one and only President Teddy Roosevelt."

"What did he mean in the letter?"

In a valiant declaration, Doctor Gilbert Greenway said,

"Let me make an attempt at it. My uncle was known to read to the love of his life, Sandy and Kenneth would spend their evenings, full of thoughts, hand in hand, by the warmth of a fire."

"Sweet couple."

In confidence, Doc paced the room in thought. "He understood the world through the eyes of his own heart, laboring in his passion for fruit through endurance, good and bad, and living out the pleasure for more than a mighty sensation, but in action, rough and yet with tenderness, for that was Roosevelt's description of courage."

"I read how Leonard Wood and Teddy Roosevelt founded the Army Rough Riders on the internet. But how did Kenneth Greenway get the saddle design? That's what started his legacy."

"His father designed it for Teddy Roosevelt. They were best friends."

"Wow! No wonder you want to keep it in the family."

Ringo handed him his eggnog and understood.

"Speaking of family, it's Christmas Eve, what did you get Sarah Ann for Christmas?"

"Cowboy boots and a trip to the Biltmore Estate."
"You want her to run away, Ringo? Come on, man."
"What's your bright idea, Doctor Loverboy?"

Handing Ringo a custom-made leather box, Doc nodded. "I think she'll like this better than another pair of boots and a trip to a place she's been to a dozen times."

"Wow! What a heck of a gift, Doc. I'll pay you for this?"

"Pomona and I are ringing in the New Year at The Carousel Bar, would you and Sarah Ann join us in New Orleans? That would be payment enough for me. Chuck will meet us there."

"She'd love to see the Carousel Bar."

Disappearing on Christmas night, Doc and Pomona danced the night away in Charlotte, she never left his arms and he spun her like an old vinyl record. For the first time in years, they were together again and in love.

Opaque and fine, snow fell on the happy couple. Being a true gentleman, Doc leased a condo in the tallest skyscraper in town, and by the warmth of a fire, they made love.

A week later, dressed like Hollywood movie stars, Doc bought Pomona, Sarah Ann and Ringo, the most expensive outfits they could find in New Orleans. Surprisingly, they found four seats together at the Carousel Bar on New Year's Eve, too. Ten minutes before midnight, Ringo dropped on one knee.

"Oh, my God, what are you doing, Ringo?" asked Sarah Ann.

The bartender turned off the spinning Carousel Bar for the first time since Hurricane Betsy hit New Orleans. Pomona hugged Doc and cried. The good doctor was proud of Ringo when he saw him hit the floor and reach in his pocket.

"Of all the shooting stars in the sky," said Ringo, holding out the leather box Doc made, "I just caught this one with my cowboy hat before it disappeared and thought of you."

"O' my, Lord," Sarah Ann cried, "that must be two carats?"

"Well," Doc whispered to Pomona, "it's 2.03 carats to be exact, round cut diamond, sparkling in platinum."

Holding her hand, Ringo said, "Will you marry me?"

"Yes! Yes, yes, yes, I'll marry you!"

They kissed for a long, long time. The large crowd at the Carousel Bar cheered and roared until seconds before midnight.

"I love you, Sarah Ann."

"I love you more, Ringo."

More people crowded inside the small room to see the love birds kiss, smiling, and admiring what Ringo had done. Having no pictures of her son as a teenager, Pomona snapped a hundred pictures that night of true love, and beating hearts, in the flesh, something new and rare.

"Let's celebrate!" shouted Doc. The Carousel Bar began to spin again.

"I'll have Cliff's Old-Fashioned with olives and High West Bourbon." Sarah Ann told the bartender.

"Then I'll have Cliff's Old-Fashioned with cherries and brandy." Ringo handed him a large bill and thanked him for stopping the bar for his proposal.

A lady screamed, "I love the way he says my name."

"Brandi!" said Sarah Ann.

"Tipp?" said Ringo.

After midnight, Chuck told Doc how much it meant for them to be brothers again, hanging out in the Big Easy.

"Happy New Year, Chuck."

"Happy New Year, Gilbert! You won't see my face again until I buy you and Ringo beignets and coffee at Café Du Monde. Make it 10 o' clock in the morning," hugging his brother, "Happy New Year, Big Brother!"

"See you at breakfast, Chuck."

Dressed in a shiny blue suit and polished shoes, Chuck escorted a beautiful brunette into a black limousine. He stood tall and waved at Doc. Then left.

At a quarter past eleven the next morning, Chuck was nowhere to be found. Ringo grabbed the newspaper.

"Look, Doc!"

"Oh, man, no! God help me. Charles Luke Greenway, 46, was shot to death, outside the Pirate Bar after midnight. Witnesses say Greenway was defending the new owner, from a man under the influence."

"It's Harley "Showman" Wagoner's picture on the front page," said Ringo. "He's dead."

Scanning the newspaper, "My brother must've returned fire after Showman shot him."

"I liked your brother, Doc. I'm so sorry."

Rubbing his chin and staring at St. Louis Cathedral, Doc knew his brother wasn't an angel, but loved him, anyway.

"For the first time ever, Chuck told me he loved me last night. He was planning to move to Barringer next month and get married at Little Joe's Chapel."
On the 2nd of September 1998, born to the proud parents of Mr. and Mrs. Ringo Bare was a beautiful baby, nine pound and eight ounces. Under a full Carolina moon, Doc was the second man to hold the baby with sky blue eyes and cleft chin.

"What's his name, Ringo?"

"Ringo Gilbert Bare." He told his father.

"Being a father is the best part of my life."

A surprising voice sounded from the hallway,

"I want to spoil him first."

"Le Joie?" said Doc.

When Frank entered the room behind his sister, his brother handed him a big red apple, Gilbert and Frank wept on Le Joie's shoulder.

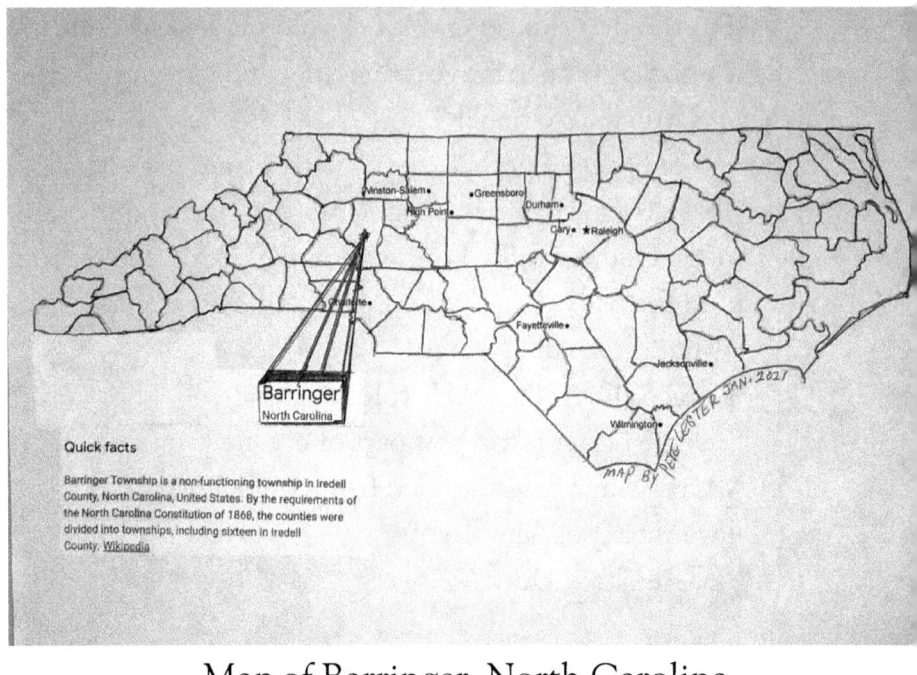

Map of Barringer, North Carolina

Barringer Stew

- Prep time: Takes about 30 minutes.
- Cooking time: 60 minutes
- Serving: 10-12, depending on appetite.

Optional: Wear a cowboy hat and boots for authenticity.

Top-Secret INGREDIENTS:

2 pounds of ground beef.

3 teaspoons ground cumin

1 tsp salt

½ tsp pepper

4 cups of water (North Carolina water is preferred)

2 pounds of kielbasa sausage (cut ½ inch thick)

2 cloves garlic (minced)

1 large onion (diced)

2 cans diced tomatoes

4 large potatoes (peeled and cut into ½ inch pieces)

30 ounces pinto beans (do not drain)

2 cans of whole kernel corn (drained)

1 can of diced tomatoes with green chiles

1 package frozen vegetables

DIRECTIONS: Let's get cooking.

Saddles of Barringer

- Turn the stove to medium-high. Crumble and brown ground beef in a large skillet. Drain and set aside. Add 2 tablespoons of oil to the skillet and add the onions to soften and begin to caramelize, then the garlic when onions are nearly finished. Transfer beef, onions, and garlic to a large stewing pot.
- Add remaining ingredients to the pot. Cover with lid and bring to a boil. Once boiling, lower temperature and simmer for 60 minutes. Stir as needed.
- Serve with crackers or cornbread.
- Enjoy Barringer Stew from the novel, *Saddles of Barringer*.

About the Author

Pete Lester *a.k.a* Tennessee Gunns is the author of *The Tobacco Barn*, an international novel that made the top #600 books on Amazon Book during August 2020. The first novel in his Hearts and Heroes series. *The Tobacco Barn* is found on the author's website at Tennesseegunnsnovel.com.

You can also find books by Pete Lester/ Tennessee Gunns online at Barnes & Noble, Walmart Books, Amazon Books, Kindle and wherever books/eBooks are sold. Book reviews are on Good Reads.

Pete's memberships include The F. Scott Fitzgerald Society, Hemingway Society and The Romance Writers of America of New York City, New York.

Pete's third novel, *Andy Oliver*, a soul-searching, multicultural journey of the heart, is slated for publication in mid-2021. Known for his uncanny humor and likeable characters, Pete's novels are Southern Fiction and referred to as Friendship Fiction, threaded with spiritual and inspirational romance. Being an Army veteran, Pete often uses military references within his stories, along with a strong sense of historic imagery and moral/ethical leadership as well.

Carson's Pickle Story

Carson has a passion for PICKLES! He also has autism and is learning disabled. When thinking about his future, Carson feared he would never be able to get a job. His crippling anxiety about the future and dread of limited workforce abilities encouraged him to begin thinking about being his own boss. Inspired by a school project, Carson started his own pickle business.

Carson's pickle adventure has given him to not only grow in confidence but to also improve both academically and socially. We are thrilled for Carson and his success!

Our hope is that Carson's hearten others to believe in and support DIFFERENT-ABLED individuals.

Tastypicklesbycarson.com

www.ingramcontent.com/pod-product-compliance
Lightning Source LLC
Chambersburg PA
CBHW071224290426
44108CB00013B/1286